Trauma Doesn't Stop at the School Door

Strategies and Solutions for Educators, PreK–College

Karen Gross

TEACHERS COLLEGE PRESS
TEACHERS COLLEGE | COLUMBIA UNIVERSITY
NEW YORK AND LONDON

Published by Teachers College Press,® 1234 Amsterdam Avenue, New York, NY 10027

Cover photo by blueflames / iStock by Getty Images.

Library of Congress Cataloging-in-Publication Data

Names: Gross, Karen, 1952– author. | Teachers College Press.
Title: Trauma doesn't stop at the school door : strategies and solutions for educators, PreK–college / Karen Gross.
Other titles: Trauma does not stop at the school door
Description: New York : Teachers College Press, 2020. | Includes bibliographical references and index.
Identifiers: LCCN 2020006453 (print) | LCCN 2020006454 (ebook) | ISBN 9780807764107 (Paperback : acid-free paper) | ISBN 9780807764114 (Hardcover : acid-free paper) | ISBN 9780807778678 (eBook)
Subjects: LCSH: Students with social disabilities—Counseling of. | Students—Mental health. | Students—Mental health services. | Psychic trauma in children. | Post-traumatic stress disorder in children. | Schools—Sociological aspects.
Classification: LCC LB4065 .G76 2020 (print) | LCC LB4065 (ebook) | DDC 371.826/94—dc23
LC record available at https://lccn.loc.gov/2020006453
LC ebook record available at https://lccn.loc.gov/2020006454

ISBN 978-0-8077-6410-7 (paper)
ISBN 978-0-8077-6411-4 (hardcover)
ISBN 978-0-8077-7867-8 (ebook)

Printed on acid-free paper
Manufactured in the United States of America

Advance Praise for *Trauma Doesn't Stop at the School Door*

"Karen Gross has authored a remarkable book that paves the way for each of us to become trauma-responsive in our own lives and in the daily life and future of the schools, institutions, and communities in which we live and work. It is a treasure trove of ideas and strategies that teachers, parents, students, and leaders of any organization can leverage to make positive transformational changes."

—**Martha J. Kanter**, Executive Director, College Promise Campaign; U.S. Under Secretary of Education (2009–2013)

"*Trauma Doesn't Stop at the School Door* is a treasure trove of information on trauma as well as thoughtful recommendations for schools, from pre–K through college, to counteract negative consequences of trauma in their students."

—**Kathleen Ross**, President Emeritus and Professor of Cross-Cultural Communication, Heritage University

"This book is highly recommended to all educators and administrators who are interested in exploring strategies on policy, program, and practice in trauma-responsive education. It is a book for the 'Generation T' in the context of our time. The book offers strategies for quieting the hyper-aroused stress response system."

—**Ed K.S. Wang**, M.S., Psy.D., Massachusetts General Hospital

"With *Trauma Doesn't Stop at the School Door*, Dr. Gross helps educators and student advocates become trauma-aware and charts a course for teachers and schools to become trauma-responsive."

—**G. Gill Hunter**, professor, Eastern Kentucky University

"Karen Gross gives her readers perspectives and resources that should be added to every teacher's toolbox in order to move beyond the delivery of content and become more cognizant of obstacles that can affect learners under their charge. A must-read for anyone that practices the art of teaching."

—**Ivan Figueroa**, educational consultant

"Applying the principles from *Trauma Doesn't Stop at the School Door* to my work as a teacher in a trauma-sensitive elementary school has transformed the way I think, plan, and teach my learners. Karen Gross gives all educators the necessary tools to facilitate student success."

—**Allyson Hoffman**, library media specialist, Molly Stark Elementary School, Bennington, VT

"Because trauma in our society lives in the shadows, is rarely discussed, is often misunderstood, and is actively hidden, we often misread the sequelae of trauma. Karen Gross' book offers a light in the darkness. If we apply her model to our learners' recovery, we will go a long way toward helping individuals heal."

—**Marie A. Cini**, chief strategy officer, ED2WORK

To the many students and educators who shared their stories with me. This is your book.

Contents

PART II: TAMING

Preface

An aircraft of a major U.S. airline loses its front engine with a loud bang, generating smoke in the cabin, and then makes an emergency landing, which injures several passengers.

A small middle school in Wisconsin is the site of a mid-morning shooting when a student's parent is gunned down on the school's front steps by the school security guard.

A well-known tennis coach is arrested for sexually abusing female athletes on his NCAA Division I team for a period of 10 years and is only now, when the issue has become public, dismissed from the university.

Floods demolish homes in California; damaging mudslides could occur next, along with the threat of earthquakes; more rain is expected in the near term.

A 1st-grader tries to sleep with the sound of gun violence in the background while holding his hands over his young sister's ears so she won't cry from all the noise.

A 5th-grader frequently witnesses her mother beating her stepbrother with a belt and locking him in his room from the outside with a lock the witness cannot reach.

These six vignettes are drawn from real life and describe events and experiences that result in trauma. Some of these events are repeatedly covered on the news and in social media, often for days at a time and with accompanying visual imagery. Think, for example, how often the video of the collapse of the Twin Towers was and still is played and replayed, even so many years after the disaster of September 11, 2001. Experiences that are personal and private and perhaps embarrassing are witnessed by others, regardless of whether the witnesses perceive what they are seeing as traumatic. In short, we are surrounded by trauma in the United States, exemplified in these six vignettes. In this book, they are stand-ins for the omnipresence of trauma in our nation and beyond our borders.

A central feature of trauma in today's world is its lack of geographical constraints. Disasters in one part of our nation, and our world, are quickly reported elsewhere. Since families and friends live in diverse locations, local events and experiences have tentacles that spread far and wide. Trauma's impact, then, can be felt locally, regionally, nationally, and globally. Trauma is not confined to those who experience it firsthand; it can be felt by those who were not physically there for the events. Even the threat of trauma (like the possibility of being quarantined due to a viral pandemic) can be traumatizing for some. In addition, vicarious and secondary trauma (the latter being somewhat like compassion fatigue), the impacts of which are described in greater detail in Chapter 5, is often not recognized. We assume that distance lessens trauma's reach. It doesn't. Even though secondary trauma can be addressed and treated more easily than first-degree (primary trauma), it can be transmitted back to those with first-degree trauma or passed along to those not even within the range of the initial trauma. Trauma knows few boundaries, physical or psychological.

The experience of and exposure to traumatic events can produce lasting, life-changing symptoms, harming individuals and communities. Sometimes these symptoms are recognized by the individuals experiencing them and by outsiders who learn about them. At other times, individuals in trauma's direct path or others dealing with its aftermath experience its symptomology[1] without conscious awareness. In either case, trauma reveals itself in relationships in homes, workplaces, schools, and wider communities. Trauma is carried forward in time through its symptoms, and it can be retriggered by subsequent events—even seemingly minor ones—as time marches forward.

Recognizing trauma's symptoms requires a critical skill set. As described in more detail in Chapter 3, the traditional approach is to see trauma's effects as *biphasic*, namely, as outsize behavior that is often disruptive, as in anger or tantrums, or, alternatively, as isolating behavior. The outsize behavior is often termed *dysregulation* and is situated at one end of the behavioral spectrum, with isolation at the other. That said, in the interest of accuracy, some experts see dysregulation as any symptomatic behavior at either end of the "normal" spectrum.[2]

However, as described here, I believe there is a third, rarely identified group of trauma symptomology: *overregulation*. Students displaying these symptoms perform well. They engage with others and progress through grade school and higher education, often through cultural pressure. Their compensatory mechanisms are so effective that the trauma is hidden, even from themselves. Their display of these newly identified *triphasic* symptoms will be detailed in this book.

Trauma's triphasic symptoms are regularly hinted at or revealed in full view in our educational system, where students of all ages and at all stages spend so much of their lives. And students can display one or more of the categories of symptomology at different times, even in the same day. Think of schools as trauma-holding pens, although the trauma does not stay in its pen. Students walk into these locations (or access them online) daily, carrying their traumatic experiences with them. Educational institutions are a prime site where trauma symptomology rears its head.[3]

In the education environment, those exposed to trauma symptomology—teachers, professors, school staff, coaches—are a fortiori engaging with traumatized students. But they are often not trained to understand what they are seeing or how to address it in classrooms, hallways, and dorms, on the athletic fields, and in libraries and cafeterias, as well as in themselves. They have not reflected on how trauma affects their role as educators. Administrators are similarly situated. They also often do not see the transference of the trauma to themselves, and if they recognize it, they may be unsure what to do to ease what they are feeling.

Trauma symptoms are often missed, particularly in overregulation, or mistaken for other issues that fill diagnostic buckets that are misguided or misinformed, as with dysregulation. And the proffered solutions for affected trauma survivors often miss the mark. No shock there, because the solution doesn't match the real wrong or source of the behavior. We make assumptions—well-intentioned but poor ones—about what accounts for student failure and lack of progression. And we make, perhaps not oddly, assumptions regarding students who succeed masterfully, as if trauma were never a part of that student's life experience. We should heed the message of Daniel J. Siegel and Tina Payne Bryson in *The Whole-Brain Child,* also expressed by many others: If you can name it, you can tame it.[4]

The present book seeks to provide insights into and solutions for all those who occupy our educational systems, from early childhood to adult. The solutions cover a lot of territory for students of all ages and at all stages, from systemic cultural change to architectural and design change, to classroom pedagogy, to student transition strategies. If you are enrolled or work in any educational environment, this book is about you. It explores trauma as it affects students and those who work with them. It provides concrete approaches for responding to what can only be described as an educational pandemic.

Further, my hope is that while this book is directly focused on trauma in the educational arena, its approaches will benefit a wide range of readers: physicians, social workers, policymakers, legislators, community leaders, judges, and scholars, among others. It is, sadly, a book for our time. And for once, unlike for many other societal issues like poverty and racism, we have effective, deployable tools to better the lives of many in the near term.

That promise of solutions—the promise of a better understanding of and approach to ameliorating trauma in the trenches—drives this book. Join me on this journey.

Scope and Coverage

No single book can address all aspects of trauma, particularly a book delimited to trauma's impact on our educational system. While this book references and notes the importance of the medical aspects and neuroscience of trauma symptomology, the neurocognitive impacts of trauma, and the epigenetic transmission of trauma from one generation to the next, it does not delve into these topics in detail. It does not deal with the polyvagal theory (focused on activating and deactivating the vagal nerve), microglia (brain cells that can be activated to help or hurt immunological responses), or neuroception (describing how our neural circuits identify safety and threats). Although many illnesses and addictions may be triggered by trauma, as can suicide, medical consequences of trauma are not this book's main focus. This said, the limited focus here is not meant to undermine this reality: Childhood trauma affects our workplaces, our relationships, and our community engagement. Trauma's reach is deep and wide.[5]

Our educational system is a siloed and complex system for educating children and adults, all of whom can be affected by trauma.[6] From early childhood through adult education, trauma raises its head and directly influences the effect and effectiveness of educational outcomes—and for the most part not in a positive direction. (The positive impacts of trauma—yes, they exist—are discussed at length in my book *Breakaway Learners*.[7]) If the negative outcomes of trauma are not ameliorated, many children in the education space will experience failure and not progress to and through high school and postsecondary education.

There is increased effort in the United States (and elsewhere, to be sure) to become more trauma informed, and trauma's power on adults and children is beginning to receive the attention it deserves. The first congressional hearing on childhood trauma and the need for a federal response was held in July 2019.[8] The American Institutes for Research issued a report on creating trauma-sensitive schools, and the introduction of the federal Trauma-Informed School Act aimed to establish a nationwide effort that recognizes the prevalence of childhood trauma and the need to find solutions.[9] Such efforts are vital, and information must be gathered. That said, trauma information garnered in the educational arena, while a starting point, is hardly enough. Our efforts cannot stop with providing educators with information about trauma and its impact. Educational institutions must move toward being trauma responsive and trauma skilled. This ratchets up the task before us. We need to move to concrete, implementable solutions in the educational landscape in the near term to ameliorate trauma's impact, recognizing that trauma is never erased.

This is not a pipe dream. We actually do some things now without realizing they are trauma responsive, although they are often limited to the lower grades: the establishment of homerooms where children have a place to keep their things and where there is a consistent adult; the inclusion of animals in the classroom that require care and attention; the use of hands-on learning with activities that engage students and their senses; the implementation of civic engagement programming that fosters an awareness of the larger context in which events occur; the offering of programs in music and art that allow self-expression and make use of different brain pathways; the looping of teachers, whereby the same teacher stays or multiple teachers stay with a group of students over a period of at least 2 academic years; and providing team sports where there is camaraderie and shared goals and consistent, repeated meetings, events, and training.

Additional approaches and activities can be implemented in the educational environment to lower autonomic nervous system responses and address other manifestations of trauma. These include pop-up courses; roving professors and teachers; changed pedagogies, including at the start of each class; sensory activities specifically designed to lower the autonomic nervous system response that trauma activates; altered classroom management strategies; deployment of processing in place where therapeutic interventions happen in school with broad participation; revised school calendars and different use of time during the school day; revised systems of punishment and discipline for student behavior; and co-leadership opportunities.

But we cannot stop there. We must do more than describe doable solutions in the education sphere. We need to make them happen and with what I call "stickiness," meaning durability over time. They cannot come and go as leadership, teachers, professors, or staff change. We must change the culture of our educational system, our assumptions about student behavior, our thinking about the role of educators, the place and space in which education happens, and our approaches to measuring educational success. Lest one worry that too much time, attention, and money will be spent on traumatized students (despite their high numbers), the suggested approaches geared to those experiencing trauma help all students. Think of the adage "A rising tide lifts all boats." What we need is for the tide to rise and stay risen.

Structure and Approach

This book is structured in three parts. Part I defines and then addresses trauma and its symptomology in the educational system. It offers a diagrammatic way of understanding trauma's many parts and nuances. It recognizes the difficulty of nomenclature, including the word *trauma*. Part II is solution focused, centered on how schools and colleges can develop trauma skills to enable more of their students to succeed academically and psychosocially. It identifies and explores concrete strategies and how to implement them in institutions, even those settings initially reluctant to change or respond to the call for addressing trauma. Part III suggests that the prevalence of trauma experienced in the United States opens the door to naming a generation—Generation T or Gen T (with the T standing for truama)—and examines what supports this movement and why it matters as well as its more controversial features, including the naming of and focus on trauma. The name draws attention to the issues that have been hidden and gives readers and educators a shared language to describe what is occurring in and outside our classrooms and educational institutions.

This book uses real-life examples and solutions from my own professional experiences in classrooms, community-based and nonprofit organizations, and disaster sites across the United States. Other examples are from my own personal trauma experiences, which inform who I am and what I do. There are several reasons for injecting this storytelling approach. First, this book is not a narrow theoretical text, though grounded in studies and data from the trauma literature; its audience is intended to be wide and deep and not to be used only occasionally. This book is intended to be tested in the lives and workplaces of those who engage with it most particularly in our abundant and diverse educational institutions.

Second, the book is born in the trenches across educational institutions, from preschool through graduate school. My hope is that the stories shared, and the emotions and honest feedback embedded in them, allow the solutions proffered to strike a chord that is personal, professional, or both. Trauma is not an easy topic to navigate. Human stories show trauma as it happens in real life and, in this way, may permit easier access to the points being made.

Third, this book links to and engages with *Breakaway Learners*, my earlier book on student success. The latter book develops a concept termed *lasticity* that, with its five foundation elements (elasticity, plasticity, pivoting right, reciprocity, and belief in self), facilitates and explains how students progress through the educational pipeline. The two books share a goal and an approach: enabling student success because of an understanding of *who* our students are, *why* they behave as they do, *where* we can foster improvement, and *what* we can accomplish in building on their strength while handling their negatives differently. *Breakaway Learners* focuses on the attributes that breakaway students and the institutions that serve them possess—lasticity—and how to foster and ensure the presence of these attributes. By contrast, the present book focuses on students and institutions that are *not* lastic. It offers approaches to help these students break away and later become lastic. Think of the two books, then, as "sidequels," speaking simultaneously to both different students and different institutions operating in the same time frame: *Breakaway Learners* speaks to success (through lasticity), and the present book speaks to how to find a pathway to success for those who are not yet lastic. Finally, the two books share an answer to the *when* question, and it is that we need to make changes *now*.

A Trigger Warning

Some educators use trigger warnings in higher education to alert students to sensitive issues to be raised in readings or in-class discussions. These warnings are controversial, and some individuals object to the very word *trigger* as it has connotations related to guns that are themselves a trigger for many. Those using these warnings are ofttimes, and quite separate from those with concerns about guns, accused of creating *snowflakes*, namely students who cannot deal with the world around them.[10] Indeed, we don't live in a trauma-sensitive world. But for me, trigger warnings serve a critical purpose tied to trauma and its impact. Some topics in the educational arena reactivate trauma; as this book will explore, trauma does not disappear even with quality treatment or remediation. If an educator can anticipate the retriggering of trauma in students (which can occur in a nanosecond, making the word *trigger* quite apt and appropriate), quality learning can be fostered. Trigger warnings lower activation of the autonomic nervous system, decreasing key effects of trauma. Through such warnings, educators can ameliorate trauma's impact; this is a new way to justify their usage.

Thus this book comes with a trigger warning, to achieve a goal similar to that intended in colleges and other settings where they are used, to let readers know that what lies ahead is sensitive and difficult and may arouse thoughts and feelings in those who have experienced trauma—whether or not they know they have been traumatized. Indeed, one of the most difficult aspects of trauma is that we often do not recognize it in ourselves, as noted above, despite reactions that are right at the center of trauma's wheelhouse. With this trigger warning, this book is actually doing what it describes: enabling readers to better gain access to the topic of trauma and how it affects individuals in the educational system. Echoing the trigger warnings offered by educators, I advise readers that this book may touch chords that hit your psychic trauma–activated tuning fork, and if you know that in advance, you can manage the tuning fork sounds more effectively. If you can name it (trauma), you can begin to tame it.

With that trigger warning in mind, onward, despite the many hurdles that are ahead as we seek to enhance how we address trauma in the educational system. For the record, there is no constructive place to which to go other than forward.

Acknowledgments

Books don't write themselves. This book has been deeply enriched by many remarkable people, most particularly the trauma survivors and those who work with them, all of whom have shared their often painful stories with me. This includes many students and educators. It isn't easy to deal with primary, secondary, and vicarious trauma and its symptomology. Yet many individuals exposed their memories of difficult personal and professional situations and experiences to me. I hope I have done justice to the trust they placed in me. The book also benefited from, and I am grateful to, the many experts who graciously read drafts of the manuscript and offered their wisdom to me.

A special thank-you to Brian Ellerbeck of Teachers College Press who believed I had a second book to write on education and enabled me to bring it to fruition. Thanks also to the editors and designers, all of whom improved this book and the illustrations within it. They helped make the book accessible, including most particularly for visual learners. Finally, since much of my own trauma history is revealed here, I want to thank several individuals for their unwavering support throughout the process of completing this book. They not only heard me but also believed me and enabled me to disclose parts of my past that had been hidden, even from me. And perhaps even more important, they helped me to move forward with both an understanding of my past and hope for the future. To MW, GK, and PR, words are not enough.

Part I

NAMING

CHAPTER 1

What Is Trauma?

Since this book has trauma as its topic and has the word in its title, one might logically assume that a universal definition of trauma exists that would link this book to the many others on the subject, that we should be able to look in a popular dictionary and find a clear, unequivocal definition of *trauma*. But nothing could be further from the truth. Remember the U.S. Supreme Court test, articulated by Justice Potter Stewart in 1964, on identifying pornography? He said, "I know it when I see it."[1] While this may be true for pornography, it is most assuredly not so for trauma. Often trauma goes unseen. It is not seen even by those experiencing it and is not identified by third parties who are in a position to observe and engage with it. A better adage for trauma is "We don't always know it when we see it; it is often, though not always, invisible to the eye."

The absence of a universally accepted definition of trauma leads to confusion on myriad levels. Psychologists and psychiatrists use different definitions from one another and from those used by physicians in addressing physical injuries from accidents and natural disasters. Social workers, child advocates, insurers, and the military also use differing definitions of trauma. Organizations that deal with people who suffer from trauma or that conduct research on trauma have their own definitions, too. While we don't need a universal definition applicable to all situations, we do need to be clear about which definitions are used in what context and the reasons for the differing definitions as well as the shortcomings of some common ones.

We are presented with the following four realities, which will be described in greater detail later:

1. Some of the approaches to and categorizations of trauma now in use in defining trauma are deeply flawed, debilitating our efforts to address trauma treatment effectively and recognize and perceive trauma.
2. If we can't agree on defining the term *trauma*, agreeing on treatment and healing options as well as their outcomes is problematic.
3. If we don't have consensus on what trauma is, assessment devices to detect or confirm trauma in an individual are at once confusing and

overlapping, hampering data-informed decisionmaking and further research.

4. If we put physical trauma in one box and psychic trauma in another, we miss how each informs the other and how engagement goes in both directions. Trauma affects the body; physical injury affects the mind; and subsequent events can trigger either the psychic sphere, the physical sphere, or both.[2]

At Least We Can Agree That . . .

To steal a phrase from James Ryan's inspiring book *Wait, What?*, there are at least three things, before we turn to definitional differences, virtually everyone agrees on across the disciplines and American society about trauma.[3]

However we define trauma, it has a profound impact. First, we know that traumatic events experienced by the young usually have the greatest psychic impact because the brain develops rapidly in early life.[4] Thus, addressing trauma from early childhood through the elementary school years is critical. Our interventions at this stage can make a profound difference, especially in a threatening environment. Raids by immigration officers can be terrifying to children, who pick up the sense of danger through their parents, communities, and television. These children anticipate the loss of their parents or caregivers and they feel, and indeed are, threatened. Stability, structure, safety, subtlety, and someone to care for them are jeopardized. These latter five elements, which I call the five *S*s, will be addressed at length later in the book when we examine their importance and how to foster their presence in an educational setting, which is particularly significant if they are missing in the home environment or larger community.

Second, we can all agree that trauma happens *to* someone; it is not something a person inflicts on him- or herself and for which one is responsible. As expressed by Mona Delahooke, we miss this very point because we assume that children who act out have volitional control of their actions.[5] We need to remember children did not choose their parents; they did not choose their socioeconomic status or their race; they did not deliberately put themselves in harm's way; and they did not choose their ethnicity or religion or gender. They did not select their schools. Instead of blaming trauma survivors, then, for the harmful, difficult, or tragic circumstances in which they find themselves, we should steer them on a path forward where they are not blamed, made to feel guilty, or punished. The use of the word *victim* here might seem appropriate, but it is too charged a term; perhaps we can agree to use variations on *trauma*, describing affected individuals as *those traumatized*, *those affected by trauma*, *trauma-affected individuals*, or *trauma-affected students*. Despite our seemingly general agreement that children are not responsible for their adverse circumstances, our behavior often contradicts such a belief, including most vibrantly in our educational system.

As to this last point, we often make assumptions about behavior, though we know better, and fail to ask the *why* question, another James Ryan insight. We witness untoward, outsize, out-of-the-norm behavior and do not ask the person—in the most thoughtful, nonthreatening way—"Can you share why you did that?" Just asking the *why* question is a good starting point for reflection. Many traumatized people who "act out" and are then asked the *why* question before any intervention can provide an answer. They may not know the complete reasons for their actions, but they likely can share something about what is happening in and to their lives. People struggling can sense the answer to the *why* question.

Third, we can also agree that trauma can be transferred: People who deal with traumatized individuals or traumatic events (such as emergency medical service workers and teachers following a school shooting or legal staff representing and defending detained children) become traumatized themselves. Adult-onset trauma, such as that of a parent in the military who returns from a war zone, affects the family of the traumatized person.[6] Another example of trauma's tentacles. Let's be blunt. The fact that trauma often goes unnoticed, unlabeled, and untreated does not mean it does not exist. Sometimes it hides from us; other times we do not have a name for what is happening to us or those around us.

On These We Should Agree

There are other topics, of which six are identified here, about which we *should* agree but do not:

How to treat individuals acting outside the norm. Educational establishments, mental health facilities, the justice system, and community and social service organizations too often treat noncompliant individuals with reprimands, punishments, or other kinds of discipline, to point out to them the distinction between right and wrong and the need to *pivot right* (i.e., move in the right direction), a term explored in depth in *Breakaway Learners* and used positively through choice architecture, the latter being an approach for enabling better decisionmaking through nudges and role modeling among other options.

By way of example, traumatized individuals (all individuals actually) are threatened with surgery for not losing weight or not being medically compliant when instead they need a helping hand. In a personal example, when I refused to take statins, the cardiologist said, "You're a stroke waiting to happen, and I don't want to take care of something you can control," despite my risk of stroke being lower than that of the average person over 10 years and with so little plaque in my arteries that it could not be precisely measured. Might he have acted differently had he known that I had suffered from trauma that resulted from untimely and unfortunate loss and separation? Might he have recognized how threatening his words were to me? Suppose he had taken the time to know me personally and conduct a trauma history. To be handed a ticket to die (an invalid one at that) by a professional is not exactly trauma sensitive, to understate the situation.

Adults who are traumatized and act out are sometimes considered for placement in a mental health facility because their behavior is seen as aberrant and intractable, when what they need is a trauma-sensitive therapist. Traumatized students are suspended from school when school is exactly where they should be. Sending these students home exacerbates the problem and enables a repetition of the troubling behavior within schools for days on end. Young students are placed in lower or remedial classes when what they need is teachers' recognition of their strengths, not their weaknesses. Those who act out are denied access to services and told to return when they can "behave"—and they are told this at precisely the moment when those services are so central to their well-being. Here's just one statistic that should frighten us: Every day 250 preschoolers are expelled from their schools.[7] Ask yourselves: What did these youngsters do to lead to such a draconian outcome? I can't even imagine.

Traumatized people should not be stigmatized. We ascribe negative connotations to trauma. People who have experienced trauma often hold it within themselves, as if sharing it will reflect badly on them, be embarrassing, or otherwise change how they are perceived. Ponder how this stigma is similar to how cancer was, and sometimes still is, perceived. If cancer patients share their condition, they were/are concerned that others will look at them differently, forgetting who they were before their diagnosis. Some worry that people will shy away from them because they have the Big C disease. They think, "Who wants to deal with someone who is dying?" Also, cancer patients are often suffering enough. They do not want others' sympathy or pity; rather, they want love and attention and connections. They want to be treated as "normal." And there is the blame game. If the person did not smoke or work in an asbestos-ridden factory or come from an unfortunate gene pool, he or she would not have cancer. Guilt comes into play.

In a distinction worth observing, though I suspect it is not in the minds (at least consciously) of those who engage with traumatized individuals, we know that a cancer patient who shares his or her illness is not sharing the disease itself. Perhaps it was different decades ago. Now we know that cancer, unlike many other diseases, is not catching. It does not move from person to person through contact. (Yes, it may be genetically transmitted.) However, trauma *can* be transmitted—those who engage with traumatized individuals can experience the trauma themselves, particularly if they have the psychic equivalent of an overactive immune system. If teachers, social workers, psychologists, or physicians have themselves been traumatized, their encounters with a traumatized person can retrigger responses in them. That risk is not ephemeral. That said, at least at a conscious level, I do not think that is the major reason that we shy away from traumatized individuals, and that's because we don't recognize secondary and vicarious trauma risks sufficiently, as discussed in Chapter 5.

Trauma is not curable. Some have argued that post-traumatic stress disorder need not be a lifelong state. In a sense, it is like cancer in that it can go into remission, only to reappear.[8] Indeed, many say trauma cannot be "cured"; it can be managed. Unfortunately, we assume that trauma is unlike cancer and is like a broken leg or a gallstone that once properly treated goes away. Little or no residual effect. Some psychiatrists even see post-traumatic stress that way. We approach an affected person as if he or she could be restored to the pre-trauma state. We make this mistake with soldiers all the time. We believe that their psychic injuries can be cured in the same way their physical injuries can be. Then we are shocked when they struggle with readjusting to civilian life—and we are shocked by veterans' suicide rates. We are shocked by military families that can't adjust to the return of their loved one after months away.

The conclusion that trauma can be cured is damaging and untrue. Stated simply, trauma does not go away. It is deeply etched in our psyche and evidenced in permanent changes to our brain structure. Yes, the brain is plastic and does workarounds—remarkable ones—but trauma is always with us literally and figuratively.[9] That is not always a bad thing, as discussed later in the book in Chapters 3 and 4. But make no mistake: There is no going back once trauma strikes. The immediacy of symptomology may wane or go undercover, but one owns one's trauma forever.

The preceding observations indicate that we need a shared understanding that trauma is more than a moment in time in which behaviors are exhibited and intervention is provided and then we are cured. Instead, we must recognize that trauma is a concept, a state of being, which stays with a person. Trauma travels with a person from early childhood through the educational system and through adulthood. Think of it as a suitcase that people carry everywhere, an image repeated in this book. Further, trauma is cumulative, and it can and often is retriggered and intensified by fresh traumatic events, which in turn reactivate older trauma.[10] In essence, the trauma suitcase grows heavier. For children, with their lives ahead of them, the opportunities for retriggering trauma are multiple. A student can experience trauma again and again; it is not as if the student starts with a clean slate when he or she enrolls in a new school. Students carry their suitcases to college and into the workplace and relationships.

Reflect on the confirmation hearings for Brent Kavanaugh for U.S. Supreme Court Justice.[11] For many students who are women and girls (and some males, too), the hearings revived memories from their own sexual past, including early childhood sexual abuse. We now know, too, that girls and women experience trauma differently from and suffer PTSD more frequently than their male counterparts.[12] Questions of memory, consent, early sexuality (voluntary or involuntary), and interactions with fellow students all surfaced and resurfaced, meaning that the processing of the actual hearing for listeners was not confined to present-day issues of who should sit on the U.S. Supreme Court. Schools and colleges had to deal with these issues, although many were underprepared to address trauma symptomology and its recurring impact. I recall offering to write on this (which I did in the *New England Journal of Higher Education* in October 2018), and one prominent higher education publication rejected my piece and suggested that the effects of the hearings would not be felt for years, that the hearing held no immediacy for listeners. Wrong. Just plain wrong.

We need to talk about trauma. We hold many assumptions about human behavior, and those of us who work in educational institutions or medical facilities too often fail to attribute behaviors to trauma because we have not defined or focused on trauma as a cause. Maybe we worry, unconsciously, that trauma is too close to our own psychic home to engage with directly. Perhaps, too, we fear that addressing it head-on will worsen the impact; even just using the word will have a negative impact. Such trepidation is misguided, and resembles how we feel about suicide and handle talking about it to someone who is suicidal. We think, "Best not to raise the subject or use the word." However, raising it is an established quality intervention. Indeed, one remarkable means for ameliorating trauma symptoms is human reciprocity—engagement, the precise opposite of what we tend to practice, out of fear, lack of knowledge, or respect for privacy.[13] Human reciprocity is also a central feature of lasticity and, as noted in *Breakaway Learners*, a component of student success.

We must approach trauma differently. Since many turn a blind eye to trauma, our responses and approaches—generated by institutional, societal, and governmental culture—need to be modified if not overhauled. Trauma survivors can't enact that massive overhaul; it is the obligation of those working in institutions, government offices, and other workplaces, and in both the public and the private sectors, to make changes. In the educational sector, the onus is on educators and their organizations, not on students. Students did not cause the trauma, and while they can work to help themselves, they need a culture that is geared toward helping them to not just survive but thrive.

No one professional discipline owns trauma treatment. This final point is one on which we should but do not have a shared consensus. We should acknowledge that, to paraphrase an overused and underappreciated adage, it takes a village to deal with trauma. It takes psychologists and psychiatrists, doctors and nurses, educators, religious figures, family, and social service providers. Trauma treatment is multidisciplinary. One wonders if it is out of convenience or more like the children's game hot potato to slot it into a single silo. And reflect on where traumatized students spend most of their time: in school. Ignoring how schools deal with trauma is a massive missed opportunity.

The Word Itself

We begin our quest for a definition of *trauma* by looking at the origins of the word and then, after examining numerous definitional approaches, conclude with a definition tailored to the educational arena and used throughout this book. One might ask, Why not just start with the definition of trauma used here and skip all the rest of the different definitions from different disciplines and perspectives? If we did that, we would be cheating ourselves out of what can be learned by assessing how these are flawed and misrepresent or fail to capture the complexities and difficulties of adverse experiences.

The word *trauma* derives from the Greek for "physical wound." Many dictionaries distinguish between the medical definition of trauma (physical injury, befitting the word's Greek root) and the psychological definition (emotional injury). This dichotomy is problematic from the get-go, because it treats brain science as if it was not a part of medicine and suggests that psychic trauma is separate from physical well-being, when these spheres are deeply connected, and most assuredly in the context of trauma.

The Medical Definition

Medicine sees trauma as physical injury caused by an external force—whether nature, an object, or other human beings. Thus we categorize hospitals based on the level of trauma they treat.[14] If one is severely injured physically, one wants and needs access to the highest level of trauma care, at a Level I trauma center (the most expensive provider, too). The four levels generate considerable debate about how many of each we need in given communities and which designations should be adjusted upward or downward based on preset criteria.[15] Add to this that we distinguish between adult and child medical trauma care, and a medical facility could have different levels depending on who is being treated—Level I for certain patients and Level II for others.[16]

The medical definition—physical injury per se—is *not* what this book addresses, though physical manifestations do result from psychological trauma. Indeed, we cannot ignore the physiological impacts, as they affect not just individual well-being but also the costs of health care delivery into the future. Heart disease, COPD, and diabetes are expensive. Further, those with massive physical trauma, the kind treated at a Level I trauma center, can develop psychological trauma both immediately and later on as a result of their medical trauma. So if you once experienced acute physical trauma and later needed medical care in a hospital setting for something "non-traumatic," that care and its effectiveness can be affected by the earlier trauma. If doctors recognized the prior trauma through trauma-informed care, the patient would benefit.

To be clear, this book does address the physical symptoms and effects of psychological trauma; making a sharp distinction between physical and psychological trauma creates a false dichotomy.

A Psychological Definition

In reflecting on the psychological definition of trauma, we need to start with this question: Are we bound to the precise definitions in the *Diagnostic and Statistical Manual of Mental Disorders* (*DSM*), which have changed over time?[17] I think the answer, at least for this book, is no. We are not looking at the requirements to be met for medical insurance reimbursement; nor are we necessarily confining trauma to being an identified mental disorder, something of a stigmatizing term. We want an approach that recognizes trauma syndromes, toxic stress, and psychological distress, whether or not they fit the *DSM*'s strict categories and subcategories.

The point of this book is not to see trauma as a mental disease, a disorder, or stigmatizing. Indeed, I would argue that many responses to trauma are not emblematic of a disorder at all. They are, at least in some instances, highly understandable and predictable behaviors that are not aberrant or disordered in the least. True, they are impactful in many ways that can, if unremediated, produce ongoing hurdles that interfere with successful functioning. But there is a reason the *D* came off the acronym PTSD (post-traumatic stress disorder) in military and some psychiatric circles.

Trauma and Traumatic Responses

We need to start with an important distinction: There are traumatic events and then there are individual responses to those traumas. (We will develop a more nuanced approach to the concept of events and a method for categorizing them that improves our understanding of trauma.) This distinction matters, even before we reflect on the types of symptoms generated in individuals, the subject of Chapter 3. Not every person exposed to or experiencing trauma exhibits a response, and not all responses rise to the level of trauma symptomology. In essence, there are three parts to the trauma equation: (1) traumatic events (though not for all); (2) responses to those events (though not for all); and (3) some of those responses leading to and manifesting as trauma symptomology. If one has all three—if we add the pieces together—then treatment and remediation are needed.

Responses to traumatic events differ from person to person, as does the symptomology, when exhibited. What *should* be our focus is not based solely on the presence of traumatic events per se (the number of hurricanes or the amount of drug addiction or the likelihood of contracting a dangerous virus), but rather on the categorization of responses, if any, that individuals have to these events. Indeed, perhaps one could go as far as to suggest that something is *not* traumatic for a particular individual if it does not produce responses that can be identified as trauma symptomology. In essence, if the just-described three-part equation is broken, intervention is not needed. The necessary corollary to these observations is that subjectivity reigns supreme in the context of trauma. A big event—say, a plane crash or a school shooting or the fall of the Twin Towers—may not be traumatic for everyone, in different locations, although it certainly is for those in direct proximity (physically or through connections). Conversely, a small event—such as receiving a caustic verbal response, a nasty online comment, or a bad grade—can be traumatic for some individuals because of their preexisting life experiences and current circumstances.

Look again at the vignettes in the preface. An airplane engine blowing out and then an emergency landing with injuries can be experienced very differently by different people. Not everyone on that plane would necessarily be traumatized, deserving a diagnosis found in the *DSM*. For some, it would be seen as a lucky outcome, in that the passengers and crew were mostly safe. Some passengers, though, would focus on the injured persons on the plane, and for those passengers, who may have had previous experience with unexpected and disruptive injuries, the impact of the event would have been great. If individuals experienced the mishap as a trauma, their manifestations would be different. For someone with separation anxiety or for whom death is a particularly difficult issue, there could be a response of fear. For an individual with deep religious convictions, the event might signal hope. For someone who had recently been in a car accident or a natural disaster, this new event with the plane could retrigger memories of the prior events.

Now reflect on the 1st- and 5th-graders described in two of the vignettes. Exposure to violence and a decrease in personal safety have an effect on a child. They lead to a sense of threat, and a child's actual brain architecture is changed as a result, leading to profound aftereffects that can be seen in the home, in school, and later in adult relationships. Think changes in neural pathways for starters, including the failure of some pathways to even be created, let alone later pruned. Unlike with the airplane incident, children who are subject to abuse may not know that what they are experiencing is trauma, especially if the abuse is cumulative and commonplace in their home. For these children, what others see as trauma is normal to them; they've normalized the abnormal. That is where the term *gaslighting* comes into play; some children have been so exposed to traumatic behavior that they think that is how all people live and feel and do not see any distinctions between their homes and the homes of many of the other children in school. These children live in a state in which their autonomic nervous system is always on full alert.

In sum, responses to traumatic events are diverse, nuanced, and sometimes impossible to predict or recognize. It's just not like pornography à la Justice Stewart.

A Flawed Distinction

People have often divided trauma into big *T* trauma, namely, events that are single major disasters, like floods, hurricanes, school shootings, and war; and small *t* trauma, day-to-day accumulated negative events, like homelessness, food scarcity, and parental drug addiction, that affect well-being.[18] Although I have used this very distinction in *Breakaway Learners* to better understand the experiences of students, I see it as increasingly problematic and facile, albeit convenient and commonplace.[19] Look at the events described in the preface. The first four are arguably big *T* trauma, and the last two are small *t* trauma. But these distinctions don't hold.

Here's why: The big/small distinction is soft at the margins, and perhaps even at its center.[20] Is sexual harassment or rape a big *T* trauma or a small *t* trauma? Are the distinctions between repeated step-parent sexual abuse of a child and a single instance of date rape worth labeling differently, the former as small *t* trauma and the latter as big *T* trauma? Does it even matter which label a particular trauma receives? Small *t* trauma, despite its diminutive-sounding label, is anything but small in impact. As one author observed, there is no such thing as "little trauma."[21] It's like saying one is a little pregnant. An event occurs and then we attach a label to it: *trauma*, not a touch of trauma as one would say about a cold or the flu (I have a touch of a cold is a possible characterization of one's physical health). Indeed, some have argued that small *t* trauma is more impactful long term than big *T* trauma, although I suspect that conclusion is both situation and person dependent. Certainly, small *t* trauma is often present in students in the earlier grades. Moreover, a person can experience both big *T* and small *t* trauma simultaneously or sequentially. Cumulative trauma of any sort is debilitating. To plant a seed for a set of ideas that are forthcoming: Reflect on ACEs (Adverse Childhood Experience scores) as a measure only of small *t* trauma as that test is presently configured.

Returning to the examples in the preface, the initial three are arguably big *T* trauma, although the consequences will not be big for everyone. But the last two items, while definitionally small *t* trauma, are big for virtually any child. And rape, as discussed, has aspects of big *T* trauma and small *t* trauma. The college student who is raped repeatedly is experiencing small *t* trauma by definition, but the amalgamation of the rapes leads to big *T* trauma for the entire campus.

Here is what is truly problematic. The individuals with the small *t* trauma, in the last three examples, may experience the first three examples as big *T* trauma, and that reality will affect their response. It is not as if big *T* trauma affects only those who were previously untraumatized. And those who experience small *t* trauma are not immune from big *T* trauma. At that point, we have to ask if the distinction has any meaning, except in the most generalized context. Stated another way, what is big for one person is small for another, and given the subjectivity of trauma responses, we'd be wise to limit the categorizations of big *T* and small *t*, lest we become confused over what matters.

An Alternate Approach

What if we replaced the notion of big *T* trauma and small *t* trauma with a new schematic that focused on events and their categorization and then, critically, the consequences that flowed from particular categorizations? That is, the basic terminology remains stable, namely the word "event." What changes is how an individual responds to the event.

Start by dividing events in life as Events (big *E*) and events (small *e*). Events (big *E*) are those that will, without question, produce a traumatic response, and they will then, in the vast majority of cases, lead to trauma symptomology. Easy examples of a big *E* event are plane, train, and bus crashes with many deaths among the passengers. For surviving passengers, this is an Event. It may also be an Event for families, friends, and others who connect to the incident. A nuclear attack or missile strike is a big *E* event. Its impact will be felt as a big *E* event for those near and far, as it presents real risks to personal safety. A massive flood with loss of lives, homes, and communities is a big *E* event for both those in the region and people connected to these individuals and the region.

Big *E* events also include events that are one-time or repeated circumstances that lead to the disruption of a sense of safety, attachment, and stability (especially for a child). Among the examples are sexual abuse, including rape (a single incident or multiple rapes or rape by multiple attackers); homelessness; food scarcity; and the mental illness, imprisonment, suicide, or fatal illness of a parent or other caregiver. Bullying and harassment, whether based on sexual orientation or difference in ability or physical difference such as weight, are big *E* events for the child or adult experiencing them. Notice that in the commonly accepted categorizations described above (big *T* and small *t*), bullying and harassment would be small *t* trauma, but they are not small events, as noted. Calling them "small" leads to misunderstandings and maladaptive resolutions. They are big in every sense. This approach moves the items on ACE tests (as discussed later) from little *t* to big *E*.

Stated simply, big *E* events cause responses that usually produce and are emblematic of trauma symptomology. Hold that thought.

Now turn to small *e* events. These are plentiful. These are events that occur in our day-to-day lives that may or may not be traumatic, depending on circumstances, the life experience of an individual, and context. Assume that a student gets a bad grade anywhere along the educational pipeline, a common event. For some students, this is no big deal. It does not cut them to the core, it does not destabilize them, and it is not internalized as a deep personal failure to meet personal and external expectations. However, for some students a bad grade can be devastating. It may be evidence that they are a failure, it may lead to parental punishment, it may threaten participation on an athletic team, it may lead to a change of classes, and it may eliminate a career option. For nursing students, failure in the course Anatomy and Physiology likely means they will never progress along a nursing curriculum and graduate. For another STEM (science, technology, engineering, and mathematics) student who is taking the course as one of a host of fundamental courses, it has no long-term career consequences, as the course can be retaken and the student can learn from the experience.

A nonfatal car crash is commonplace and is another small *e* event. For many, while inconvenient and a pain in the proverbial rear end (pun intended), this is not a big deal. The car can be repaired with relative ease, a loaner car can be arranged, and everything will return to normal shortly—albeit with a likely increase in car insurance rates. No biggie. But if one is 16 years old and has just gotten one's license, a car crash feels enormous. There is a feeling of guilt and the memory of the horrific sounds of the collision, and one's parents may take away one's license. And if the crash involves someone who recently lost a parent or had a friend die in a car crash or for whom this is the third accident in a short period of time, it is experienced as a big *E* event, even though it is not so in any objective schematic.

With this new approach in mind, think about Figure 1.1., demonstrating visually how Events/events play out in the context of trauma responses and trauma symptomology. What this chart demonstrates is that some things are traumatic for everyone (virtually) and produce traumatic symptoms. These are big *E* events. Other events are traumatic for only some people, not others. These are small *e* events, where the outcome is subjective. That does not convert small *e* events into big *E* events. No, what happens is that what is experienced because of a small *e* event differs from person to person. Unlike the big *T* and small *t* distinction and division, this Event/event characterization is based on the nature of the events, the likely responses to them, and the possibility that some events are not problematic for everyone. In practice, Figure 1.1 demonstrates the complexity of trauma but also the difficulty for teachers or physicians of knowing enough about their students or patients to identify what they are feeling and experiencing.

Figure 1.1. Categorizing Trauma

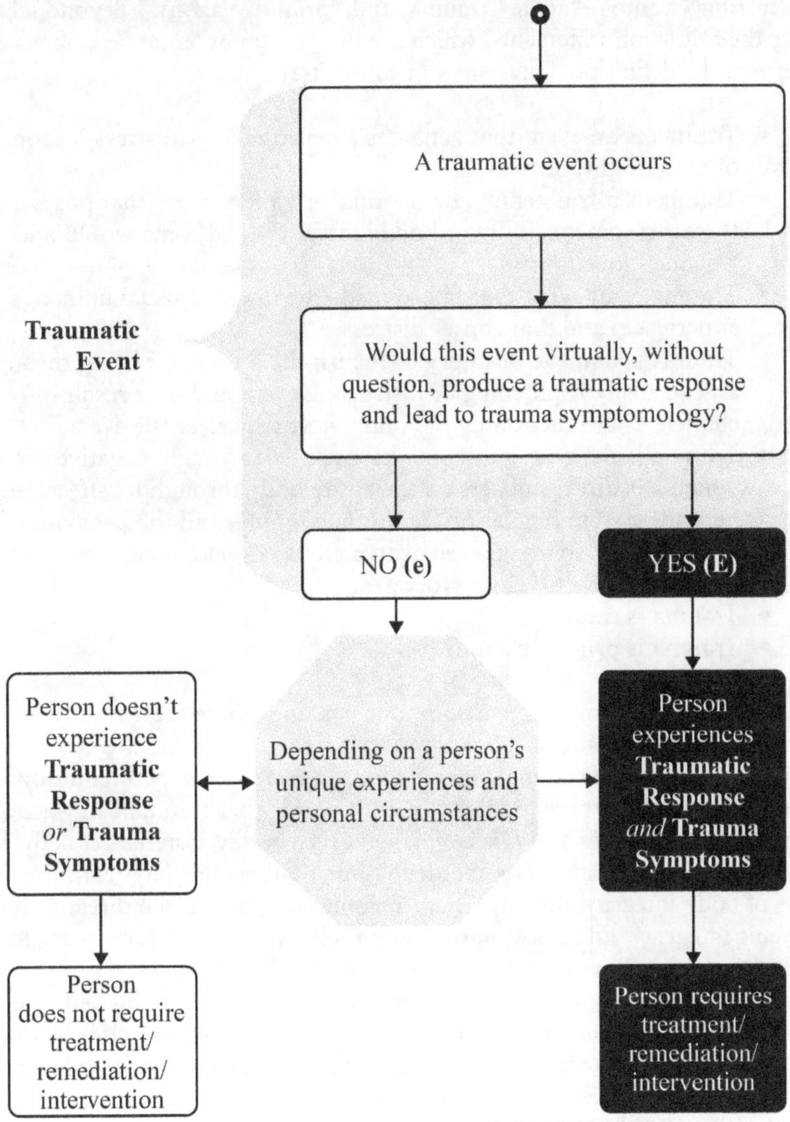

Definitional Diversity

Moving away from big *T* and small *t* trauma, other labels exist. Some highlight differences between adult and child responses. Others get at big and small and constant or cumulative through still other labels. Consider the examples of "complex" trauma, "massive adult-onset" trauma, "developmental" trauma, "recurring" trauma, "acute" trauma, and "primitive agony." Beyond labels, take the following statements, which are by no means comprehensive, as evidence of the definitional diversity of trauma itself:[22]

- Trauma is an event that activates a neurobiological stress response of fight, flight, or freeze.
- Trauma is a frightening, dangerous, or violent event that poses a threat to someone's life or bodily integrity (and some would add "to one's loved ones").
- Trauma is an event that falls outside the range of usual human experience, and that causes distress.
- Trauma is damage or injury to the psyche after one's living through an extremely frightening or distressing event and may result in challenges in functioning or coping normally after the event.
- Trauma is the body's internal response to a strongly negative event, which has direct impacts on the entire body through its effects on nervous system regulation, brain functioning, and the behavior of other body systems, as well as to a child's development, sense of safety, and identity going forward.
- Trauma is trauma.
- Trauma is primitive agony.

Without going into great depth, one can appreciate the vast differences between these definitions. Some are too narrow and some are too broad. Some miss aspects of trauma. Fight, flight, and freeze are only three autonomic responses, when there are many more *f* words that trauma can generate, among them *flocking* and *fainting*, when other bodily systems get activated moments or hours later. For the definitions that require physical injury or loss of body integrity, there is a huge missing component: the threat to one's psychic integrity and safety, one's sense of self. Not every trauma is frightening, dangerous, or violent, as the discussion of Event/event shows; trauma can be generated by other causes, such as humiliation, loss of self-esteem, or distrust. Then some of the definitions suffer from being self-referential, defining trauma by using the word *trauma* as if its repetition provided clarification. Surely we can see that not every distressing event is traumatic. We can be distressed by the weather, wearing the wrong clothes to an event, giving the wrong gift, or forgetting a birthday or anniversary. These are small *e* events—unless they become big *E* events because of an individual's personal experiences and context.

Finally, trauma is not limited to primitive brain responses. The first response to trauma is not located in the brain exactly—it is situated in the autonomic nervous system, our system of sympathetic and parasympathetic nerves, with added messaging through hormones delivered by the bloodstream. The fight, flight, or freeze responses originate in this system. Later, trauma symptoms are evidenced in different parts of the brain, often beyond our control but not autonomic in the same sense as that of the nervous system. Trauma affects, then, different parts of the lower brain, the limbic system, and cognitive function but not necessarily all together and often in a sequence in which initial responses are followed by later symptomology.

A Definition for the Educational Context

There is no perfect definition. What matters here is that our definition addresses the impact of trauma on our *educational system*. This means it needs to be broad enough to cover a wide range of students, from the very young to adults. And it needs to encompass the secondary and vicarious trauma that educators can experience from the work they do with children or adults with trauma. It needs to be narrow, in the sense that it does not need to cover extensively or in detail trauma that is caused by the workplace. Nor does it need to address the epigenetic transmission of trauma. For the purposes of this book, therefore, I provide the following definition:

> Trauma is any significant psychologically distressing experience, including acts of omission and commission and regardless of whether these experiences are recognized by those who encounter them, occurring at any point or points in the life of a person that have the probability of disrupting his or her learning success and quality educational outcomes in an ongoing manner throughout the person's participation in the educational system.

Assessment Devices and Definitions of Trauma

Notwithstanding the definitional issues just described, there are more than 30 different tests, quizzes, and other diagnostic devices to determine if an individual is likely to experience or is currently experiencing trauma.[23] Some of these assessment devices are predictive of the likelihood of trauma symptomology over the near or longer term. Others measure current trauma symptomology to determine whether an individual is traumatized and needs intervention. Some are designed for adults; some are geared toward children; some must be administered by medical personnel; and others can be used by trained (or even untrained) social workers, community-based workers, and educators. There are lots of cautions in administering these assessments, particularly in unintentionally creating situations that retraumatize individuals by ignoring race, gender, ethnicity, age, context, and trust, among other variables.[24] Sadly, too, we mistake a predictor with a definitive statement of an outcome.

ACEs

Leaving aside for the moment issues of personal privacy, storage of the results of assessments, and cyber- and other security risks, there is a test that has attracted enormous attention in many circles: the Adverse Childhood Experiences (ACEs) questionnaire. This test, developed decades ago through a partnership between a private insurer and the federal government, presents 10 questions to adults about their childhood. In essence, the test measures small *t* trauma, a problematic categorization, as noted. It measures family-based, continual, cumulative adverse events like sexual abuse within the family, absence of sufficient food, and physical punishment, also familial.

As will be addressed below, this is a test that, despite its shortcomings, should be taken by every educator in the United States, regardless of the age of the children or adults he or she is educating. (Note: The assertion here is *not* that every teacher or administrator should give it to every child.) The score is self-generated and, based on existing and duplicated quality research, determinative of the risks the test taker has in various arenas: medical issues; educational outcomes; success or failure in relationships; and potential for psychological disorders leading to addiction, depression, or suicide. As I will describe later, the findings are frightening. Remember, though, that the ACEs produce predictive, not definitive, findings.

One important additional note before revealing the test outcomes: The initial test takers of the ACE questionnaire were predominantly White, middle-class individuals with some college education who were able to pay for private health insurance. They were offered the test because standard efforts to reduce obesity were not working well, and the insurer offering the test wanted to determine why these individuals (as a group) were struggling so mightily with their weight. The population that was originally tested has led some to conclude that the impact of ACEs on low-income, diverse populations with low educational attainment levels would be even more devastating, so the data presented needed to be viewed as minimums, not maximums.

The test, which is available to take online, has a scoring system in which one wants a lower score—the higher the score, the more exposure one has had to traumatic events that **can** (not will) lead to adverse consequences long term. Any score over 4 (the highest score is 10) increases the likelihood of adverse outcomes. In the original test, 12.5% of the test takers had a score of 4 or higher. One could call the test a predictive device, showing how higher ACEs reflect a higher probability of negative outcomes. Estimates are that almost half the children in the United States have at least a score of 1. Slightly over 20% of children have at least a score of 2. The numbers go up for those in the lowest socioeconomic quartile (income of less than 200% of the poverty level). Nadine Burke Harris's book summarizes these findings, and they are readily available online as well, including at www.

acesconnection.com/blog/got-your-ace-resilience-scores. For the record, as I have publicly disclosed, I have a score of 7.

Delving into these scores, we see disparate impacts within socioeconomic groups and among different races. Gender can affect outcomes too, as can demographic data that are unmeasured by ACEs, like ethnicity, age, and the community context. So ACE scores are far from a complete measure, and there have been movements to expand and alter the questions to make the results more comprehensive. While the test is generally administered to adults (new parents are a key cohort), there are efforts to have teenagers take a version of it. Some are even suggesting that it can be given to children, even young children.

Despite the shortcomings of the ACE test including that it pathologizes trauma, it does yield valuable data. Here's a sampling of that data for those with a score of at least 4, without statistically regressing for protective variables that can affect outcomes materially (note too that many of these numbers reflect co-occurrences):[25]

- Twice as likely to be a smoker;
- 7 times more likely to be an alcoholic;
- 390% more likely to have chronic emphysema;
- 1,200% more likely to attempt suicide;
- 10 times more likely to have injected street drugs;
- 240% more likely to have sexually transmitted disease; and
- 460% more likely to become depressed.

If you have an ACE score over 6, there is a likelihood that your life span will be shortened by 2 decades.

ACEs Caveats

An increasing amount of work is being done to counter the effects of ACEs with an investigation of curative or protective factors that can decrease the risks and ameliorate the outcomes of ACEs.[26] Some suggest tests that measure only protective factors (positive childhood experiences, or PCEs, detailed in Chapter 12); others suggest PACEs (Positive and Adverse Childhood Experience score), a test that combines the original ACE questions with protective questions.[27] The theory in part is that this will ease the difficulty and sense of doom that can accompany taking the ACE test and the ways in which it has been used.

Notwithstanding criticism of the ACE test, some states are mandating that it be administered, an effort to improve childhood outcomes but one fraught with interpretative and policy implications.[28] Some states are pushing for the use of the ACE questionnaire or a variant of it, particularly in physicians' offices, for teenagers and new or prospective parents.

In sum, for a goodly number of people, the ACE measures are the unassailable gold standard.[29] They aren't. But—and that's a big but, as now detailed, they can provide powerful insights.

Educators

The noted child trauma scholar Christina Bethell observed, "Just last month, in another state, out of a room of 600 early care, home visiting, special health care needs specialists and health system and education professionals, fewer than 30 raised their hand to my questions on whether they had ever heard of the ACEs study."[30] I have experienced similar situations. I have spoken to educators in a state where a major trauma had just occurred. Many had never heard of ACEs. I have conducted trauma workshops in schools with an at-risk population and have found that few teachers are aware of ACEs. And in higher education, the lack of awareness of ACEs is astounding, as it also is among highly educated professionals in criminal justice, social services, and nursing and other health fields. Among community service workers, there is also little recognition of ACEs. Perhaps the only field in which I have seen remarkable, consistent progress, not legally mandated progress, in addressing ACEs is that of social work, in part because social workers are front-line soldiers in efforts to help others in need.

Yes, the ACE test is not the be-all and end-all of assessment tools. But it offers a critically important opportunity for educators to self-assess and then see the score they themselves receive. If teachers read the questions and understand that they may have experienced one or more adverse childhood events, this could dramatically shift how they view both themselves and their students. My experience of taking the test and watching others take it has allowed me to better appreciate students' situations. Personal light-bulb moments. In a sense, a self-awareness of trauma makes educators cognizant of not only their own trauma but also the trauma of others, most particularly their students. Once one starts seeing trauma, whether in oneself or others, and reads some of the key data on the effects of that trauma, one is changed. From what previously was an uninformed lens on one's students, one develops a new perspective. Teachers will start to see their students differently; ask questions about their homes; listen differently to their stories; and look differently at their writing, playing, art, movements, and expressions.

The obvious temptation is to administer the test to students and to their parents. I am often asked whether we should do this and if not, why not. For starters, many teachers are not trauma trained. So administering the test is not in their wheelhouse, let alone interpreting the results and understanding the needed interventions. I worry about how the results will be used (I worry about that for all tests), I worry about whether they will remain in a student's permanent file, and I worry that children with high scores will be stigmatized or grouped together or subjected to disparate treatment.

But if educators just read the test (and perhaps now the PACEs version), they would be better able to ask the right questions, observe behavior differently, and handle students in a new manner. Both can be found (without automatic scoring) on this website: probaway.wordpress.com/tag/pce-positive-childhood-experiences/. Teacher recognition of this sort is really a first and major step in transforming a school into being trauma informed—on its way to becoming trauma responsive and skilled. Call ACE measures a door opener—as in one's seeing light one did not know existed before. And as one or before one reflects on the stories in Chapter 2, my suggestion is that readers first take either the ACE or the PACE test, remembering that a score is not destiny.

The focus on ACEs notwithstanding, here's a caution: Let's not redefine or replace the words "trauma aware" or "trauma sensitive" with "ACE aware" or "ACE sensitive," as ACEs miss way too many aspects of trauma to be viewed as a term identical to and substitutive for trauma, even if the acronym is better sounding.

We now move to three short vignettes detailing trauma in the educational arena, allowing us to see how the definition laid out in this chapter can be applied, reflect on how to identify the trauma responses that the Events/events would generate, and then project how trauma's symptomology is evidenced—in our brains, bodies, and thoughts—and why.

CHAPTER 2

Trauma in Action

Consider the following three scenarios with which I have been involved, albeit in different roles. At first blush, they appear quite similar, but when deconstructed, they demonstrate different aspects of trauma in an educational setting and our responses to them. They also set the stage for Chapters 3 and 4, on trauma symptomology—its origins and manifestations—and then enable our progression to Part II, which develops usable approaches for trauma amelioration.

Scenario 1

We habitually have drills for fire, shootings and other threats to safety to prepare for impending disasters at every level across the educational pipeline. If you are in California or other earthquake-prone states, you may experience the once-a-year specialized earthquake drill, the date of which is announced in advance. With the exception of the Great California ShakeOut Drills (www.shakeout.org/california/) just mentioned, drills typically occur more than once at various intervals during the academic year and without warning. The drills are regulated by state mandates, with some notable differences between the states. For virtually all drills, a sound (such as a harsh, intermittent buzzer) is heard and then a voice (often prerecorded) comes over a public address system, telling everyone to vacate the premises of the school or college. The no-nonsense voice is firm and clear. These are real-life drills—not virtual experiences.

I experienced one such drill at an elementary school where I have been the artist in residence for 4 years. The affected students all went out into the Vermont winter and stood on the school's circular driveway, right next to the large school building. Had there been an actual fire emergency, we would all have been burned to death or been hit by debris, but such realities are not experienced at the conscious level. The students went out without their coats (teachers shared our shawls and sweaters). School personnel with clipboards checked that all the students in attendance that day were present, noting if a student was in a different group from that indicated for him or her in the paperwork. When we reentered the building some 20 minutes later, it was back to class, as if nothing had happened. No conversation was held about the drill.

Scenario 2

Students from PreK to 12th grade become familiar with the sound of the PA system. It is often fuzzy or laced with static, and they hear the bells or buzzers that signal the end of one period and the start of another. Sometimes there are multiple buzzers: One signals a one-minute warning, another marks the end of a class period, and another starts a new period. Kids take to the halls between these periods, rushing to get to the next class on time. PA systems with their bells and buzzers are just considered part of the fabric of the school day.

Assume that a horrific disaster has occurred, such as that outlined in the opening to the preface—the shooting of a student's parent by a school guard on the school's front steps. Assume, too, that it took place between the end of the 2nd period and the beginning of the 3rd. On the day of the shooting, the PA sounds continued as usual throughout the lockdown and before students were sent home. In the days, weeks, and months following the shooting, the same buzzer sounded to signal the end of classes and the start of others. This included a buzzer at the end of the 2nd period and the start of the 3rd, the same moment when the shooting had occurred. The buzzers continued even though administrators and teachers were well aware that the sound and the timing coincided with the shooting.

Scenario 3

It is common practice in many schools to send notes (often only in English) home in students' backpacks to parents or guardians to announce upcoming activities at school, such as parent/guardian–teacher meetings, musical performances, and athletic events. In addition, notes are sent home about field trips, often requiring an adult signature to allow a student to go. Notes also go home if a student has misbehaved, has not done assigned homework, or has received bad grades; these notes also require the signature of a parent or guardian. Notes go home about career days and fundraisers. This form of communication requires several steps for the desired action: The student has to bring the paper home; the student needs a parent or guardian to able to read and then sign the note (this raises the issues of literacy, familiarity with English, and availability of the parent or guardian); and the student needs to feel that the note will not generate negative feedback (and fear) at home, which would make some students reluctant to divulge that notes have been sent from their school.

In some schools, notes are sent by email or text. This assumes that parents/caregivers have a computer, access to the Internet, and a cellphone; that they know how to send and receive messages; that they have a printer, so they can print the note and sign it if needed; or that they know how to sign digitally. There is an assumption that recipients of the notes understand the information that is being communicated and are willing to respond to it in the manner provided. What if they have questions or concerns? And there is a deeper assumption that all children have someone who fills the role of "parent," something that is not true for some youth.

Small e Events

All three scenarios describe small *e* events. In Scenario 1, fire drills or other, similar disaster preparations are, we surmise, needed to ensure safety for students and educators. Whether they actually work effectively as a form of protection is a question for another day.[1] Some of us remember bomb shelters in our homes and schools in the 1960s; we can question the effectiveness of these as well.[2] In my own case, it was in the boiler room of our home, so were a bomb to actually fall, we would have been killed by a boiler explosion. In Scenario 2, buzzers or bells are used to notify everyone of when one period ends and another begins. Announcements over loudspeakers provide an easy way to convey information. Whether the actual time periods for classes make sense and are optimal is another issue, raised later in this book.[3] In Scenario 3, notifications of a wide-ranging sort are needed to provide communications and transparency in educational settings. The note-in-the-backpack approach is only one system; as stated earlier, others are digital.[4] Both physical and online communication have real benefits, but they do not reach everyone, for reasons that are complex.

Small e Event Reactions

With the possible exception of active shooter drills, which are increasingly viewed as traumatizing, all three scenarios reflect happenings that are not traumatic per se (they are not big *E* events). But these same scenarios can be used to demonstrate the absence of trauma sensitivity, because for some students, one or more of the events can trigger a trauma response. Their reactions can be misunderstood, mischaracterized, or ignored. We turn later in this chapter and then in Chapter 5 to how educators are affected, through direct or vicarious trauma.

For Scenario 1, we generally do not consider the impact of these drills or their warning sounds on individuals in an educational institution, particularly one that has not been subject to a natural or human-made disaster. However, for some students who have experienced trauma in the past, such as repeated yelling or objects[5] being thrown in the household by parents or others, loud noises activate their autonomic nervous system. Disruption of the daily routine is triggering also for some students, as they like the order, structure, and stability that schools provide. For students who have experienced building fires or natural disasters that have touched their family, drills reactivate trauma from the past.

Many educators are unaware of the triggers caused by fire drills. If students refuse to leave the building, do not keep quiet during the drill, or are upset by the drill and struggle to settle back into the school routine when they return, educators try to get them to "behave properly." During the drills, I have seen educators telling children to be quiet, to get into the right line, and to stop misbehaving. When these students return to class, some will be overactive and disruptive, while others will feel silenced and become unengaged. Think about drills this way: We are in essence playing music (the buzzers and the bells) that does the opposite of calm people—which is what music can and often does do positively. In this context, the "music" reactivates trauma.[6]

In Scenario 2, the buzzers and bells take on a stark meaning between the 2nd and 3rd periods in the times following a tragic shooting on campus. For some students, there is no awareness that the buzzer is activating their autonomic nervous system. For others, the buzzer is like a neon sign—*danger, a shooting, memories*. Both the sound and its timing are troubling. In that school, when requests were made to shut off the system or change the sound of the buzzer to a different, less triggering sound, the administrators responded that the system was old and changes of any sort were not possible. When I later became involved and the buzzer issue was again raised, I asserted that the answer that had been given had to be wrong. At a minimum, the school needed to remove the system and broadcast handheld bells over the intercom. Or walk the halls with cowbells. Or it needed to immediately bring in a technology expert to adjust the system. Daily retriggering, whether or not folks knew that it was affecting them, was having an influence on education. There was the anticipation of the sound and then the sound itself and then the aftermath of the sound. In other words, it was not the just 10-second buzzers; it was what happened before, during, and after.

In Scenario 3, we interpret parental/caregiver failure to sign notices, read emails, or attend events as disinterest. I have talked with teachers and principals at many schools, trying to understand and increase parental and guardian engagement, so these adults would not be afraid to attend school events or sign papers for school trips or go to parent/guardian–teacher conferences. I made what I thought were good suggestions that fell on deaf ears. Then, some teachers shared that parental/caregiver so-called disengagement from school was not evidence that these adults did not care. For some parents/caregivers, school raises negative memories, and entering a school building is fraught for them. This is not uncommon among minority groups where the students and their parents (particularly those who were non-native-English speakers) were not welcomed or not regarded with respect. This is also true with respect to Native American families, likely and understandably as a result of Native Americans being sent off to boarding schools for decades to become "Americanized," an aspect of American history unknown to many. For other parents/guardians, addiction interferes with their behavior. They say they will come to school, and mean it at the time, but when push comes to shove, they are unable to. If you want poignant examples of this in high school, watch the movies *Step* and *Raising Bertie*.[7] Parental absence generates sadness and disappointment and unmet expectations in children. Add to all this that many parents and guardians work more than one job, many students are latchkey kids, and other students may not have a stable home. No matter the cause, the absence of adult involvement in a student's schooling has lasting negative impacts.

There Are Solutions

In Scenario 1, consider whether warnings of an upcoming drill, at least for some students, might ease their autonomic nervous system response to the event. I suspect that warnings would not reduce the effectiveness of the drill. When students refuse to stand in line, perhaps it is because they have been triggered, and yelling at them to try to effect compliance is not likely to help the situation. What if, instead, teachers set out to calm the kids who were acting out during a drill? Bring puppets outside or broadcast calming music on outdoor speakers. What if one teacher were assigned to observe and then respond to students who appeared to be struggling outside—either by acting out or isolating themselves? And it goes without saying: Teachers need to work not to create panic; instead, they need to create calm, something that would also be needed if the fire or other threat to safety were real.

And when students return to the classroom, why are we so keen on picking up where we left off, without addressing the drill that has just happened? I get that there is a sense that time in the classroom has been lost and that it seems best to get back to the academic material at hand. But in truth, that all-important content will not sink in for some students if their autonomic nervous systems are on high alert because of the drill. No matter how good the teaching, those students are not "in the moment."

There are a number of options for dealing with this. One possibility is to talk about the drill, discussing why it was done and praising how well it went. Just raising the issue and creating a sense of calm around it can be effective. That is much better than acting as if it had never occurred. And why not anticipate the future after the completed drill? Try saying in class, "I know we'll have other drills this year, but you're getting very good at responding to them. Well done." What if the teacher asked, "What would make these drills easier for you all, other than canceling them? Let's share ideas."

Another approach is to delay returning to the material that was interrupted by the drill. Instead, do an exercise that deactivates the autonomic nervous system and settles students back into the routine. This can be any activity that uses the senses, a topic to which we will return in Part II. Consider having students get up behind their desks and stretch to music—using their bodies. Consider having them sing a song they enjoy (e.g., the hit song "Baby Shark") or try a tongue twister. Drawing or coloring may help, especially if students use markers that are scented. The point is to give them distractions, as detailed processing, central to learning, is not possible right then.

In Scenario 2, the sounding of buzzers and bells that are normally small *e* events feel like big *E* events following a school shooting (a big *E* event). Noises at a particular pitch become triggers for students and educators alike. What if one did away with them for a while? Would the school day totally disintegrate if a new method of signaling the end of one period and beginning of the next were instituted? Picture the head of a school walking up and down the halls ringing pleasant-sounding chimes or playing a harmonica or a triangle. (Avoid drums.) The point is to build new memory pathways and close off damaged ones. This is *positive* learning, akin to operant conditioning and learning where positive behavior is rewarded.

Trauma-skilled teachers can also alert students to triggers and explain how they work. This is not a bad thing: Contrary to what may instinctively be believed, it will not make matters worse—it is silence that makes matters worse. If the unease of those who have trouble recovering in a big *E* event's aftermath is not acknowledged, they are left to feel isolated and inadequate, as if everyone has fully processed and recovered from the event or been untouched by it—except them.

In relation to Scenario 3, we should recognize that getting reluctant adults to feel comfortable in school, erasing decades of bad memories, is not a quick process. Consider instead holding school conferences or other meetings in a nearby community center or religious venue that holds no bad memories. I just learned of a school where not only do kindergarteners have their classes outside but parent/family meetings are held outside at a campfire. Simply changing the location, with leaders and teachers going to parents as opposed to parents coming to them, has enormous value.

Next, consider how notes sent home are structured. Are they scary? Is the text too dense? How about positive notices with positive imagery and a small amount of text? Sometimes less is more. How about using laminated placemats with school events embedded in them as opposed to paper that can be easily misplaced or torn?[8] For notices about a particular student's behavior, what is wrong with a call or an email instead of sending a note with the "offending" student? What if the call or email were nonthreatening and couched in terms of helpful intervention? Yes, a call or email can activate the autonomic nervous system of parents and guardians. But tone of voice and choice of words are critical. Instead of saying, "I'm calling because your son has failed to meet expectations," what about saying, "I'd like to talk with you about how we can help your son succeed in school"? How about home visits by teachers and school counselors, perhaps in teams and ideally speaking in the language of the family and bringing a culturally appropriate small gift?

Transferred Trauma

Critical distinctions exist between the three scenarios. Scenarios 1 and 2 affect students through the fire drill or PA buzzer. Scenario 3 affects students who need to take notes home and parents and guardians who are asked to respond to the notes. But—and this is critically important for our subsequent discussions on vicarious trauma—educators are affected by all three scenarios. Some educators might experience primary trauma in each of these scenarios, as individuals, not as educators per se. What if educators had a prior history with natural disasters, particularly forest fires? Suppose they hailed from California or another state prone to wildfires. If so, drills could be a trigger for them. If educators had dealt with prior shootings in schools that used buzzers, hearing buzzers again later could be triggers for them. If an educator had parents who were unable to read English or attend school events, sending notes home and noting the absence of the parents at those events could be triggers for that educator.

Now, what has not been addressed is how trauma gets transferred from students to educators. The teachers of students affected by events in Scenario 1, which students then proceed to act out in class and become hard to manage or fail to integrate into the classroom, themselves become affected. What is affecting them is not the drill per se; it is the symptoms displayed by the student who is traumatized by the drill. If the behavior of this type of student who acts out or isolates him- or herself becomes habitual in the classroom for one period a day or every period every day, then this teacher or all the teachers working with the student will experience trauma.

We addressed that buzzers marking school periods in Scenario 2 have a primary effect on students and teachers, but we have not addressed that the teachers have to deal with students' responses to this repeated trigger (as well as their own responses). The trigger can activate students' autonomic nervous system and produce other symptomology that makes the process of education difficult: acting out, not engaging, daydreaming, memory failure, classroom fights, unwillingness to listen to (or hear) instructions and directions. Teachers dealing with that trauma as well as their own trauma have tough sledding.

In Scenario 3, teachers begin to make assumptions about parents/caregivers and their lack of engagement. Some teachers take it personally, as if they are failing their students, when, in fact, teachers have nothing to do with the parental/caregiver absence. This is primary trauma. Then, when students become scared or disappointed by parental/caregiver involvement (or noninvolvement) and are keenly aware that other parents/caregivers are not behaving similarly, they act out or isolate themselves in class. If teachers pay particular attention to students the day after notes go home or when there is an at-school event or meeting, they might observe changed behavior or catch the student's trauma before it becomes overwhelming to the student and teacher alike.[9]

A key distinction can be made here, one explored in Chapter 3. For some students, a reaction to notes home and school events may be autonomic. Students may be afraid that their parents' behavior may make teachers treat them differently (not a wholly unrealistic observation). For other students, their symptomology affects their classroom performance, behavior, and engagement. They may become class clowns, announcing that school doesn't matter and parents aren't needed. Alternatively, such students may become isolated when other students talk about their parents' attendance; the students without involved parents feel different.

Next Steps

The three scenarios presented here reveal the possibility or presence of trauma in small *e* events in educational settings that feel like big *E* events in certain contexts or to certain individuals. Scattered throughout this chapter are references to different types of trauma symptomology that often go unrecognized by those experiencing them and those who work in educational environments. Indeed, the failure to see and later memorialize trauma has negative effects, interfering with our capacity to process trauma and move forward in ways that facilitate a pathway to student success.

To delve further into these thoughts, Chapters 3 and 4 describe trauma symptomology and its impact on educational outcomes. Chapter 5 deals with secondary and vicarious trauma (they are *not* the same) in more detail. These chapters can be used to build a checklist of symptomology for educators to keep in their minds or write down in their notebooks, though no list of trauma symptomology, however thoughtfully and carefully constructed, can ever be complete.

Since traumatic events have commemorations—the date and time when they occurred are remembered—we need to pause and focus on how to deal with traumas whose dates keeps reappearing on our proverbial mental calendar. We know this from 9/11, we know this from Kent State, and we know this if we have been traumatized ourselves: We often can remember exactly where we were when the event occurred. And we remember it yearly, if not more often. In fact, when my son was in college, he remembered the anniversary of when his best friend had died in an avalanche while preparing for the Olympics. Each year on that date, my son would remember and be shocked that I did *not* remember and hence was upset by my lack of sensitivity to his particular vulnerabilities on that date. I did remember the death, of course, but not the exact date and time. He did. He still does.

That's an example of why we now turn to anniversaries.

What About Those Anniversaries?

Before addressing how we deal (or more accurately, don't deal well) with anniversaries of traumas, let's reflect on positive (and negative) anniversaries and how we celebrate or commemorate them today in our public and private lives—outside the educational arena. As a starting point, the word *anniversary* has a broad meaning. There are anniversaries of celebratory events (engagements, weddings, sobriety, citizenship) and anniversaries of difficult events (deaths, natural disasters, permanent physical ailments or injuries, wars). Generally speaking, we know how to celebrate positive anniversaries such as of a wedding or the birthday of a child or grandchild. We arrange get-togethers or special dinners. We make toasts. We give presents. We send cards. We blow up balloons. We have annual shared commemorations such as Presidents' Day, Veterans Day, Labor Day, and Independence Day. These are marked by grand ceremonies, with flags and parades and music and cookouts and speeches. We have media coverage and plenty of photographs. We even use some of these dates as computer and cellphone passwords, much to the chagrin of cybersecurity experts.

At the opposite end of the spectrum are commemorations of sad events. We have detailed protocols to mark the deaths of people who have held high office. Religions have ceremonial traditions related to death. The state funeral of President George H. W. Bush was held over a period of several days and was carefully choreographed, like all presidents' state funerals. There was a funeral procession, and his casket was placed on public view in the Capital. Flags were flown at half-staff for 30 days. The funeral service—televised, attended by many dignitaries from the United States and foreign countries, and marked by eloquent eulogies—was held at the National Cathedral. The military conducted a 21-gun salute, and there was an honor guard, flyovers with a "missing person" in a plane formation (a blank space in the sky for the plane the deceased would have flown), and a flag-draped coffin.

Such funerals and their traditions contain embedded messages. Upon the death of Senator John McCain, a war hero and former presidential candidate, the president then in office did not follow protocol. The flag on the White House flew at half-staff only after considerable controversy, and then there was a debate about how long it and other flags should remain that way, with the president seeking to broadcast both his personal and his political dislike by limiting the flag being in a position of honor.

Sometimes public events intended for shared mourning and reflection evolve into holidays that allow a day off work and some form of celebration. Consider Martin Luther King Jr. Day. Yes, there are public declarations of his life and impact, but children have the day off school and workplaces are closed—the day is not spent in reflection on race and civil rights. The "I Have a Dream" speech is not commonly read at the breakfast table (except in my home, where it was a tradition with our son). Memorial Day was designed to honor soldiers who died in wars but has become a time to celebrate the start of summer, as people gather for cookouts and drink plenty of beer. Some folks do not even know the intended purpose of Memorial Day.

We have developed shared customs to mark negative anniversaries. We visit a cemetery on the anniversary of the death of a loved one. We leave flowers or special objects. In some religions, there are opportunities to mourn at designated times after a death—at the 1-year mark and as part of annual religious holidays. In some instances, we gather to share memories, including positive ones. In sports at the sudden death of a teammate, we retire the player's number, and teammates wear the number for the balance of the season on their jerseys or shoes. For an example, look at how the Los Angeles Angels memorialized the sudden death of their pitcher Tyler Skaggs, long before the autopsy revealed the true cause of his death.[10] After canceling a game, the team went out and played. Tyler's mother threw out the first pitch—a perfect strike. Two pitchers combined for a no-hitter (and one assumes the opposing team did not tank on purpose). And as if by divine intervention, Mike Trout hit a home run at 454 feet—Tyler's jersey number forward and backward. There was a 45-second moment of silence. And if one is into coincidences, the last no-hitter in California had been on July 13, 1991, the date of Tyler's birth; the number of runs that day was 13. Tyler's birthday was the day following the game—July 13, 2019.

We often remember specific dates: the date our parent, child, or best friend died; the date we decided to leave an abusive spouse; the date we lost a job. We don't always do anything special on those dates but may think about the past. We might be sad. We might look at photographs. We might go into nature to reflect. We might talk to a friend. Families develop their own ways of remembering and grieving—dinners with special foods or favorite foods of the deceased, moments of silence, playing a well-liked game everyone used to play together, looking at photographs or videos of the deceased. It is not uncommon for soldiers remembering fallen comrades to get a memorial tattoo that they can look at on anniversaries and other days when memories return.

Dealing with Trauma Anniversaries

Despite many anniversary traditions, generally speaking, we have not planned well for anniversaries of traumas, those in our own backyard and those farther away. We know, I suspect intuitively, that simply sweeping trauma away is not a strategy. It is a default mechanism, an attempt to ignore the reality of what people are experiencing, even when it is unvoiced. We may not want to remember even as our minds remember. Consider how we commemorate a school shooting, something for which there is often disagreement. Buildings may be torn down and gardens or other memorials created. A moment of silence may be organized.

But here's the question: Do we pause to reflect on how to deal with anniversaries of big *E* events—hurricanes, tornados, repeated sexual abuse, shootings—*in our schools*? The simple answer is that, as a general matter, we don't. We should. We need to start reflecting on how anniversaries of traumas could become important and curative, not disruptive and disquieting. Indeed, ironically, silence is disruptive and deeply disquieting. We are so scared of awakening ghosts that we fail to deal with the ever-present ghosts. Anniversaries can be "healable" moments.

To arrive at suitable approaches in the educational arena, we need to recognize that there is no one approach to all traumas in all schools. Traumas differ from one another, as do the cultures where they occurred and how they were originally addressed. And surely we do better if trauma anniversaries are handled and controlled by those who experienced them, not by the media, which regularly reminds us of bad things that happened. Take a school shooting. The media will cover the anniversary of Sandy Hook, Columbine, and Parkland. Kent State has had this issue for decades now. But how can the individuals involved in and living with and through these traumas remember those fateful days? For some, the intervening months or years will have been difficult, but for others, the events are deeply buried and unprocessed in the psyche.

Planning, Teachable Moments, and Control

Start with the idea of *planning*. Spontaneous events may have value, but there is remarkable power in planning how to address an anniversary. Thoughts from students, parents/caregivers, teachers, and survivors (family members, including siblings still in school) need to be considered. Ideally, the media could cooperate—something not so easy to arrange. Then reflect, since we are dealing with educational settings, on how to create ongoing healing moments that attempt to or do engender greater understanding and context for the horrible things that have transpired. The old adage "Knowledge is power" takes on real meaning in the context of trauma. If we can regain some sense of *control* over a situation, we are better able to handle it in the moment and afterward. So as we reflect on approaches, consider planning, healable moments and fostering control as the guideposts and foundations for the effort to recognize and memorialize trauma.

Kent State and New York Law School

Let's begin by examining the remarkable ways in which Kent State University planned for the 50th anniversary of the May 4, 1970, shooting on campus that killed four students and wounded nine others. The event was captured in an iconic photograph of a distraught young woman kneeling next to the body of one of the killed students. (We deal with this woman's responses in a later chapter.) It is a photograph, for better or worse for the woman pictured in it and the parents of the deceased student, that has continued to capture our nation. I know about the extent and seriousness of the planning, which began years in advance of the 2020 anniversary, because I spent time talking to one of the professors who was centrally involved in it—a remarkable man with a hugely difficult task, and one tinged with considerable controversy.

Kent State did not initially embrace its history and only later saw the importance of what occurred on its campus and the messaging about freedom across the nation and the world that can now be shared. Indeed, the site of the shooting, through the university's efforts and that of others, is a National Historic Landmark, listed on the National Registry of Historic Places. One can think of this status as a permanent reminder on campus. Consider another example of recapturing and owning one's negative history. Georgetown University has been a stellar example in taking its history of slave ownership seriously, recognizing its offensive institutional behavior, and taking concrete steps not only to remember but also to recompense the slaves' descendants. Healable moments.

The decision Kent State made was to not have a single day to remember the anniversary on May 4, 2020. Instead, it planned a year of educational programs, exhibits, and other events, along with more traditional memorials, culminating on the anniversary—all healable moments. A website detailed the events.[11] Individuals could write their own reflections on the site, and a video shows two former students (now married to each other) who were present at the fateful events and one of whom was shot. The event is becoming owned, and the institution is regaining control—telling its own history, a deeply painful one.

In my own personal experience, I along with other faculty, staff, and students were challenged to respond to the events of September 11, 2001, at New York Law School—eight blocks from the Twin Towers. The planes hitting and the towers falling were all in our line of sight. The school closed for 2-plus weeks and reopened to intense smells, with trucks rumbling past and sirens blaring, as emergency vehicles drove by on the two streets that bordered the law school. Collectively we wrote a book called *Eight Blocks Away*, containing the memories and thoughts of those on campus that day and those who were connected to the school but were not there then. Self-published, it was placed all over campus, there for the taking, available to students, faculty, and staff. It was reissued on the 10th anniversary of 9/11 with an added preface. I have always had a copy in my office or home. The book is available now as a download—yes, free of charge.[12]

After the tragedy, we ran educational symposia on how different legal disciplines respond to a world in which the rule of law is undermined. At one point the institution had a choice: It could either not emphasize its location (particularly to prospective students), or it could own its history and the steps it took to give meaning to that history. These presentations were converted into articles and published in the school's law review.

Planning, healable moments, and ownership. These three features were present.

I vividly remember the piece I wrote for one of these educational programs and still refer to it from time to time.[13] It was about the "Portraits of Grief" series that appeared in the *New York Times* and explored the lives of the survivors and how they would handle the monies (of differing amounts) they received to recompense them for their loss. I still read obituaries and I still think about survivors. But as an educational institution, we used the events as healable moments and made them a part of our history. We did not deny where the law school was located. I am often asked on anniversaries of 9/11 if I watch the videos of that day. I have one response and it has not changed since 2001: I do not need to see the videos; I have a permanent video etched in my mind.

Some Lessons

The examples described above demonstrate the need to have trauma commemorations—to mark what has occurred. Critically, when we are dealing with educational institutions, we need to be sensitive to the age of the students; the nature of the trauma; and the many directly affected parties, including those who are not on campus, like family and friends and alums. The planning process itself is therapeutic. It is the beginning of gaining control over horrific events, to counter having the events control the institution or those in it. The opportunity to explore possible teachable moments depends, of course, on what happened and why. These events are limited only by our imagination and capacity to reflect on what will better the lives of the many affected people. Survivors should draw on their own talents. Bringing in outside speakers, even famous ones, is not nearly as powerful as having individuals who were there speak or write about what happened. There is nothing more authentic, assuming people are willing to express their deeply held feelings and reactions.

A critical aspect of our trauma anniversary responses is that they are opportunities for creating structure, stability, and safety, three of the *S*s that trauma takes away. Commemorations on campus enable processing in place—a remarkable approach discussed at length in Part II—and keep trauma amelioration in its home rather than in a disconnected setting like a large auditorium or other public space, however gorgeous such a setting might be. Setting up a tent on campus is much better than heading to some large space off campus.

Material Goods as Memorials

To reflect on what is the best, most appropriate way to memorialize a trauma, I want to transport some ideas from the non-trauma arena. In a fascinating article, Joseph K. Goodman, Selin A. Malkoc, and Brittney L. Stephenson focus on consumption choices to honor special events. They look at whether consumers favor experiences or material objects. After examining key studies, they conclude that individuals mistakenly favor experiential opportunities and give short shrift to the enduring memories generated by material objects. The authors state, "In sum, we propose that when consumers are marking special live events or achievements, material purchases reveal an advantage over experiential purchases as time passes. Further, we propose that consumers do not predict this material advantage, as they fail to appropriately consider the permanent nature of material goods."[14]

Can we interpret these findings to suggest that engagement activities related to trauma are not, despite their seeming appeal, as powerful as permanent material representations to commemorate a trauma? We have a proclivity for memorial services or other events. Indeed, in the examples of Kent State and New York Law School, there were transient experiences—educational healable moments. But there were also material objects: the university registered as a National Historic Landmark, a published book on community responses, law articles tied to the trauma.

Tangible Evidence

Think about mementos from our travels or a wedding—something tangible we can hold on to going forward. Gift-giving cultures recognize the value of tangible, enduring objects—necklaces, seedpods, ornaments. My own leadership style involved giving to others on campus. This messages on a go-forward basis. Folks could keep the gifts on their desk or in their homes.

If a trauma occurs, are there material objects that can help traumatized individuals move forward more effectively? For anniversaries of traumas we should consider material, permanent memorial objects as a way of remembering and processing. In a sense, we can think of material objects as creating object permanence in a world where permanence was disrupted materially and psychically. Objects restore permanence, and to return to three of the *S*s, they restore stability, security, and structure. This is an idea that stems from theories about the development of object permanence in healthy children, something that is disrupted through trauma.

We have memorials—consider the lit chairs in Oklahoma City, the Pentagon's water benches, and the Vietnam Wall. At a university on an

Indian reservation, there is a permanent teepee, honoring Native Americans and decrying the effort to annihilate their heritage (the teepee is, not without irony, at an institution named Heritage University). What if in the context of schools where shootings or other traumatic big *E* events have occurred we considered concrete, visible memorials, both large and small? Ponder initiatives for installation art that involve the community. They both are experiential and can be permanent.[15] Schools can have tiles or murals that are enduring. Painted stones have been used. Consider planting trees. Consider creating gardens, messaging growth and future crops. These are beneficial and may provide solace since one can return to the location. But these larger memorials cannot literally be carried forward with students and their families when they leave that particular school. And although they progress to other schools, they are not shedding past trauma with the move; if anything, the transition to a new location may reactivate a previous school trauma.

We need to consider smaller, portable objects. These can be beneficial, as seen in the published works previously mentioned in the context of New York Law School. Consider coins, akin to those used in the military to honor certain deeds. The coins can be carried in a wallet or backpack, and they are small enough to be ignored if desired yet large and heavy enough to have an impact. Faculty and students could design them together. They could travel with the child, so to speak, like a transitional object that young people use to increase their sense of comfort and safety as they move forward in time. With young children, we hope that sense of safety becomes internalized, doing away with the need for the object. But in the case of trauma, the transitional object can be useful for years, even decades.

In addition to coins, consider objects that individuals affected by trauma can hold and carry with them. I have been struck by the many uses of *Kimochis*, feeling objects made of stuffed felt and produced by a company in California.[16] One particular Kimochi has remarkable power. It is a heart within a heart ("nesting hearts"), and when one person goes away (not through death), the departing person takes the small heart with him or her.[17] Those staying behind have the larger heart into which the smaller heart fits. It messages that "I have your heart with me (reciprocally), and there is a place for your heart when you return."

Picture the creation of something similar given in the aftermath of trauma. What is created depends, of course, on the type of trauma. What works in one situation may not work in another. That said, here are some suggestions for Kimochi-like material objects that can be delivered post-trauma, adapted for each situation: small stuffed creatures holding hands (suggesting the importance of staying connected) or bendable blocks or cubes that one can fidget with to calm one's nervous system but that are linked to the event in terms of color—no, not red for blood, but, say, school colors or calming colors if the school is near water or shades of green if the school is near mountains. Perhaps they could even be photographs laminated on cubes or blocks. The order can be arranged (stability) or moved but then returned (consistency). Kintsugi pots are another example, explored in more detail in Part II.

One question many may have is whether these material objects (or experiential activities, for that matter) will keep retriggering trauma. Yes, that is possible. Coins or images can serve as reminders, which can become triggers. The objects may need to be put away if they are too painful. But having the object—whether or not one sees or touches it—has value. Eventually, perhaps someone will touch that object and that will begin to facilitate the ability to process the trauma. We know that hiding trauma or pretending it does not even exist is a flawed approach, as the trauma comes back strongly when another event occurs. Holding the trauma inside has physiological consequences that lead to illnesses.

For others, material, tangible objects can function in positive ways to celebrate and commemorate events. They can keep memory alive with positive thoughts. Remembering a loved one, remembering a community coming together, remembering people who helped one another, remembering that over time traumas find a way of being incorporated into who we are and how we act and think and feel. Connections.[18] True, these can be negative in some instances, but trauma can also help us be empathetic. It can enable us to see the good in some people and allow us to see that, over time, our brain allows us to process negative events. For those whose feelings have been frozen in time, these objects can enable thawing.

Onward

In Chapters 3 and 4, we engage in a detailed investigation of trauma symptomology in the educational setting. We start with autonomic nervous system responses, what generates them, and the damage they do to students in the near and longer term. Then we turn to other trauma responses, situated in our brains and bodies, responses that also affect students in the present and into the future. We examine the triphasic responses to trauma referenced in the preface. Finally, we note how secondary and vicarious trauma express themselves.

These chapters also prepare us for Part II, which focuses on how we lower autonomic nervous system responses and how we can alleviate other trauma symptomology. Before we can improve our educational responses to trauma, we need to see how trauma expresses itself in schools and colleges—in classrooms, in residential areas, in cafeterias and dining halls, and on athletic fields. The symptoms are hurdles we encounter as we move forward. Onward, hurdles notwithstanding.

CHAPTER 3

Acute Symptomology Is Autonomic

Given that one could write whole books about trauma symptomology, what follows in this chapter and in Chapter 4 are not intended as a complete rendition of trauma symptoms or their causes and effects in all contexts.[1] But what is offered is, I hope, sufficient to enable us to better understand some of the behaviors that our students exhibit in the educational arena if they have experienced trauma. (Educators can self-identify symptoms in themselves, too.)[2] Even with a limited scope, it is hard to capture trauma's educational impact, given the breadth of enrollment of students at differing ages and stages in the educational system, from early childhood through adulthood. But absent some shared understanding, we can't develop and justify solutions like those contained in Part II of this book.[3]

Trauma symptomology can be subdivided into categories based on such factors as its origin within the body or brain; its impact on human functioning at all levels; its duration in time; and its medical implications, short and long term, referred to earlier in regard to the ACEs literature. I want to start with yet another categorization, because it is best suited to the educational context: symptomology based on *when* it occurs relative to a traumatic event. I want to target the very first evidence of trauma. Given our focus on students, I want to begin with the way trauma symptoms first appear in a school or university; in some instances one student is affected and shows symptomology, whereas in other instances multiple students are affected and the symptomology (while varied among individuals) is widespread. We do need to recognize that there is no one exact moment we can identify for every student in every situation; responses differ based on each person and the context.

First Appearances

Start here first. Indications of trauma appear immediately following big *E* events or when small *e* events feel like big *E* events. For ease of explication, let's call this *acute symptomology*, because it is immediately tripped off by something and it is intense.[4] It is the first thing we see when something traumatic has happened. Workers in disaster relief encounter acute symptomology and must address it in locations where survivors are gathered. It can be triggered repeatedly over time, relating back to the original event or caused by a new event that revives feelings from an earlier event. In a sense, a sequential look at trauma symptoms follows how an educational system operates: It is progressive, starting at the earliest stages with acute symptomology and moving forward to delayed symptomology (addressed in Chapter 4), like students moving from grade to grade.

Acute symptomology is housed, as we'll discover, primarily in our nervous system, although it can lead to other symptomology in other bodily systems and in our brain, short and longer term. Since these symptoms are triggered and retriggered over time with the occurrence of current and future events, the nomenclature used here, *acute symptomology*, is apt. It can be felt physically, and in some people the response is intense. For others, there may be no awareness of the acute symptoms because for these individuals it is their normal state (chronic), and they need help identifying what is occurring in their bodies.

When acute trauma occurs, the brain, while involved, has shut down its emotional and cognitive functions. A person is responding to a stimulus that starts in the nervous system. The brain is not completely absent in these events,[5] but it is not the higher brain functions that are at work. As we'll see, what occurs may initially have protective functions and has historic origins physiologically from the animal kingdom, but it is debilitating on a number of levels. Reflect for a moment on those fleeing the nightclub in Dayton, Ohio, where there was a shooting. A photograph of shoes left behind was reproduced regularly on social media.[6] Removing shoes was not a reasoned decision. Victims did not think, "Oh, let me ponder whether my shoes will slow me down as I flee." Instead, they took their shoes off or could not keep them on as they fled, without deliberating on it.

One added note: Since acute symptomology can be repetitive, we develop a propensity for the symptomology to be reactivated; we create a pattern of easy reactivation. Yes, the pattern differs in intensity from person to person. Consider the situation in New York's Times Square after the shootings in El Paso and Dayton. A motorcycle backfired and there was mass panic as people feared it was another shooting, with El Paso and Dayton fresh in their minds, and they began to run.[7] Off went the autonomic nervous systems of thousands of tourists and New Yorkers. Among people who had previously fled other events (9/11 or hurricanes or domestic violence), the response was even more intense.

A second, more persistent trauma symptomology usually appears in the aftermath of acute symptomology. Some suggest that any symptoms that occur after 30 days are converted from acute symptomology to delayed symptomology. Delayed symptomology, explored in Chapter 4, affects every aspect of what we do (or don't do), feel (or don't feel), and think (or don't think). Teachers witness this daily in their students, although they may not be able to identify what they are seeing. It affects our hard and soft brain wiring. Both children and adults can feel the impact but, like acute symptomology, it is most harmful and the damage most severe when it occurs in young children, as their brains are still developing.

Think of early trauma, whether acute or delayed, as akin to what can occur in building a home. If construction on the floors and walls starts before a building's foundation has firmly set, the building rests on a weak base. So it is with the brain; people affected by trauma in infancy retain its effects for their entire lives. Reflect on infants ignored in orphanages or other institutions, not given regular human contact and left to cry.[8] No hugging, no coddling. Neglect. These infants, even when adopted by loving families, struggle to connect with and attach to others.

One key point: One can have acute symptomology that does not progress to delayed symptomology. Or one can experience acute symptomology that does progress to delayed symptomology and then, on a go-forward basis, either or both can be exhibited and not necessarily sequentially. Delayed symptomology and continual acute symptomology, as opposed to one-time acute symptomology, can reduce our capacity to have fruitful relationships, our potential to succeed in school, our ability to find and maintain employment, and the opportunity to find pleasure and enjoyment in daily life and have a long life with good health and less chance of chronic illnesses (mental or physical).

Before turning to specifics, it is worth repeating that neither acute nor delayed symptomology arises in the absence of a big *E* traumatic event or a small *e* event that becomes traumatic for an individual (see Figure 1.1).

Acute Symptomology

The more formal scientific definition of acute symptomology is "activation of the autonomic nervous system," a phrase that is not self-evident to many. Some label it the "stress response."[9] Some refer to a "high allostatic load."[10] The title of this chapter, containing the word *autonomic*, is meant to have readers slip between or mistake the words *automatic* (common) and *autonomic* (less common, unless one is a physician or focused on trauma). That is because it is easier to understand and remember the second term if we understand the first.

Both words begin with the prefix *auto*, a Greek root meaning "self." Words that start with *auto* refer to things that are self-acting or self-reflective or self-moving, as in *autobiographical*, *automation*, and *autofocus*. The root of the suffix *matic* means "willing," as in "willing to perform." So an automatic car is one that performs without the need for a human to shift gears. An automatic coffee maker makes coffee once it is set up to do so and can be programmed to process at a particular time. The second part of autonomic also derives from the Greek, in the root *nom* or *nomo*, meaning "laws or a system of laws." So "a self-operating set of laws" is a way of describing autonomic in the human body; the laws are those of the human nervous system. The word autonomic is rarely used in English outside the field of physiology.

At the simplest level, we could say acute symptomology is automatic. It is—but that word does not cover the source of the trigger, namely, a set of laws (or a system). The set of laws that we need to learn about are those of the human nervous system (although animal physiology has been helpful in increasing our understanding).

Nervous Systems

The autonomic nervous system is composed of three distinct nervous systems that engage with one another much of the time, a fact that came as news to me. I must have missed this in premed biology or never learned it well enough (more likely).[11] We have the *sympathetic nervous system*, which operates through a connected series of neurons, in both the central and the peripheral nervous system. These neurons get activated and release various chemicals, including, if there is prolonged activation, norepinephrine and adrenaline. This is what causes what is often referred to as an "adrenaline rush," which one feels when the sympathetic nervous system is revved up. The released chemicals attach to the peripheral tissues. What this all leads to is the *fight-or-flight response*, a familiar phrase. We'll return to what fight-or-flight means in greater depth momentarily.

Then, we have the *parasympathetic nervous system*, which mediates the sympathetic nervous system and calms it down. It is often referred to as the "rest-and-digest system," an odd nomenclature, since the third nervous system also deals with the gut. What the sympathetic nervous system speeds up (breathing, heart rate, blood pressure), the parasympathetic system slows down. Think of them as mirror images. What worries us initially with trauma is the imbalance that is created, and that imbalance produces numerous symptoms that are normally in a checks-and-balance status—homeostasis.

Here's an analogy: When functioning well, the autonomic nervous system works like the three-part checks-and-balances system of American government, composed of the executive branch, the legislative branch, and the judicial branch (when it is working well, which it presently isn't, in the eyes of many). When one system overrides another, the balance goes off and sizable consequences occur, which can be lasting. In government, a life appointment to the Supreme Court can change the court's philosophy and decisionmaking on critical issues affecting individuals, corporations, and our entire nation. In the body, a traumatic event can overwhelm the balance of the entire system. This can produce changes in the structures deep within the brain, among them the hippocampus and amygdala.

The third system, the *enteric nervous system*, is limited to our digestive processes, that is, our gastrointestinal tract. It can act independent of or be influenced by the sympathetic and parasympathetic nervous systems. It is often called the "second brain." It can operate even if something as significant as the vagus nerve is cut off. Research suggests that trauma can and does affect the enteric nervous system, likely with the biggest impact on the youngest children.[12] The *Canadian Journal of Psychiatry* probes whether gut microbiomes can explain part of post-traumatic stress.[13] The research is still preliminary and way less advanced than that on the sympathetic and parasympathetic nervous system in how they are affected by trauma; there is surely still much to learn through advances in scanning and understanding chemicals in our bodies.

The Three *F*s

The most common autonomic response to trauma is one of the three *F*s, *fight*, *flight*, or *freeze*.[14] The first two, fight and flight, are basically touched off in the sympathetic nervous system, which overrides the parasympathetic nervous system to create the responses. Also activated is the adrenal-cortical system, which delivers its messages through the bloodstream (as opposed to the nervous system). To enable this release and transport, our brain is transmitting messages. Be aware: This is not the brain directing our actions or inactions in any emotional or cognitive sense; rather, it is the body responding, with the brain acting more like the traffic signal at a complex intersection. One can't think one's way out of acute symptomology. The brain stem makes sure of that. Call it our survival brain if you like, distinguishing it from the thinking and feeling brain (which are part of the capacity to learn).

The third reaction to trauma, the freeze response, which actually has many layers and complexities, occurs when the parasympathetic nervous system becomes overactive, the inverse of what was just described with the sympathetic nervous system. Sometimes referred to as the "deer-in-the-headlights response," freezing can take the form of freezing physically or freezing psychologically. In a sense, it is the most complex and common of the responses to trauma.

Human beings sense which of the three autonomic responses will be most effective for self-protection in a given situation. Yes, there are people for whom this doesn't work, as a result of some nervous system or brain dysfunction. For example, think about the movie *Solo*, where the central figure, the climber, does not experience stress or fear; his autonomic nervous system differs from that of most individuals.[15] He does not experience fight, flight, or freeze. Before fixing on this lack of response as a good thing, recognize that the climber lacks other capacities, too—empathy, love, and expressions of care for himself and others.

Commonly, freezing is the best way to survive, and given the difficulties an infant would have in fighting or fleeing, it is the most common initial response. Whether the enteric nervous system freezes remains unclear. We know that nausea is often connected to trauma and flight, and one has to wonder whether the gut system is also triggered as part of the trauma response. The early research on the enteric nervous system has focused on delayed symptomology, not acute symptomology. We await further research on whether freezing affects our digestive system, but personal experience and seeing others in a state of freezing suggest to me, intuitively and anecdotally, that there are digestive implications.

The *F* Words

While acute symptomology—fight, flight, or freeze—is autonomic, I have the sense that we have created assumptions about and moral assessments of these states. Rather than attributing positives to them in the name of self-preservation, we come up with negative interpretations or justifiable deviations that hurt individuals and skew our perceptions of what trauma survivors experience. We render value judgments based on how someone reacts to trauma as if one autonomic response is better than another. That's a flawed approach, since one cannot choose the autonomic response that occurs, although one can learn to tame the responses once they occur.

Here are some examples of these phenomena and their impact: We generally discourage fighting and other kinds of violence as forms of dispute resolution in the United States. But we accept that self-defense has a place when someone's life is threatened, and we even regard fighting in the context of self-preservation as a defense in criminal law. Through this justification, we accept behavior that is normally considered to be bad. Think about how many perpetrators of violent attacks, including those resulting in murder, claim they carried them out in self-defense. What we don't say, and what would be beneficial to say to children who are traumatized and exhibiting aggression, is "I understand why you are fighting."

To be sure, not all fighting can be justified. Think about then presidential candidate Gary Hart and his fight for his political life under the revelations of his having been with a woman in his Washington, D.C., home, depicted in the movie *Front Runner*.[16] In his situation, fighting did not benefit him; indeed, it was viewed as defensive and arrogant. Yet what motivated the anger was autonomic rather than planned. Similar anger was displayed by Brett Kavanaugh at his nomination hearings for a seat on the Supreme Court when he was questioned about his youthful indiscretions and possible commission of sexual assault.[17] The photographs of him almost spewing venom that appeared virtually in all news feeds are hard to forget, and the issues haven't gone away.[18]

We criticize those who run away from a troubling scene as if they were chickening out, but we know that fleeing from danger is a way to protect oneself, whether from another person or from the effects of a natural disaster. We see people fleeing following involvement in a car crash and later trying to justify why they did not stay at the scene of the accident. One explanation is that they knew they were in trouble and wanted to avoid being caught, a negative take on behavior. Another explanation is that they had an acute symptom—flight—that enabled or caused them to flee from the trauma of the accident. There are people who flee who cannot remember fleeing and cannot report how they got home after the accident. Some of these individuals regain an awareness hours later and turn themselves into the authorities.

This is not an effort to justify Ted Kennedy's behavior at Chappaquiddick, for those who are reflecting on this in light of the movie of the same name.[19] This is not an effort to justify the flight (literal and figurative) of a U.S. diplomat's wife after she struck and killed an individual with her car in the United Kingdom.[20] Yet we punish those who leave the scene even when their leaving may not have been in their control. In the United States, we have a negative view of sidestepping fear. Our culture favors overcoming our fears and moving forward. Even fighting is better than fleeing. To that end, reflect on the childhood taunt "scaredy-cat." It is used to describe a child who is acting cowardly. We make having fear something bad. And flight is not a chosen pathway; to repeat, it is autonomous.

Perhaps most damaging, we think poorly of those who could not act at all, as if their immobility was in their control and even evidence of consent. The American way is to think, at least to do something. Actually, freezing *is* doing something—in the case of trauma, nothing is something. Remember that there are longer-term physical and psychological consequences of all three *F*s. Ponder the response of victims of sexual harassment or rape. Often they do not report the incident right away, or even ever. They do not fight their rapist; they may lie there seemingly passively. Police and lawyers who defend alleged attackers comment on a lack of bruises as evidence of consent, ignoring the traumatic response of freezing, which would have avoided such bruises. We have many examples of disbelieving witnesses for this very reason. People assume that survivors of assault would have scratches and bruises when, in truth, freezing might be the very response that saves one's life.

One only needs to recollect the responses of Christine Blasey Ford in her testimony at the Kavanaugh Supreme Court confirmation hearings, despite her scientific explanation for her memory lapses.[21] People asked: Why had she been silent for so long? Why were her memories imperfect? Why didn't she run away sooner or fight? Why didn't she have physical evidence from the incident, whether on her body or in photographs? Why can't she recollect who else was in the room and the house where the incident took place, even with prompting? And how can she not remember how she actually got home, which was some distance away?

Think for a moment about a child who is being sexually abused. The child could try to fight but would not be able to physically overcome an adult. The child could try to flee, but this would be impossible if an adult had the child pinned down. That leaves children with the option of freezing, their most common response to trauma. I often pretended to be asleep when Harold, our house caretaker, came into my bedroom. That way, he would be less likely to put his hands down the sheets to feel my youthful breasts. And for the record, this happened to all three female children in my household, and none of us said anything to each other about this until many years had passed. My sisters, though, were successful in sharing this with my mother, so she acted to dismiss Harold; my efforts to get a change went unattended to and, more debilitating, disbelieved.

Let's get more specific about freezing, as it can occur at many levels. One can freeze physically, as one becomes immobile or hides. Crawling under a bed or into a closet is a combination of flight and freeze. Or one can freeze physiologically. Breathing and heart rate greatly slow down in the body's effort to become less detectable. One can surely freeze emotionally, not reacting by crying or screaming or calling for help. One can literally be immobilized in every way. An extreme form of freezing is fainting, another of the *f* words, a last-ditch effort to play dead, so to speak. As a survivor of a shooting explained from her hospital bed, she just acted dead. She did not move or make a sound.

All these freeze responses are automatic and autonomic. We can't control them. We don't mentally debate: Shall I faint or not? Shall I run when my legs can't move? Shall I shout when I have no voice?

What Happens to Our Bodies?

There are commonalities among acute symptoms, and they are often paired with opposites because the sympathetic and parasympathetic nervous systems are out of whack; one or the other is overactive and its functions are then exaggerated in our bodies. We can call this out-of-whack state *deregulation* (to distinguish it from *dysregulation*, which occurs in delayed symptomology). Our heart rate goes up or goes down. Our chest feels compressed or tight, or not. Our breathing speeds up, or it slows down. Our capacity to move is sped up, or it is slowed. Our blood pressure goes up, or down. We release stored sugar. Our adrenal glands release adrenalin, or they do not. Our cortisol levels rise, or fall. We tune out nonessential information and pay close attention, or we do not. Our muscles get ready to engage, or they do not. Our senses are activated, or are not. We are keenly aware of our surroundings, or we blank them out.

When an individual has a fight, flight, or freeze response, his or her nervous system is on alert—whether it is being alerted to rev up or rev down. Regard it as having green and red neon lights inside your body and these lights have no off switch. The green lights (sympathetic system) can send us out with myriad bodily sensations, leading to fighting or fleeing; the red lights (parasympathetic system) freeze our responses. But it is not an all-green or all-red situation. Both lights can shine at the same time so that some bodily systems are quiescent while others are raging.[22]

Thus far, our words have failed to capture fully what the autonomic response feels like to the person experiencing it. It is a whole other level to actually describe the sensations. Think of it as trying to describe labor pains if one has never given birth. For those who have experienced one or more of the fight, flight, or freeze responses, the sensation is usually very uncomfortable and scary. First, it represents a strange duality. It happens outside our control but inside our body. It is as if the body has a mind of its own—which it does in these instances. Second, it is difficult in those moments to know with any sense of certainty when the symptoms will evaporate. A few seconds of terror can seem like an hour. And even when the symptoms stop, the cessation can be temporary or incomplete. Stated another way, the lights on the traffic signal may change, but the car is slow to move forward or stop. All this is exhausting. One's body is working hard—extremely hard—to manage a situation. And remember, this is not the brain managing. This is our internal nervous and endocrine systems working in tandem to save us.

I am going to assume that most readers have experienced one or more of these symptoms in their adult life. If you experienced them as a child, the symptoms were stronger and felt more powerful—in part because they were new, in part because you did not understand them, in part because they were so out of your control. There is a reason children vomit or urinate when stressed. Their nervous systems—all of them—are sending rapid-fire messages. In fact, infants and young children may actually struggle, without success, to impact fight and flight. Despite our efforts to mitigate the systems, the effects of all three autonomic responses are clear: hyperarousal or its opposite, silencing.

Here's a personal example from outside education, one that was traumatic for me, and my response was mischaracterized as a sign of immaturity by others, including my mother. By way of background, I had spent lots of time dealing with separation and loss in my early years. Maternal neglect was present (thank goodness for a remarkable grandmother and quality babysitters). My parents separated when I was a year old, and I was shuttled between them (Boston–Chicago) at a time in the 1950s when air travel was uncommon and expensive and planes were poorly pressurized. Children on planes were a rarity, especially traveling alone, something I did after age 5. Then, when my mother remarried, we moved to a new neighborhood and I became, and stayed for decades, a close friend of the girl across the street, Gail. When we were in 1st grade, it was common for Gail to stay overnight at my house. I never went to hers; separating was hard for me. Finally, we all decided (me included) that I should stay at Gail's house one night. Her house was across the street. You could walk there with your eyes closed. I knew her parents and her sisters. I thought I was ready. After I went there, within an hour I started feeling a tightness in my chest and shortness of breath and I vomited (in their bathroom, thankfully). Home I went. The adult response was, she's not ready yet. She's immature. She's maladjusted.

Actually, had anyone known about trauma, they could have said she was having acute symptomology.

One more caution: It is hard work to shut down the reactions of the autonomic system. They are tough and enduring, and even when we think they are eliminated, vestiges may remain.

The Autonomic Nervous System in Action

Let's return to the vignettes in the preface and focus on the impact of acute symptomology in schools and colleges. Before I give examples, if you are an educator, pause and reflect on whether you have seen these responses by children or adults in your classroom or elsewhere in the school building and whether the symptoms were recognized and then treated as trauma by you or others.

Start with one of the vignettes. A young person sees her brother getting hit by their mother, and she can't do anything to stop it. Suppose the hitting occurs right before this young person heads off to school. And for the sake of simplicity, assume that this is the first time this child has witnessed this type of abuse. Now, what happens when this student enters school? Likely, her heart is beating rapidly. She may feel compression in her chest. She may have trouble concentrating. She may not relate well to her classmates. She may not even say hello. She may pick at her fingernails. She may revert to sucking her thumb. Perhaps she may ask the teacher for work to do before class begins to take her mind off her thoughts, which does not endear her to classmates, who see her as a goody two-shoes. Her teacher may not witness what is happening; after all, some 25 children are entering her classroom. Or she may write off what she sees as evidence of a child's bad night's sleep or poor mood. Or she might see the request for work as a sign of diligence and the qualities of a good student. The teacher may assume, since the student's parents are well educated and well off and her father is a professor at a famous university in town, that all is well at home. Just a bumpy beginning of the day.

That she was me. I actually remember my 2nd-grade teacher repeatedly calling me a worrywart, when what she was seeing was a traumatized young child, fearful of failing, fearful of being left out, fearful of not doing well on the systemwide placement test. I was hypervigilant too, a symptom we will explore in Chapter 4.

Now turn to the fire drill example in Scenario 1 in Chapter 2. Assume for our purposes that the home of three of the students in the school (all siblings) had caught on fire and was burned to the ground. Assume that no one was hurt, but fire engines arrived, the family's belongings were lost or ruined, and they were living with relatives in the next town until they could find a place to rent and their original home was replaced or a new one purchased. Assume, too, that the family had inadequate home insurance.

For these three students, the fire drill at school sets their autonomic nervous system on high alert. That is because the drill retriggers memories of the house fire and all the feelings associated with it. It is worth noting that the three children may behave differently from one another. One may not move; that student could be frozen in his seat. The next sibling might go outside and start punching everyone in line and running around as if high on some substance. The third sibling might be silent, sitting alone on the edge of the driveway with her head down. Each child is exhibiting one of the three acute symptomologies: freeze, fight, and flight (in that order). When these three students return to their respective classrooms, they may not be ready to launch back into the materials presented by the teacher. Their acute symptomology may still be active. For their teachers, re-engaging them and getting them to concentrate and focus will be hard. But the teachers may not know the reasons for the exhibited behaviors, and they may not know strategies that can calm the autonomic system effectively. And the strategies are not identical for fight, flight, and freeze symptomology.

Return to the student who had experienced her brother being beaten. For this student, the fire drill, with accompanying loud voices, disruption, and sense of risk, may trigger symptomology. The lack of stability and consistency is disquieting and reminds her of the lack of stability and safety in her own home. Since a fire is obviously something unsafe and a drill is disconcerting, this student may again feel her heart rate pick up, her chest tighten. She may start picking at her fingers. She may struggle to join in the group outside. When she returns to class, she may have a hard time settling down. She may start to fidget or ask for more work. Her stomach might be in knots. Her memory might be weakening.

Now return again to the vignettes, this time to the child who is falling asleep at his desk following an evening of little or no sleep in a gun-ridden neighborhood. When this child enters school (although this is unlikely to have been a one-time occurrence of trauma symptomology), his parasympathetic nervous system is overactive, tamping down his sympathetic nervous system. He is drowsy. He cannot concentrate. He isn't engaging. He isn't fighting or fleeing; he is experiencing a kind of freeze where his body is automatically protecting itself from intrusions. It is also letting him sleep, meaning his sympathetic nervous system has been quieted (one cannot sleep when the sympathetic nervous is activated).

I remember seeing many children asleep like this in schools in which many children of low income from violent communities were enrolled and asking why their teachers didn't wake them up and get them involved in the activities. I was concerned that they were not learning. Hard to learn when you are asleep. The response from teachers was near universal at one excellent school. They replied that these young children couldn't engage. They needed to sleep. You cannot learn if you haven't slept or eaten. Good points, and well taken. I learned.

A lesson shared earlier in this book is worth repeating. Children should not be asked when they fight, flee, or freeze what is wrong with them, because they did nothing wrong. Instead, they should be asked what happened to them. That's another way of asking the *why* question. Sadly, we don't focus on the *why*s often enough.

The Impact of Repetitive Acute Symptomology

Real, measurable, negative physiological changes, including those in the brain, take place when the autonomic nervous system is repeatedly put into a state of high alert or, worse, is regularly in that state. Thus, absent interventions, the outlook is bleak. The impacts are greatest among the youngest of our children, suggesting that in a world of scarce resources, we might want to direct our time and money toward helping these young people. Trauma travels, as we've noted, with a child like an expandable suitcase, and if it is not treated, although it never disappears, it will stay with that child through elementary, middle, and high school and into postsecondary education. And the suitcase will expand as more events trigger the symptoms.

The brain of a child is plastic and can recover dramatically from the overuse of the autonomic nervous system; the brain can do workarounds, often in ways the body cannot do. Neural pathways can be rerouted, whereas a damaged lung cannot regrow. The shrinkage of the hippocampus and amygdala can be offset by adjustments made by the brain. A rise in glucose levels that bathe the body and set the stage for diabetes can be mitigated. Even fetal brains can be affected by maternal stressors, so you can't start too young to enable quality brain health.

Here is a list, not in order of severity, of some of the empirically verifiable consequences of repeated activation of the autonomic nervous system (recognizing that trauma's long-term impact can be mediated): obesity, diabetes, heart disease, cancer, COPD, liver disease, difficulty concentrating, trouble coping with negative emotions, weak impulse control, negative self-image, attachment disorders, addictions, risk-taking behaviors, and depression. The parts of the brain affected by trauma include the amygdala, the hippocampus, the prefrontal cortex, and the neural pathways.[23]

The changes described play out through different pathways when children are in school. There is dysregulation, an inability to regulate emotions. We treat many of these children as if they had attention deficit disorder. They experience problems with maintaining attachments and have difficulty connecting to others. They may sit by themselves or not look people in the eye. They may not trust others. Attachment disorders affect one's ability to form relationships throughout life. Some view children with this profile as being on the autism spectrum. Nope, they have been traumatized.

We can add dissociation to this list. Students who experience this may not recognize their symptoms. Their sensations may seem normal to them;

they may not notice they are disconnected from their own thoughts. Call this an internal silencing effect that, until awakened, leaves children unable to alleviate what ails them. To awaken understanding, we need trained individuals who know what a child is experiencing when the child him- or herself cannot identify it.

For all children (and adults) affected by trauma, memory and information processing are impaired. It is hard to sleep if one's heart is racing. Stated another way, parts of the brain are cut off by trauma, and the primitive brain becomes dominant. The limbic system and cognitive aspects of the cortex come into play only if you can get beyond the impacts of the autonomic nervous system. Until it is quieted, not much else that is positive can happen. The older a child gets, the more the responses to trauma directly affect learning and the school and college experience. Further, as we will see in Chapter 4, delayed (or cumulative) trauma symptomology has profound effects on student learning, socialization, emotions, and behavior, and physical health. This is true even when an individual's personal foundation was not flawed or damaged.

A child who refuses to go to school because he or she has a tummy ache may be met by the reaction of parents and guardians who deny the condition, saying, "You're just trying to stay home," "You're just trying to get more time to watch video games," "You're faking it," or "You must have a test today." Perhaps the child is experiencing the activation of his or her autonomic nervous system. Perhaps the child heard, saw, or dreamed something horrific. In elementary school, there are children who regularly go to the nurse, with a tummy ache or a more generalized "I don't feel good." Yes, the child could be sick independent of any trauma—or the child could be feeling ill because his or her autonomic system is on full alert; the child hurts. The presence of the nurse as a caring figure, the opportunity to get out of a stressful class setting, or the desire to withdraw may be a factor. Were we to study why children head to the school nurse, we might find that trauma is a major contributing factor. And sadly, we do not have enough school nurses, let alone trauma-trained ones, to deal with this situation. If only all school nurses could develop responses and tools to address the trauma responses suffered by many of the students who enter their offices. And, for the record, we don't have enough school psychologists and school counselors either.

Adult Physiological Responses

Here's an example of what can occur in adults if their childhood trauma is not processed well and mediated. Call it a look forward. Without early intervention, this example will be repeated over and over, to the detriment of the adult who is still harboring vestiges of his or her past. Such adults may be unaware that the symptoms they are feeling result from their autonomic nervous system being on high alert. It is a common situation among those who experience relationship abuse. Remember, too, that there can be massive adult-onset trauma, something well beyond the scope of this book, though it certainly can be experienced by educators.

Have you heard the expression "I feel like I'm walking on eggshells in my own home?" This type of phrase is often used by those in abusive relationships. Their autonomic nervous system is always on high alert because they never know when they will be physically or emotionally attacked. To prepare for the coming trauma, their autonomic nervous system revs up in anticipation. It is not something they control. Their mind and body know they are at risk—eggshells can crack at any time.

One of the consequences of having one's autonomic nervous system on alert at all times is that the heart pumps blood through the system more rapidly. In fact, it is pumping so fast that when the blood reaches the fork in each of the left and right carotid arteries, it bangs into that fork and causes the formation of plaque—hard plaque. This is not the plaque one gets from high cholesterol (soft plaque) or some genetic proclivity toward plaque growth. No, it is the body's response to being attacked. It is like scar tissue, which can break off and cause a heart attack or a neurological event. It is now thought to be more dangerous than soft plaque (the one statins treat). Some of this can be measured by looking at the C-reactive protein. The more protein, the higher the risk of a heart attack. In my case, after years of living with a spouse with Alzheimer's disease who exhibited abusive behavior from yelling to verbal assaults to physical restraint to throwing objects to physically hitting me caused by drug-induced dreams in the night, I decided to get my heart checked. Instinct, I guess. I was told I had this horrible scar tissue plaque and that the stress my body was experiencing was damaging. I had other body systems fail as well, but let's just say, simply, that the body was most assuredly keeping the score. Then, and I remember the date, I decided my eggshell days were over, and I was getting so sick I needed to remove myself from the abuse. Not an easy decision. About 9 months after I went off on my own, I returned to the physician. "Remarkable," he said. "The scarring plaque is gone." And all the indicators of health were trending in the positive direction. I guess my body knew the eggshells weren't under my feet any longer. I share this story because the damage the autonomic nervous system causes can be severe, and with aging it can be life-threatening. But there is good news: The damage can be reversed if one takes steps to shut the system down. I have paid a price for my decision to leave—a distant son, for one thing, but I am healthy and happy.

We now turn to nonautonomous trauma symptomology. A warning: It is even worse than what has been described thus far. A warning, akin to the trigger warning in the preface, seems like a wise choice at this juncture. It's hardest for those of us with dissociative disorders because we may be totally unaware of what is happening in our minds and bodies. Pretty scary stuff.

CHAPTER 4

It's Actually Triphasic

As noted earlier, after an initial trauma, symptoms can persist and be retriggered, described by the overarching term *delayed symptomology*. The symptoms can be behavioral, emotional, cognitive, physical, and existential, and as discussed, they can easily be mistaken for other conditions or maladies. The symptoms are more damaging if they occur in younger children and can and often do have lifelong impact, including on learning and thus on successful progression through the academic pipeline. They are housed within the brain, distinguishing these symptoms from those described in Chapter 3. The impacts occur within the limbic (emotional) and cognitive parts of the brain—the midlevel and higher aspects of our brains. While deeper discussions of brain functioning are well beyond the scope of this book, we can make certain observations to explain the behaviors that will be detailed below.[1] It is vital to foster certain protective factors, which we develop in Parts II and III.

Acute symptomology, as discussed, can be differentiated from delayed symptomology because of the physical systems that are activated. However, important bridges link the two types of symptomology. When there are reactivated or prolonged acute symptoms, this results in the release of cortisol, as referred to earlier.[2] Studies show that cortisol disrupts neurodevelopment as well as the immune system.[3] This accounts in part for the autoimmune diseases that can be experienced by some adults with a history of childhood trauma (as evidenced for example by high ACEs). There can also be temporal lobe damage. Brain weight (cerebral cortex and cells) can decrease with trauma. Some suggest that there is damage to our capacity to be empathetic. The neural systems are shaped by our emotional, cognitive, and physical experiences. Because trauma is a negative experience, it damages our neural pathways, and while our brains remain plastic through life and neurodevelopment is continuous (a good thing for late learners), there can be harm when the brain keeps responding to trauma through hyperarousal and detachment (both described below).

Think about it this way: The brains of traumatized individuals are changed, and if the changes are not mitigated or protective factors are not available, the damage can be severe, affecting health, learning, well-being, happiness, relationships, and overall functioning. Crucially, the damage is not limited to one part of the brain.[4] Trauma can affect the amygdala and hippocampus, the limbic system, and the prefrontal cortex. These areas modulate how we act, feel, think, remember, problem solve, analyze information, create new ideas, and generally engage in creativity and innovation. Our trauma responses are culture sensitive, and people dealing with traumatized individuals should have a deep cultural awareness that can address everything from responses to bodily injury to religion to traditions to ceremonies to symbols.[5] As further research is conducted and neurobiology and neuroimaging expand, we are uncovering other ways in which trauma affects the human brain. Since some of these studies begin with animals, we will need to wait considerable time to verify and understand the impact of the effects on human behavior.[6]

The "Traditional" Delayed Divide

Many describe delayed trauma symptoms as *biphasic*.[7] There are traumatized individuals who exhibit dysregulation, what we could call "outsize behavior."[8] For young children, this may be evidenced by behaviors like aggression such as hitting, pushing, or throwing things; hostility; or failure to attach to peers or adults in any meaningful way. Even older students periodically lose control when there are relational problems with friends or a lover or family members. In addition, conflicts (even manufactured ones) and irritability may be evident. There may be a failure to concentrate and easy distractibility. Do you recall the expression "That child has ants in his pants"? That can be attributable to trauma, not attention deficit hyperactivity disorder. School-related tasks (in and out of class) may not be started, let alone completed. Older individuals, say, college students, may not concentrate during class, may not complete assignments, and may be hard to get along with in class or at parties. It might be easy to make them angry. They may act out, throwing things or shouting at authority figures.

For young and old alike, there can be finely tuned vigilance—hypervigilance, whereby these individuals are always on the lookout for the next alarming or problematic situation.[9] They can detect mood changes in individuals and alterations in classroom dynamics. Consider this example in younger children: A child stands near the door and then darts from place to place in the classroom, staring at peers, the teacher, and out the window. That child is always aware of who is where, who is missing from class, why something is different in the classroom, and what changes have occurred in the landscape. Teachers often say, "Paul, pay attention. You are not focused here." Ironically, the child is actually hyperfocused—just not on the teacher's assignments. *Hyperarousal* is an overall descriptive term for these types of behaviors.

Standing opposite hyperarousal are detachment and dissociation, which are often confused (as explained below).[10] In a state of detachment, traumatized individuals are feeling the opposite of hyperarousal. Those who are detached may isolate themselves. They may refuse to participate in activities or engage with peers or adults. Just going out to recess or to another classroom for art or music may be stressful. They may be nonverbal and unengaged. They may feel shame. They may have an absence, not an overabundance, of feelings. They may refuse to get close physically or psychologically with others. Those operating in this isolation mode may avoid conflict, repress feelings, and have a lack of control over their circumstances. These are individuals for whom engagement is not comfortable, despite the efforts of educators to encourage it.

Among young children, such behaviors are displayed by students who sit alone in the corner, don't respond when called upon, or fail to join in games or educational activities. The teacher who sends a child to a corner can be feeding directly into a trauma symptom, making things worse. And surely, the old-fashioned approach of putting a student in a dunce cap may itself be traumatizing. Keep this in mind as we rethink how we can discipline children in ways that are trauma sensitive.

Older students have different ways of exhibiting these behaviors. They may stay in their dorm room, eat alone, fail to attend class or school activities, or eschew academic support groups or social functions. These students are loners, not joiners. In class, they may fail to pay attention, focusing on their laptops or cellphones—anything to avoid listening to the professor. They may gaze at the ceiling or lower their heads to avoid eye contact and express disinterest, although they may well be hearing and absorbing the material. They may be perceived as drifting off, leading some professors to ask, "Laura, are you with us here?"—hardly a therapeutic response.

At first blush, it might appear as if these categories of trauma responses are in sharp contrast to one another—at opposite ends of the behavioral spectrum. True. However, one individual can display trauma symptomology that does not stay within one category; behaviors can be hyperaroused, detached and disassociated at different times during a single day. For teachers, this is highly problematic because they cannot find any comfortable space in which to engage with the child.

Whether a student exhibits one or all of the symptoms, there are consequences of these behaviors. Many students with delayed symptomology have attachment disorders. It may be hard for them to form lasting relationships—friendships, romantic connections, familial ties. For example, some children may complain that they have no friends. Others may answer the question "Do you have a favorite teacher?" with a blank stare. Relationships with at least one person are crucial in navigating trauma, so difficulty forming attachments has profound effects on trauma responsiveness.

I once had the idea that upcoming graduates at the college where I was president should send a letter to a teacher from their school days who would be pleased to learn that their former students were graduating from college—a teacher with whom these students had had a lasting connection and for whom the letter would have meaning. The effort was a dismal failure. Students could not come up with the names of those teachers, whether from elementary, middle, or high school. Never once did it occur to me that the project presupposed attachment, and many students at this college, who had high ACEs based on anecdotal and some concrete information and low predicted college graduation rates, had some form of attachment disorder resulting from trauma. The project presumed attachment. My failure was to not understand fully who our students were.

Dissociation, yet another delayed symptom, is an attachment disorder related to oneself, distinguishing it from detachment, which is a lack of attachment with others. Dissociation occurs when individuals are unaware of their own feelings and thoughts. They do not own their thinking. Dissociative symptoms range across a wide spectrum, from the very mild to the totally disruptive of a person's full functionality. Individuals with dissociative symptoms may be highly functional but may not see a physician for an illness because they do not feel they need to. They may not share with a teacher that they do not understand the material. This is not the same as freezing, one of the autonomic responses addressed in Chapter 3. Dissociation is not short term and is recurring.

People who are disassociated may also have problems understanding their feelings. Picture the child who says to the teacher, "Sally doesn't like me." Now, that statement could be true, but it could also be the child's *perception* of how Sally feels, and that could be totally fictionalized. In another example, individuals may assume that all people feel and think like they do; they do not see the distinctions (positive and negative) between themselves and others. Thus, they have trouble seeing how their thinking relates to and differs from that of their peers, making analytic thinking and problem-solving more difficult.

Disassociated individuals may put ideas into cabinets in their heads, so to speak, closed off from themselves. Call it a protective barrier. While helpful in some ways, the cabinets can be opened accidentally (by a teacher or a professor), and a person has trouble dealing with the contents that come spilling out unprocessed; or, alternatively, the cabinets are so stuck shut that the issues within them are not processed but do affect behaviors and feelings seemingly with no apparent cause. An example of this are students who can't understand how to protect themselves from others who are harming them or stop working when they are in fact maxed out. They can't see limits because the limits are walled off. We all know many students like this.

Add to this that dissociation may be a complete loss of memory, a disconnection with something negative. Individuals who do not know they were abused or are living with toxic stress may be disassociated, as with the narrator in the book and movie *Glass Castle*.[11] Members of certain religious cults show signs of dissociation, unable to distinguish between reality and the cult's belief systems.[12] Technically, we distinguish between depersonalization and derealization, both of which are intrinsic to dissociation. For our purposes, we are looking at trauma-induced dissociation as a whole, though the origins of dissociation are not fully explicable.

But There's More: Think Tri

We assume that people with delayed symptomology show evidence of trauma, even if we do not recognize it as trauma. Teachers and professors come across students who are hyperaroused or detached or disassociated or failing to attach. Educators may miss the causation and lack strategies for resolution, but they are seeing or sensing something.

I think there is a forgotten third category of delayed symptomology that has not been identified, let alone addressed. I'd describe this as the condition experienced by students of all ages and at all stages: *hyper-regulation*. These individuals do everything that is asked of them and then some. They arrive on time, and they do the assigned tasks and even take assignments and expand on them. They show caring for others and immerse themselves in wide-ranging activities. These are children who can engage with peers and adults alike. They are accommodating and likable and often filled with ideas and energy and a willingness to please. For teachers and professors, these students are gems, the ones they view as highly engaged, willing to learn and grow and flourish. Many such individuals, because of their responses caused by hyper-regulation, have found a different approach to dealing with trauma. They are experts at sensing what is needed to meet and exceed expectations. They do not disappoint. They are not called out for disobedience but instead for being extraordinarily compliant—overcompliant. They do not rebel except in very circumscribed ways.

Teachers and professors rarely question what motivates these students. They do not see their behaviors as compensatory. They do not see that they are very good at avoiding conflict and complaints to minimize disruption. They cannot tolerate raised voices, aberrant behavior, or disorder. They do everything they can to keep order and keep themselves and others calm. But in the privacy of their homes or rooms or minds, these individuals may be struggling mightily. Their trauma has driven them to succeed, but at a very high price, and if and when they express distress and trauma or assert that they are actually shy, no one believes them. No one supports them or asks them why. These individuals are so good at acting as expected that those around them falsely assume they are perfectly happy and comfortable in their worlds.

Often, nothing could be further from the truth. There are many examples of this. Return to Christine Blasey Ford, who asserted that now Supreme Court Justice Kavanaugh sexually assaulted her decades ago. She is an established and successful scholar. She is married and has a home and children. She is well regarded among her peers and has friends. Nonetheless, as she disclosed in her testimony, her internal life was not completely in order, despite her success. Many observers said she could not have been assaulted, given that remarkable success. They did not see her hyper-regulation as yet another symptom of trauma—delayed symptomology. Similar comments could be made about Anita Hill. Here is a woman, a law professor, of remarkable achievement. Yet when she testified, she was disbelieved. People could not reconcile her achievements with a past riddled with abuse by her former employer, Clarence Thomas, who was being nominated and then was ultimately confirmed for a seat on the U.S. Supreme Court. Think about the many female athletes under the aegis of USA Gymnastics who won gold medals after being sexually abused by their team physician. No one suspected they were anything but happy; they worked hard; they attended meets; they practiced. They were hyper-regulated, and only after the abuse was disclosed did they reveal their anger, their fears, their sense of betrayal.

If it is hard for educators to identify acute symptomology and the traditional biphasic delayed symptomology, it is much harder to identify and recognize *triphasic* symptomology. Which teacher or professor looks to his or her best, most well-behaved students and sees trauma? What educators see is success, and they erroneously mistake that for a sign of happiness instead of seeing it as a symptom of trauma. I know this from personal experience. I remember going to my high school chemistry teacher and asking her for more oxidation-reduction problem sets on which to work. I did this for weeks. Did she wonder, What is wrong with this student? No, she assumed I adored Chemistry and gave me more and more problem sets and watched and helped as I worked through them. As a college president I attended many networking events across my state and the nation. I was good at networking, meeting people, and sharing the college's story. If I had expressed that I was shy, people would have laughed at me, protesting that I was the opposite. Little did they know that networking was hard work for me and that I paid a steep price for it internally. Attempts by educators to understand their students rub against many assumptions. Understanding trauma symptomology requires that we set aside long-standing and commonly applied preconceptions and reflect differently on trauma's impact—because that impact takes forms for which we lack training, experience, and knowledge.

If Part I of this book alerted educators to trauma symptomology and increased their awareness that their own standard operating procedures are missing deep understanding of the students they serve, then it will have achieved at least one of its major goals. If it makes teachers look at student behavior differently and ask the *why* question, then we will be making progress.

Before turning to solutions for both acute and delayed symptomology, that is, practical ways in which educational institutions can become more trauma sensitive and responsive—improving the lives of students and educators alike—I want to conclude this chapter with two true stories pertinent to delayed symptomology. Having read this far, readers should find that these stories make sense and, hopefully, provide a smooth transition between identifying symptoms and addressing them systemically in our educational system, from early childhood through adulthood. Through these stories, we can probe the embedded challenges to the effort to respond differently and more effectively to the inevitable trauma that occurs in educational settings. And through these stories, we can learn how to change school culture as well as educator behavior to better respond to the trauma evidenced in students. Student success depends on our capacity to do it. Now.

Story 1: It Is Dark at Night

The Southern Vermont campus had an upper and lower campus, with most academic and administrative functions on the upper campus, along with the library, a popular evening student gathering area. The road linking the two locations was bumpy and the lighting was poor. And in the winter, it got dark early.

One evening, as I finished my day, I offered a ride down the hill to several female students from New York City. They accepted with alacrity. Once they were in the car, I asked why they were so eager for a ride down the hill. One exclaimed, "We're afraid of the dark. It's so dark at night here compared to home." Another said, "I'd never walk to the dorm alone." I responded, a tad too fast, "Are you expecting bears or other creatures to leap out onto the road?" They answered quickly and in slightly different words, but they were all basically saying, "You never know what happens in the dark."

I raised the issue at the next senior leadership meeting. My colleagues' responses varied. Some thought the students were just lazy and did not want to walk in the daytime *or* at night; it was a distance of maybe half a mile, considerably less if one went through the woods. Another remarked that the students were probably in a hurry to get back to the dorms for some social event. Yet another suggested that this was part of a larger issue where many students wanted a van to run up and down the hill, especially at night, to increase transportation and ensure safety. Costly, yes, but in response, we installed both lights and a van system, doing so really as an accommodation to student demands; and we did it without fully understanding the real reasons and ascribing reasons that were, in retrospect, wrongheaded.

Some years later, it dawned on me: The students were truly afraid of the dark. In their own communities, bad things happened in the dark, and they feared bad things in the Vermont woods, despite repeated assurances about rural safety and bears and other creatures not meandering onto college pathways. They wanted lights on the road. They wanted rides. They were not venturing, and certainly not alone, into the dark. Their autonomic nervous systems were on high alert.

Yet my response was anything but sympathetic or understanding. In their own communities, people were shot in the dark of night and women were attacked and raped. At night, there were sounds of violence. Perhaps most of them had experienced such traumatic events or knew someone who had. In short, whether they were traumatized directly or vicariously, the darkness of the Vermont night and the shadowy trees provoked a fear that was not grounded in current reality, and that took on a life of its own. In my earlier book, *Breakaway Learners*, I would have described these students as *lastic*; these were students who had progressed into higher education despite the odds. They were elastic and plastic and had pivoted right (moved in the right direction). They must have experienced reciprocity and had belief in self. But even with those foundational elements and academic success, they had not left their past behind them.

I might add that I was once walking at night in a strange city with my partner, and we got lost. Totally lost. We ended up at a homeless shelter in a terribly dangerous neighborhood. Police were all around. My partner was calm. I, on the other hand, was panic-stricken. Yes, I had my cellphone. Yes, I was with another person who cared about my safety and well-being. But none of that mattered. I was sure I would be attacked. And the more lost we got, the more panicked I became. My autonomic nervous system was in full swing—my heart was racing, my body sweaty, and my breathing much too fast and heavy. Why did I react this way? Well, the easy answer is that being lost reactivated childhood fears of being lost and abandoned when I traveled by airplane alone in the 1950s between two biological parents living in distant cities, as referred to earlier. Since that time, being lost has had ramifications for me. I get uncomfortable when not knowing my way—even when, unlike in this situation, there is zero danger. Add in danger, and the results are not a surprise. The good news, I suppose, is that I was fully and keenly aware of what was happening to me, even though I could not stop the panic reaction. I at least knew where it came from, and that's useful.

Story 2: A Change of Teachers

Garrett adored his kindergarten teacher at his new school. She was warm and welcoming and soft-spoken. She was approachable and calming. Her desk had tissues and candies on it, and she regularly handed out both. There was no tension in her classroom. Everything seemed to just flow. There was peacefulness in both her room and her manner. Then, in December over the holiday break, she left the school for reasons that were unclear and not shared with students; and at the start of the next semester in January, when the children returned to their classroom, a new teacher appeared. The new teacher was dynamic and loud and larger-than-life. She was tall and had dramatic dark hair and wore red lipstick. She played loud music in class and got everyone moving about physically. She was full of energy. Garrett felt the difference between the teachers and just tuned out the new teacher. Her vivacity bothered him, and he wasn't in the singing and moving mood. So he sat in the corner or at his desk most of the time. He didn't participate in the classroom activities. He never went to the teacher's desk, as he had with the prior, now departed, teacher.

The new teacher tried to coax Garrett out of his shell. She called his name; she asked him to join in the action; she went to the corner where he sat to encourage him to move into the center of the room. None of her efforts were successful. Eventually, the teacher mentioned Garrett's behavior to the head of the school, asking if this child was usually shy and was having problems adjusting to kindergarten. The head paused and then noted how well Garrett had done with the prior teacher and could not explain the change in behavior. Then, several days later, the reasons suddenly became clear to the head of the school. Garrett's father was in the military and had been deployed, and the place Garrett had gone to find peace was school, and now, with this energetic new teacher, he had lost his quiet space. Further, the departure of his beloved teacher triggered memories of his father's departure and the uncertainty about his return. The absence of information about why the original teacher had left just added to his concerns. When the head of the school recognized why Garrett's behavior was so changed, she shared her insights with the new teacher, who continued to exert her best efforts to help Garrett adjust to her. But the task was fruitless. It was as if he was waiting for his original teacher—and father—to return.

In *Breakaway Learners*, I would have said that Garrett lacked lasticity, and I would have focused on the critical missing element: reciprocity. With the change in teachers, he lost his connection to someone in his school, and that loss was upsetting.

What the Stories Tell Us

In both these stories, our failure to see trauma and the behaviors and reactions it engenders in students is clear. While lights and a van were put in place on a college campus, it was for the wrong reasons and perhaps with some resentment from the college over the expenditure. With respect to the young student, no effort was made to share with him the reasons for the teacher's departure or to explore and acknowledge his feelings. No one said, "I understand why you want to remain alone. Whenever you are ready, I am here to help and maybe we can find a few quiet moments together during recess."

In short, we don't see trauma's symptoms, and we find other explanations for the students' behaviors. This must change if institutions are to have success with their students. Our sensitivity to trauma must increase, but we also need solutions and interventions that mediate trauma's symptoms. On top of that, our approaches are compartmentalized and segmented in education, which means longer-term effects and impacts are not addressed or followed. We lack psychologically sound and continually informed approaches for dealing with traumatized individuals as they progress along the educational pipeline. Eventually, if and when Garrett goes to college, his fears and experiences related to separation will likely recur.

Now, before we address solutions, we turn to one recognized but oft-unaddressed trauma—variously known as *secondary* and *vicarious* trauma, labels that are confused and don't fully explain things, as detailed in Chapter 5.

CHAPTER 5

Secondary and Vicarious Trauma

As we have seen, we do not focus on trauma in schools as a generalizable matter. Nor do we focus on the secondary and vicarious trauma (each of which is indirect) of those who work with traumatized students. That said, we need to get our terminology straight here, as it is easy to conflate concepts, which inhibits solutions that work. The term *burnout* is often used as a substitute for *secondary trauma*.[1] It may be a symptom of trauma, but burnout can occur in any work setting where people feel that the demands are high and they are no longer as productive as they once were. There is nothing specific to burnout that relates to those in the caring professions. There is nothing specific to burnout that relates to trauma.

I was struck by a quote about burnout, "Burnout happens when you avoid being human for too long," apparently from the musician Michael Gungor.[2] Nothing could be further from the truth. Burnout may occur precisely because one is with humans (and all their emotions) for so long and the effort is exhausting. Nevertheless, the quotation is representative of an antipathy to struggle and the seeming assumption that people use burnout as an excuse, despite repeated studies showing both its existence and its deleterious effects.[3]

The phrase *compassion fatigue* is also often used as a substitute for *burnout* or *secondary trauma*. Compassion fatigue is common in the caring professions and occurs when those who deal with individuals in need of compassion get exhausted from the repeated effort to give and give, seemingly not always getting enough in return (physically, usually, as opposed to materially, although the latter may apply).[4] Compassion fatigue inhibits one's capacity to work and is painful and disturbing because normally giving individuals start to notice they cannot do their jobs well.

While compassion fatigue may be tied to the trauma of those being treated, it is not necessarily a trauma-induced state, although it can produce symptoms similar to those of secondary trauma. Individuals helping Alzheimer's patients—whether in a facility or in a home setting—can experience compassion fatigue, as can people working with chronically ill children. For both, trauma is not being transmitted; rather, the psychic demands of the work deplete one's empathy, despite all good intentions. These caregivers become emotionally exhausted, drained, wrung out. That is why there are opportunities for respite care for those dealing with the chronically ill. One could call compassion fatigue the cost of caring.

The terms *vicarious trauma* and *secondary trauma* are used interchangeably to describe what occurs when individuals are exposed to the trauma of others—and the latter's symptomology, including both autonomic and delayed.[5] To compound the intricacies of the terminology, *vicarious secondary trauma* and *secondary vicarious trauma* have also been used. Before we fine-tune the terms, note that compassion fatigue is reflected in the caregiver; it is theirs on a primary level. And similar to burnout, it is not necessarily caused by trauma.

Vicarious trauma is an indirect result of trauma suffered by others and is experienced by people who deal with these traumatized individuals or with traumatizing situations. The impact of trauma is experienced by one group, and then that trauma is conveyed to people who work with and care for them. Secondary trauma is also indirect, and, like vicarious trauma, it is the result of work with traumatized individuals. But here's a key difference between vicarious and secondary trauma: While both groups of individuals may experience trauma symptomology, those with vicarious trauma typically experience a threat to and change in their view of life, their existential story, and their sense of hope. To be more concrete, individuals who work with abused children in foster care or youth detention centers may decide that bringing children into this world is too risky and that we will never be in an environment where children are safe and loved. Those who work in war zones may believe that peace will never come and will never be lasting and that violence is a permanent state. This type of experience—psychic change—is different from the triphasic symptomology described in Chapters 3 and 4.

In education settings, we are talking about trauma that teachers "get" through working with traumatized students—whether younger or older. The trauma that concerns us is secondary trauma, whereby educators are deeply stressed by the situations in which their students find themselves, the behaviors the students exhibit that challenge even the very best classroom managers, and the difficulties students encounter when they cannot focus or remember or problem solve. We address this secondary trauma in ways similar to how we address *primary trauma* (a term not used here with any frequency): It begins with recognition and progresses to changes small and large within educational institutions. It is for these reasons that Part II of this book, while focused on solutions for students at every level of education who have experienced trauma, has applicability for educators secondarily affected by the trauma of their students. The solutions work for those both primarily and secondarily traumatized.

Four important points:

1. Those working with traumatized people may themselves be traumatized by the events in question. Paramedics on 9/11 experienced primary and secondary (indirect) trauma. Teachers working with students after a school shooting have experienced primary and secondary (indirect) trauma. Medics working in the field with soldiers can experience primary and secondary trauma. Medical professionals working with COVID-19 victims can experience primary and secondary (indirect) trauma.
2. The severity of secondary trauma differs from person to person. Depending on caregivers' own trauma history (and not all people working with traumatized individuals are what one would traditionally call caregivers), the effects, or symptoms, may be more or less pronounced.
3. Educators can experience vicarious (also indirect) trauma, but their changed worldviews and their behaviors relative to hope for a better tomorrow, while important, are not within the scope of what we can address here in depth.
4. Educators need to pay attention to themselves and to see this as a component of their professional and personal well-being. This need may not have been on their radar when they were trained as teachers or professors. However, with rising numbers of traumatized students, educators are coming closer to resembling those who work day in and day out with traumatized populations such as disaster survivors. While not nurses or psychiatrists or certified counselors, educators are being confronted with a changing student population, one that demands that they reflect on self-care.

Here's why this matters—and each reason has enormous impact. Educators experiencing secondary trauma will struggle to do their jobs well. They may be less patient. They may sleep less well. They may feel themselves wandering off point in class. They may have personal relationship struggles. They may stop socializing. We will see greater educator turnover, which is damaging to traumatized students.[6] Teachers will stop teaching altogether after a few years, especially if the role of educator continues to expand in response to the students we are now enrolling. And for professors who have visions of themselves as content experts, greater personal demands may become an unacceptably high price to pay for life in academe. We will see some educators opting out of certain schools, perhaps the ones that need them most.[7] The "better" teachers will seek out schools where trauma is less, though sadly, departures can and do occur in many settings where trauma was not expected. Ask how many teachers and administrators leave a school or college after there has been a traumatic event or series of traumatic events? Just think about the educators working at Sandy Hook,

Marjorie Stoneman Douglas High School, Virginia Tech. The list of institutions with traumatic instances is long, unfortunately.

And here's the real kicker: We will see students who do not succeed, because their educators are not trained or equipped to handle the trauma that is so pervasive in our schools.[8] Sad truth. A reality. We cannot change who our students are. What we can do, though, is pay much more attention to the people who attend to our students and provide them with vastly better training—while they are preparing to be educators and when they are in our schools. I recently learned that some schools in Canada are considering using two school psychologists in their elementary schools, one for students and one for teachers.

Concrete Exemplars

Some educators are deeply in touch with their own feelings, and they do understand the students whom they are teaching. Listening to these educators is difficult. They are tired; they are fighting hard to assist their students in gaining success, in a struggle that often seems daunting; and they are trying to meet the demands of required testing while managing students for whom tests are suboptimal.[9] Leadership is not always supportive, consistent, and stable. These teachers share feelings like "I can't take it anymore. This is too hard. I can't wait for vacation or the weekend." Some just throw up their hands in despair.

Not long ago, I was in a classroom with students whose behavior produced utter mayhem. The entire class was in a state of disarray, and as soon as I entered the room to read to the students, the regular teacher left. She literally fled. She returned periodically throughout the hour but only to pop in and then escape. Now, it was a good thing I was an educator, as the typical children's book author might have run from the room, too. I never read my book to the students in that class that day; instead, I worked with them on how to calm themselves so that eventually a story could be read to them. And their teacher? I mentioned it to the principal and assistant principal, and I should have followed up. I, too, was rattled. I related this to other teachers, who remarked that what I had experienced was not at all unusual. Some teachers need to escape from or not be in their classrooms.

Here's another example. Observing the teachers of several classes in the library where I was reading to children, I saw that each grade came with its own teacher or two. I have been in this school once a month for over 3 years. People know me. Students and teachers and the library do not see me as a stranger. There is genuine trust and affection. So, what I write here is not meant to be critical or negative; rather, it is merely descriptive of what it is like to teach in a school where there is 100% free and reduced-price lunch and the school ranks near the bottom of a list of 175 elementary schools in the state.

Some of the teachers engaged with the children and me as I read and in other activities, including repeating words in the story and drawing a giraffe in five simple steps. Some teachers shared their drawings with me, and I called on some to recall passages or try tongue twisters. Other teachers tuned me out. They were on their cellphones or gazing up at the ceiling. They were not there, so to speak. Other teachers looked tired and bored. They no doubt were happy to be sitting down. But here's what's key: They were sitting at the periphery of the room; they were not part of the group. They were isolating themselves. Were I to take a guess, I'd see these examples as showing which teachers were experiencing something like burnout, compassion fatigue, vicarious trauma, or secondary trauma. However, being precise would require knowing more about the teachers and their experiences in the classroom, information I do not have. But the teacher responses were so different from each other that only someone seeing many teachers could identify those struggling the most. And the affected teachers need our help.

A Personal Story over Time

Having worked in one area or another of education for over 40 years, I can share how the different states referred to above (burnout, compassion fatigue, secondary trauma, and vicarious trauma) play out and how they are distinguishable. Call it one of the benefits of having been in the workforce for so long in a caring profession; there is little that one does not see or experience. Sadly, the world is filled with untoward turns and unexpected events that rattle the cages of even the most stable individuals.

At about year 15 as a law professor, I started to feel that my job was no longer fulfilling. No matter what I tried—sabbaticals, working at Legal Aid, throwing out my teaching notes, teaching new classes—I could not revive the joy I used to feel. I always said to myself that when I didn't feel jitters at the start of a semester as I entered a new class filled with law students, it would be time to reassess my situation. I'd define this as burnout. There was no trauma. There was no compassion fatigue. I was just plain tired, and my feelings were not being remediated by the usual cures: time away, different activities, new material. It was time to consider leaving. Interestingly, I was not sure my students noticed the "me" who was burnt out. In an odd way, the enthusiasm of my youth was replaced by the experience of teaching, and that must have made up for the absence of a bounce in my step.

Then 9/11 occurred. As I described in Chapter 2, the law school was blocks away from the crumbling towers, and I was there that morning. Surely, there was primary trauma. I saw the towers fall. I had white dust on my car and on me. I could not communicate with my family, and my son was just starting college. My autonomic nervous system was on full alert.

I differed from many others about how soon school should resume. I wanted to wait but was outvoted, and we reopened 2 weeks later. We were issued ID passes to enter the area. Some of us wore masks to deal with the bad air. Nothing drowned out the sounds of the ambulances, emergency vehicles, and trucks that ran up and down the streets near the law school. We brought in a team of psychiatrists from New York University, we had our own school psychologist on-site and available by phone for faculty and staff, and we had a faculty meeting I will never ever forget before the official reopening.

We were gathered in the main building's reading room, a stunning, wood-paneled space, and not the usual dining hall where we often met for faculty meetings. The dean spoke about reopening the school and then invited questions. One professor raised the topic of how we would talk to our students about the events that had transpired. How would we begin the first class back? Excellent line of inquiry. At this point, another professor (who was later dismissed for charges not worth detailing here but perhaps presaged by his complete absence of empathy) stated, "I don't get the big deal. Just open the book and begin where you left off before we closed." I sat, silent. Unbelievable to me. Let me see: We just move along as we were before we were so rudely interrupted? At last I spoke up. I said that it seemed impossible and wrong to just "pick up where we left off." Did it not make sense to take stock of what had just happened? Silence would not make the issues go away. I offered some suggestions: having a moment of reflection, changing the order of the material so it would be more relevant to the recent events, sharing a personal story, offering the help that the school had arranged, and ensuring the absence of stigma if help was sought, bringing my pet (a large sheepdog) to class.

When classes started again, I did several of these things. I switched the order of the material we were covering and explained why—which had everything to do with 9/11.[10] I brought my Old English sheepdog (who was cool as a cucumber) to school and let him roam the aisles of the tiered classroom. Students seemed comforted by his presence. I was too. No doubt, I had experienced *primary trauma*, and watching the news coverage over the 2 weeks we were closed had not improved my well-being. I was still on high alert. Just going through the barricades to get onto the block where the law school was located jarred me, having to see police and other armed uniformed officers everywhere and debris and feeling an eerie sense of doom. And there was that omnipresent smell that defies description to this day.

After 2 weeks, the faculty met again to discuss our progress, back in that same room again. It is another one of those meetings I will never forget. I remember it with the same clarity as I do the earlier meeting of faculty, as the same ungrounded, insensitive, unaware remarks came up. The same professor who had advised, "Just pick up where you left off," stated with complete confidence, "Everything is back in order. All is well in my classes, and we are operating as we did before." I was stunned. Each day, whether I taught or not, students lined up outside my office to describe the past 2 weeks, where they were when the towers fell, how they had handled the suspension of classes, how they were doing now, what they were feeling. I had the business cards of the NYU psychiatrists in my desk. I listened to the students and then said, "I'm glad you shared. I have many of the same feelings. But best to talk to someone who is more experienced than I am about how to handle these types of issues. We have therapists right here on the ground floor to help."

I must have seen 10 students a day, every day, for 2 weeks. I was exhausted. I sensed that the students benefited from coming into my office—and the other women professors had had the same experiences as I had. We were accessible, we listened, and we were compassionate. We could try a psychological explanation for why students came to us and say they needed a "mother" figure in a time of stress. And remember, back then, there were not many women law professors—perhaps 10 of us on a faculty of 60. I was worn out. Story after story, feeling after feeling. There was nothing I could actually do to help except be available and listen well. I was not trained for this for sure, and yet there seemed to be some benefit students got from telling their stories, something I now understand much better in terms of trauma solutions and connecting with others.

I called the school therapist and shared my fatigue and noted that in contrast to the outlook expressed in the professor's comments in the faculty meetings, my world was anything but normal. I was angry that his world seemed to have gone back to normal. "Compassion fatigue," the school therapist said. "Take it easy. Don't be hard on yourself. Rest." Good advice.

Fast-forward several years. I became the president of a small college in Vermont, and of the many positions I have held, despite its challenges, this was one of the most remarkable, allowing me the most rewarding professional experiences of a lifetime. I was there for 8-plus years. As one might surmise, college campuses are filled with wide-ranging problems. Many of our students were the first in their families to attend college, many had experienced childhood trauma, many were far from home for the first time, and many were struggling academically and in relationships with peers and others.

In the beginning, I felt like a firefighter on a hillside of brushfires spraying water as fast as I could. Over time and with a culture that changed for the better and new faculty and staff and increased revenue, the place started to hum. That was until the chief operating officer, who had become acting president when I temporarily took a leave from the college to work at the Department of Education for 13 months, stole money from the school. We brought in a threat assessment team, who considered him a suicide risk, raising the possibility that he could kill me and then himself. I had a 24/7 security detail. The episode ended when he killed himself in the woods near his home. It was 10:30 at night. I remember the call.

The campus adored this person. He was fun and engaging. He was helpful and befriended everyone, from the cook to the maintenance staff to the coaches to the faculty to the senior leaders. I had known him for 30 years without being aware of his mental condition, not unusual given his particular diagnosis. He had been a family friend; his wife and children celebrated holidays with my family. I had literally trusted him with my life, my son's life, and the life of the college. I felt deeply betrayed.

The faculty and staff needed to learn of his suicide before it came out in the local paper. They needed to learn it from me. Suicides are risky business on campus, where they can spread like a contagious disease. I brought faculty and staff together for an early morning meeting. They had to know something was up, despite my efforts to hide my security detail and pretend life was more or less normal. I shared the news as ably as I could. It was hard. I spoke softly. I tried to share that we never have the answers to some of life's questions. And we would never know or understand his death or his actions. Some people started crying. Some asked if we were going to have a memorial ceremony (note the irony of a ceremony celebrating a person who stole a million dollars or so from a small college). Some asked about how students would react. Some asked how we were ever going to move forward again.

In the weeks that followed, I must have walked the campus 200 times. I spoke in small groups and one-on-one to students, faculty, and staff. I visited the dining hall, I was at athletic events, and I canceled all travel. I just was there. Slowly, ever so slowly, we began to process what had happened. I defended the school and its fiscal stability in the community, in the newspaper, with the accreditors, and on campus. We were fine, I kept repeating. I defended the school before the nursing accreditors in a contentious battle and read my presentation to nursing students in their classrooms so they could hear the passion with which I was defending their program, their college, and their future.

Those events left me exhausted at some level. Nevertheless, on another level I was highly energized, working every minute of every day. No one could outwork me. But in the midst of all this, I had a crisis of confidence that I kept to myself. I wondered: Am I making the right decisions for the hundreds of people for whom I am responsible? Am I handling things optimally? Am I right to fight so hard for the school's reputation as if I were a soldier defending a nation-state? I worried that I was losing perspective. I worried that my decisions were flawed somehow. I worried that I was making a mess of things. I went to a therapist out of town. I shared the events over a period of months. I shared my decisions and my concerns. At each step of the way, the therapist said, "I think your judgment is fine. I think your decisions have been wise. I think you are experiencing a kind of paralysis born out of the events and your sense of responsibility. I have seen no evidence that you are making decisions that are bad or misguided. If anything, they are bold and sure-footed and right."

I can now put a label to what he was saying: I was traumatized. At the same time, I was experiencing secondary trauma, too. It wasn't compassion fatigue. I had the symptomology of trauma—primary and secondary. Loss of sense of self, difficulty making decisions, and questioning decisions are common hallmarks of both primary and secondary trauma. I exhibited all three phases of trauma responsiveness: I was hyperaroused, I was isolated in my own mind, and I was overworking and performing in ways that did not reveal my inner thoughts. I had a loss of belief in self.

Fast-forward again. After I left the position of president of the college, I searched for explanations for trauma's impact on children and adults in the educational system. I saw that we had little understanding of and training about something that felt omnipresent. I saw how trauma affected student success. However, students who were lastic were able to navigate forward, not with ease, necessarily, but with success. As it turned out, I was writing that book I had promised to write as detailed in the preface to *Breakaway Learners*.[11] And that book, when completed, examined in part how trauma (in others and myself) can be mediated. One could call *Breakaway Learners* the professional outlet that provided at least one solution to trauma through the development of the concept of lasticity. I began to go to disaster sites to help individuals deal with their trauma. After all, I had a wealth of experience, both personal and professional. I became certified as a psychological first aid provider. I enrolled in a program at Rutgers Graduate School of Social Work on trauma and disaster response, a program in which I now teach. And I started writing.

Disaster after disaster kept occurring in the world in general, and in my world in particular. There were natural disasters as well as human disasters. We had hurricanes and school shootings. We had friends die from illness. We had children and young adults being abused by teachers and coaches and professors. My husband developed Alzheimer's disease and became threatening and abusive to the extent I had to barricade myself in a cottage on our property. I felt the need to call the police often but resisted, to preserve some imaginary sense of normalcy. The verbal abuse was once accompanied by being hit in the middle of the night, eventually necessitating surgery. My relatives and some friends didn't seem to get (or want to get) that life was dangerous to me and my staying there with my husband was not an option. It just wasn't. No one should live feeling that his or her life is threatened, whether or not the intensity of that feeling was objectively verifiable on a daily basis. If you have a childhood of trauma, later trauma symptomology intensifies.

In short, the list of traumas was not shrinking.

I spent my time reading, writing, and speaking about trauma and traveling to trauma sites to aid those affected, as referred to earlier. I went to help people move forward—resiliency and grit don't solve problems like this.[12] I went to Las Vegas after the concert shooting. My children's books were sent to Puerto Rico for displaced students following Hurricane Maria. I spent time at a school in the Northwest where there was a shooting. I spent time with lawyers and paralegals who represent detained immigrant children. I spent time on an Indian reservation, including with young children and their early childhood teachers as well as the campus personnel charged with handling the many concerns of Native American college students. I worked with schools with traumatized populations, mostly from dysfunctional families (often with additions) and deeply entrenched intergenerational poverty. I worked with the staff of a nonprofit that served youth who had not completed high school; the staff themselves were experiencing primary and secondary trauma as the young people they worked with were often struggling, and some succumbed to addictions or endured mental illness.

At that moment, and in a world of political craziness (and I live in D.C.), I started to think about whether our world was safe,[13] whether I could help enough people, whether I was doing enough, whether we would ever live in a world where kindness reigned. I ended up spending a day with a spiritual leader in her sanctuary for a special meal, thinking that perhaps answers to this traumatic world rested in some higher spiritual approach or being. Everything at her sanctuary was white (except the people): the sofas, the chairs, the clothing, the headgear, the dishes, the walls, the room dividers, the lamps. For me, not being a religious person, this was quite the meeting and quite the setting. The sister invited me to a several-day retreat. I actually thought about attending, but in the back of my mind, the word *cult* kept coming up.

I'd say that at that point, I was experiencing vicarious trauma. I was thinking that my worldview was off base. I was pondering the impossibility of all that the world was experiencing. I reread a piece I had written while a law professor on the "Portraits in Grief" series that appeared in the *New York Times*.[14] I recalled the piece but not its poignancy. The piece is about how we will treat the victims, something that was haunting me again. I had a sudden urge, long past menopause, to have another child with my new partner—an utter impossibility. I thought about adoption. I thought about a trek to Africa or traveling to a war-torn nation. I thought about moving—apartments, cities. Little things were making me angry, reactions that were out of proportion to the situations.

Then something changed. Over the next few months, I went on a wilderness camping trip where I was eaten by mosquitoes and developed an immunologic reaction. My dog got really sick. I visited a friend in California who had been an inspiration from my youth, and we spoke Spanish together. I started planning a winter ski trip. I began writing about our world—and how we needed to speak up and out (a theme in much of my writing, to be fair, but it had new fervor). I wrote about Jeffrey Epstein's unchecked abundance of privilege that enabled his bad acts to continue for years. I wrote about President Donald Trump trying to buy Greenland and telling the Veterans Administration to purchase the nose spray Spravato as a cure-all for the 22 veteran suicides a day.[15] (By the by, if such a spray existed and was effective, it would be a solution proffered in Part II. It isn't there.) I saw the Gary Hart movie about his affair with Donna Rice and wrote about how Hart didn't own his transgressions and had poor judgment and disappointed many. I wondered how he could sleep at night—he hurt so many people, both those close to him and those who believed in his candidacy. I bought flowers for my partner. I made appointments with various doctors for October. I signed a new book contract. I got the Comcast guy to get the Internet working. I emailed some folks to whom I had delayed writing. I signed up for two new courses at Rutgers Graduate School of Social Work. I wrote a piece on aging and its benefits, inspired by the words of Frank Bruni: "You have to be awake to individuality and alert to subtlety."[16] I recognized all the work I had done, even when it felt like I had done none because I had locked it in a cabinet labeled "No longer needed or remembered." Bruni's words suggested that with age and experience come some remarkable capacities. His awareness of individuality and subtlety, not surprisingly, are reflected in the five *S*s and my approaches to addressing trauma in our educational system.

Here's what I did psychically: I unlocked that cabinet of good work, quite by accident. I received a call from the illustrator and designer of one of my then about-to-be-released children's books (*Lady Lucy's Ghost Quest*) and another children's book in the works titled *Lady Lucy's Dinosaur Quest* (www.northshire.com.). Both books have stunning artwork, a glorious quest for the multiracial heroine Lady Lucy and remarkable support from those involved in creation of these books. The conversation centered on how these two books would meet the needs of so many children across the globe and that folks were already asking for copies and to meet the author. I saw value in and felt the value of my work. I saw that small steps can make a difference, especially if aggregated psychically and in actuality. I offered to share how public libraries can be more trauma sensitive with staff and trustees while I was on a writer's retreat and to read one of my children's books while there. I never would have agreed to that weeks beforehand. The answers for me didn't rest in some spiritual leader. They didn't rest in giving up my work. No, the answers rested in recovering from vicarious trauma.

I think when we suffer from vicarious trauma, we lock the good things in some mental cabinet, and the lock is strong. The goal is to get that cabinet unlocked and the door opened, so we can return to our work and our capacity to care. When educators get vicarious trauma, it is truly time to pause and reset.

How we recover from trauma in the context of education—both primary and secondary—is the subject of Part II. I am comfortable saying this with conviction: Recovery strategies within the educational arena exist, and part of that is recognizing that trauma, once it appears in your life and that of your students, will never disappear. These solutions give me enormous hope for the future of our schools and the future of all our students—young and old. It is to these solutions that we now turn in Part II.

Part II

TAMING

CHAPTER 6

Finding Solutions

Recognizing and reducing the trauma now deeply embedded in our educational system require more than good ideas.[1] We need effective and timely approaches and practicable solutions that lead to demonstrable results. This is not the time for theoretical high-tech solutions, although practical, implementable technologies can be relevant. Nor is this the time for solutions too complex to be deployed, especially in a world of scarce educational resources.

We need solutions that will capture the interest of the many stakeholders in education—from children to adults, from educators to administrators, from parents and guardians to graduates, from school boards to wider government—and lead to their implementation. We all know that such solutions require change and that change, even needed and desired change, is hard. We tend to resist change, regardless of its merit. Embracing change as the best thing since sliced bread isn't our modus operandi. We seem to live by the adage: what worked in the past is good enough for the present; we just need to get tough.

As we will see in Part II, there are reasons to believe that the time is *now* for changes in our educational system. The tipping point—to borrow from Malcolm Gladwell—is upon us. We can't afford to wait, because the damage to our students is severe and pervasive, and there are indications that change will happen, as the preconditions for improvement are all present.

Where and How to Begin

There are lots of approaches to facilitating change in institutions, all of which recognize the difficulty of the tasks. Some people suggest starting from the bottom up, to focus primarily on what happens in the classroom, hallways, residential halls, dining halls, nurses' offices, and other areas in educational institutions.[2] Look, for example, at what is now being done at one elementary school in Denver, which the city hopes to replicate.[3] Among other things, this school has a multi-person welcoming committee at the door each day; they do check-ins with children in need; they have a cool-down room and a card that a child can show a teacher if that child needs to re-regulate. Let's call these *micro changes*, a term used in *Breakaway Learners.*[4]

Others suggest that change, particularly in institutions in which workers struggle in caregiving roles, has to come from the top down; changing the culture and organizational structure as a prerequisite to micro changes. This approach is adopted in *Destroying Sanctuary*, a book that details the failures in delivery to clients in human services facilities. Let's call these *macro changes*, a term also used in *Breakaway Learners*.[5]

I suggest a third approach, one that will be adopted here, namely, simultaneous bottom-up and top-down efforts to change how educational institutions deal with traumatized students. This suggestion is premised on how trauma actually works in affected individuals and how easily it can be triggered and retriggered in the lives of students over time (see Figure 6.1).

Suppose there is an excellent preschool trauma program across a state but the program has not been carried through consistently to all the state's elementary schools. Then assume some of the quality solutions are adopted with age-appropriate changes to the state's middle schools but not in the high schools and universities, including at the graduate level. Further, assume that few families move out of the state, though many move within it.[6]

Since we know trauma is carried forward throughout one's life, and it can be retriggered by any number of events near or far, piecemeal approaches

Figure 6.1. Change Strategy

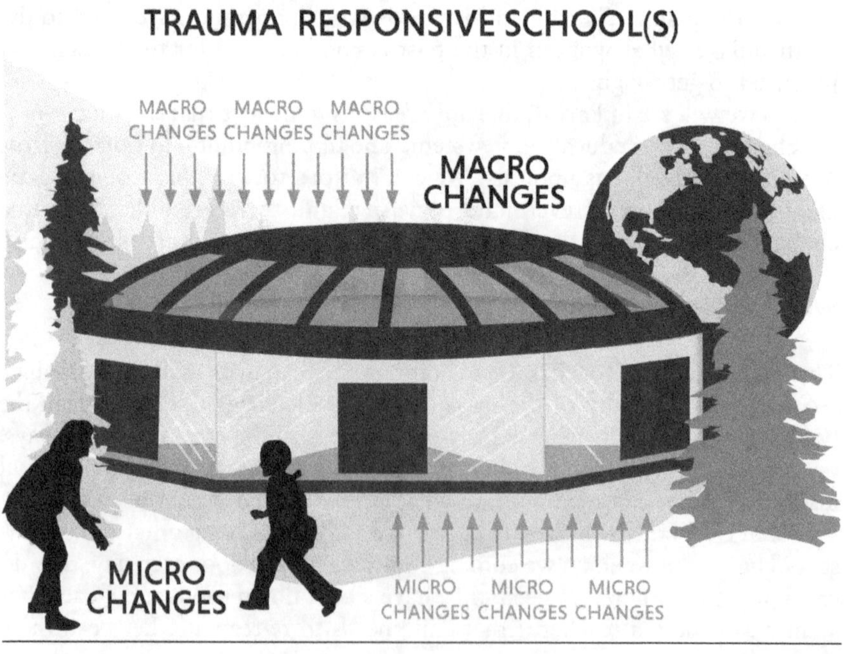

in educational settings are at best palliatives. They will not have lasting benefits. For maximum effect for affected students, the educational trauma "help line" cannot be active for some years and inactive for others. If it is, backsliding by students will be inevitable. And because other factors (deaths, illnesses, military deployments, new siblings, natural disasters) can add to the complexity of students' lives, inconsistency is even more damaging.

Consider the elementary school (true story) that is planning to open two "trauma-responsive" classrooms in a school filled with traumatized students and secondarily traumatized educators. In these two classrooms with 8–10 students each and trauma-trained educators, progress can be made. But what happens when these traumatized students join the general student population for lunch or art or gym or library time? What happens the next year when they are not in this "special" classroom? And what happens to the other 400-plus students in the school who could benefit from trauma-sensitive approaches? What happens when these students in the special classroom (stigma aside) enter middle school, where no such initiatives are in place?

These two trauma-responsive classrooms, evidencing micro approaches as the entire school is not changing, fail to smooth out the educational pipeline for the benefit of students. What we want, overall, is a set of initiatives that incorporate micro initiatives and programs but with consistency in all locations where students attend school during their lives in the educational system. Macro changes enable students to move from school to school without backsliding in their access to trauma-responsive environments. And yes, given that perfection is an impossibility, even with micro and macro changes across states or the nation, there will be kinks in the system.

Figure 6.2. Inconsistent Trauma Responsiveness (TR)

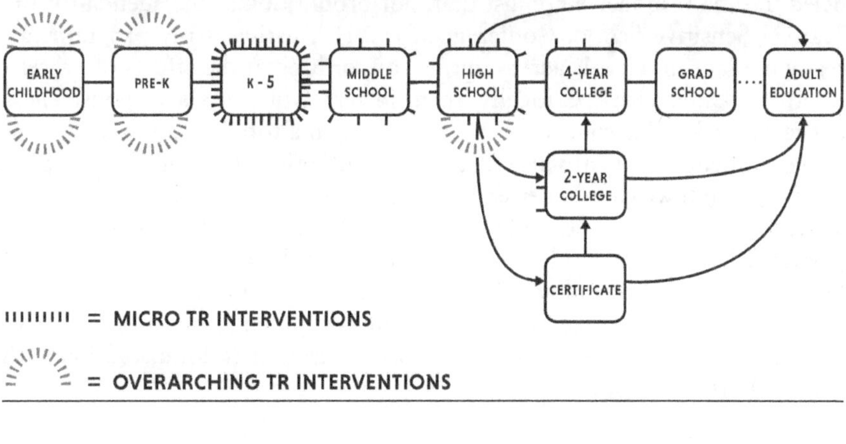

Benefits of Allostatic Load Lifting

The simultaneous bottom-up and top-down approaches represent the ideal model, but as changes are made and in the absence of perfect implementation, there will be many gaps. Rather than bemoaning their existence, we should recognize that all micro and macro interventions—even uneven or incomplete ones—help lift what is known as the *allostatic load* that traumatized students carry with them. The allostatic load is the wear and tear that people experience through continual stress. When the autonomic nervous system is on full alert, stressors act on the body and the mind, flooding the bloodstream with chemicals such as cortisol; this is harmful, as already noted, to everybody but especially young people.[7] Damage to minds and bodies is the price we pay when our allostatic load is on overdrive. Any efforts, even incomplete, that reduce that load have value, and there are tools to quantify the load reductions with interventions over a period of time.[8]

Start with this reality: Attending school does not, in and of itself, reduce allostatic load, although some of us thought it would for students with high ACEs.[9] That is why bottom-up changes to become more trauma responsive (even trauma aware or trauma informed or trauma sensitive, as we'll discuss) in some classrooms have value, even in advance of top-down buy-in or incomplete buy-in by educators at all levels. To be clear, we are talking about educational change from early childhood through postsecondary education, meaning that colleges and universities are within the scope of institutions that need to be trauma responsive.

On-the-ground implementation of trauma-responsive programs resulting in some change is already happening. There are trauma-responsive schools operating across the United States from early childhood through 12th grade. Colleges have used some of the ideas on implementing lasticity drawn from *Breakaway Learners*; these are efforts that while not labeled trauma responsive are just that. For proof, look at the agenda for the Trauma Sensitive School Conference for 2019, listing many programs already in place in schools across our nation, or look at the efforts of Eastern Kentucky University.[10] Critically, then, in terms of trauma responsiveness in the educational arena, we aren't operating on a totally blank slate.[11] Yes, we could bemoan the absence of universal adoption, particularly in higher education, and we can do better, but even partial adoption lightens the allostatic load of some of the students in some of our institutions. For children, particularly the very young, every moment that the allostatic load is lifted helps them because it allows the brain to develop and function more normally.[12] Surely we can see, though, that simply lightening the allostatic load from time to time or in certain schools or classrooms is not a solution with teeth over the long haul.

Breakaway Learners, Baseball, and Trauma

There are noteworthy similarities between Part II of this book and chapters in *Breakaway Learners.*[13] Both books seek change in the educational pipeline and the adoption of a new (or as yet unimplemented) approach. Here, the focus is on making educational institutions trauma responsive. In *Breakaway Learners*, the topic is how to replicate lasticity in colleges and universities and more broadly across the educational landscape. Both are efforts to facilitate and expand student success. I wrote *Breakaway Learners* to identify what factors enabled "vulnerable" students to succeed—because some did and greatly exceeded expectations based on high school GPA and standardized test scores. The usual approaches to dealing with breakaway learners—resilience, grit, and mindsets—lack sufficient breadth and particularization. Given this, *Breakaway Learners* moved away from a deficit model, which views students as having something wrong with them, to a positive approach, which sees what is right with the students and builds on those positives. This approach eschews efforts that focus on students who fail, drop out, or never attend college.

However, there are key differences between making institutions more lastic and making them more trauma responsive (or *lastic ready*, a term to which we will return). Lasticity is not going to be a pathway forward for all students, because its foundational five elements (elasticity, plasticity, pivoting right, reciprocity, and belief in self) will not be met, but it can be implemented without the 100% compliance of all educators across all educational levels.[14] Pieces of lasticity in place are better than no lasticity at all. And a lastic student can and does navigate non-lastic environments, including graduate school.[15]

Trauma-responsive institutions need buy-in at both the macro and the micro levels, because for traumatized students, there is less leeway for buy-in given how trauma works and how it can be triggered and retriggered by subsequent events over time. Consistency in approach is key, as we'll see in Chapters 7 and 8 when we explore the five *S*s—safety, structure, stability, subtlety, and someone(s)—that are needed for any trauma-responsive environment. This observation reveals a key difference between *Breakaway Learners* and the present volume: One was generated based on student success, and the other deals with student failures. So implementing trauma-responsive education poses a higher hurdle than does implementing lasticity. If successful, the former will help vast numbers of traumatized students who, but for these efforts, will fail to progress in education, from the early years through postsecondary education and beyond. It will be transformative for not only current students but also those in the future, as well as for families and communities.[16] Educators will benefit also, as secondary and vicarious trauma will lessen. There is real power in implementing macro and micro changes that improve how trauma is addressed in education. But make no mistake. Spotty implementation of institutional uptake of trauma responsiveness (micro and macro change) will cause many benefits to be lost. Moreover, micro changes alone will not be hugely effective long term, when students are in school and afterward.

Baseball offers a useful analogy for how implementation of trauma-responsive approaches can be understood and optimized and how it differs from implementing lasticity and other educational changes. Think about the offensive and defensive aspects of baseball. On the offense side of a team we'll call Team Success, hitters need to get on base. But if a batter gets to first base and never moves from there to second, third, and home base, a run doesn't score. To get home, the batter could steal some bases or hope other batters from his or her team get hits. Absent that, the hit to first base is, in essence, wasted for Team Success except for player stats (which do matter to some players in terms of compensation) and perhaps some benefit in belief in self for the hitter (who may have been suffering a slump or was recovering from an injury that put him or her on the disabled list). But if the base hit is to count for Team Success, the hitter who got the single needs to get around all the bases. A single only gets you so far—to first base, to be exact.

With me so far on this?

Now, reflect on the defensive aspect of baseball. If the pitcher for Team Success does not get the hitters from the other team—we'll call them Team Trouble—to strike out or hit grounders or foul balls, winning won't happen. Plus, if the outfielders from Team Success do not catch the balls and if its catcher does not tag runners, then Team Trouble will score runs and the offense of Team Success will not be enough to enable a win. The Team Success defense has to buy in to helping the Team Success offense in various ways, and if they don't get this role, then the offense and Team Success won't win. Note that this being baseball, the players on Team Success and Team Trouble play both offense and defense, something that becomes relevant momentarily.

Stated another way, to use the terminology we have applied to trauma and education, the hitters are making micro moves—hits (not counting home runs). Defensive players are working at the macro level, enabling the micro moves to have meaning. Baseball recognizes two essential issues about trauma: A hit in and of itself (absent it being a home run) is good but not enough. Without more hits and a good defense, one hit will not win the game. And winning is the goal. But if there is a hit by a member of Team Success (a trauma initiative in one school) that is followed by another hit (another trauma initiative for the same child in another school or the same school) and then another, the batter from Team Success will cross home plate. However, even crossing home plate is not enough; the defense of Team Success (the educational institution) has to take steps to create the opportunities for a Team Success win—stopping hitters from the opposite team, Team Trouble, from crossing home plate as well as getting the needed three outs. The Team Success pitcher is in essence setting the table for the Team Success offense when their turn comes up by limiting Team Trouble's hitting capacity. We can call what the defense on Team Success is doing both *protective factors* and *affirmative actions*.

And so it is with changes in educational institutions. Micro changes (hits) have value, and you can't win without them. A micro change in one classroom isn't enough in and of itself. The student needs to advance in other classrooms, and the institution (defense) has to enable that micro change to be part of a larger effort (a game) to keep that student safe and ahead across time and moving forward. Protective factors can be implemented, and there can be encouragement for getting base hits. Macro changes (the defense and other participating offensive players) need to be coupled with micro changes for impact. This isn't easy, because the offense and defense need to work together, just as the micro and macro changes need to work together. That is why we need to work simultaneously from the bottom up and the top down. Baseball teams and their managers know this; offense without defense is wasted, apart from minor benefits to the hitter. Conversely, the defense cannot win the game without the hitters hitting (although on rare occasions some games are won by pitchers walking bundles of hitters or other baseball flukes). Educational solutions need to be both micro and macro before we can claim success, despite interim benefits achieved along the way.

Before we turn to the needed micro and macro changes, we must reach consensus on what our goal is, namely, what defines a win in the world of trauma. Unlike baseball, where the team with the most runs wins, what constitutes winning is more complex in education. This complexity is increased by problems with terminology, an omnipresent problem in the world of trauma, as noted in Part I.

Name It Then Tame It

Consider these possible terms, which we will call trauma terms, for determining our end game (what is a win): *trauma aware*, *trauma informed*, *trauma sensitive*, and *trauma responsive*. Whichever words we settle on, they identify and describe the goals of this book and, more broadly, of our educational system. This matters for several reasons. For one, we want to make sure we have shared goals, and whichever trauma term we adopt has to reflect those goals or we won't know where we are going or when we get there. This is essential in any major initiative. For another, the trauma terms differ from one another in how far we need to move in achieving trauma solutions. Reasonable people can differ about their goals in the abstract and the concrete. Some may see the benefits of one long-term goal but settle for a lesser goal given real-world constraints. I see this approach as too tame, particularly when we recognize trauma's omnipresence and the effects of its symptoms on so many people, especially young people. I think change at both the micro and macro level is doable, and I feel that we have no choice but to make change. To return to the baseball analogy, a single won't do it. Trauma-trying is not enough.

Two key points before we turn to the trauma terms from which we can choose and which of these terms is deployed here. First, if we agree that trauma is impeding student success and if we see that the absence of success is hurting students as well as teachers and institutions (more on that momentarily), then from my perspective, we need the trauma term that has widest and deepest meaning, encapsulating micro and macro changes that are measurable and embedded into the future. We need the changes to travel across the educational pipeline over decades, just as the student travels along that pipeline. Otherwise, if the student moves and the progress on trauma doesn't accompany that movement, we truncate success. It would be like getting a baseball player from Team Success stranded on third base.

Second, we must recognize that it is not just the students who are traumatized. Educators are traumatized, too. In an excellent observation developed in *Destroying Sanctuary*, institutions themselves can be traumatized, and that can lead to devastating consequences.[17] If institutions are traumatized and their mission is to work with traumatized students (or clients or customers as the case may be), they cannot function. This observation leads to emphasizing changing institutional culture. Otherwise, workers will leave and customers, clients, or students (depending on the institution) will not be well served.

Destroying Sanctuary observes that with the growth of trauma and its effects, many human services providers are struggling because their clients are struggling, in part because the roles of providers are expanding and they are being asked to do more, often with fewer resources. In essence, a child-care worker must be a "parent-surrogate, educator, therapist, disciplinarian, caregiver, nurturer and security guard." Summarizing the new demands on institutions and their staff in light of client trauma, Bloom and Farragher poignantly observe, "Caught in the grip of monumental assaults upon the systems, few people [working in the system] have had the time or energy to step back and begin to look at the system as a whole through a trauma-informed lens." The authors add, "Our institutions are failing us. They are failing our clients and making too many of us sick in body, sick in mind and sick in spirit."[18]

Destroying Sanctuary contains numerous parallels to educational institutions—they fly off the page. Educators are being asked to do way more and to bear many more responsibilities. Their students from early childhood through postsecondary education demand greater skills in their educators, including some that educators may not have. All at once, the role of educator is changing (macro change), and the maintenance of classrooms and the proffering of content are becoming more difficult and demanding new approaches (micro changes). In addition, teachers and professors are being asked to engage differently with their students, and old methods of engagement, such as guidance counselor meetings with families and office hours with college professors, are not working sufficiently well. We urgently need change. As elucidated in *Destroying Sanctuary*, that change has to be "alert, fast, focused, relentless, and continuously overcoming irrelevant activities so that time for what is important is available and measures are in place to prevent burnout."[19]

Trauma Terms

Elucidating the terms that address approaches to trauma will help us formulate our path forward.

Trauma aware. Awareness of trauma is not action based; it is an intellectual achievement that gives a topic a name and then provides the meaning of that name. Naming is a key first step. It is the baseball hit. It gets the ball rolling (pun intended). And it is not that simple. If a topic is not familiar or not easily accepted, for any number of psychological reasons, then naming is more complex than it appears. A name is not just a name, to challenge a common adage.

Think about this naming through an analogy to diabetes. We need to name an illness before we can treat it. Without a name, we don't know what to prescribe. In the context of diabetes, we need to name the disease for patients. That isn't easy in real life. Once you name something, you open a big door—a door about illness, longevity, incapacity, and treatment options. That's where the danger comes in. You can't just name something and stop. If the something named has risks and heightens emotions (say, trauma), then a name isn't enough. Consider the efforts of psychiatrist Daniel Amen to see inside the brain of patients before treating them.[20] In essence, he is saying you need to name what a patient has—for real and by seeing it—before you can treat it. Naming the disorder in the brain isn't enough; it tells you what to do next. Doing nothing isn't, in most instances, an option when a patient is unwell.

Trauma informed. This formulation indicates that there is institutional information about trauma and its importance. Regard it as a notification posted on a door or printed in a brochure that says, "As an organization, we understand trauma." This would be like identifying diabetes and knowing that insulin is needed. Others see *trauma informed* as meaning much more than that. The Trauma Informed Care Project (www.traumainformedcareproject.org/) views *informed* as indicating "an organizational structure and treatment framework that involves understanding, recognizing, and responding to the effects of all types of trauma." This employs a broader use of *aware* and *informed*, given the incorporation of *responding* (as in action).[21] Importantly, it speaks directly to institutions and indirectly to those who work in them. What is particularly bothersome to me is the use of the word *effects*. *Effects of trauma* seems like a reference to trauma symptomology. *Effects*, however, is nebulous, as it does not speak to the audience—effects on whom or what? Audience matters, given the fact of primary and secondary trauma and vicarious trauma. Further, *effects* can mean financial effects and medical effects, vastly more territory than we are covering here in this book.

Trauma sensitive. A trauma-sensitive school is a school where "all students feel safe, welcomed, *and* supported *and* where addressing *trauma's* impact on learning on a school-wide basis is at the center of its educational mission" (emphasis in original).[22] Such schools "promote (a) feelings of physical, social, and emotional safety in students; (b) a shared understanding among staff about the impact of trauma and adversity on students; (c) positive and culturally responsive discipline policies and practices; (d) access to comprehensive school mental and behavioral health services; and (e) effective community collaboration."[23]

The first description above has many positives, but it limits interventions to learning, in the academic sense; and while learning is one aspect of school, it is far from the only one. We want psychosocial development and engagement, which cannot necessarily be measured on tests, at least not the tests we now administer. The second description is broader, as it includes not only action but also culture change and community involvement. However, some troubling words are embedded in the second description, and it is missing some items. The word *discipline* bothers me, as we need to move away from a negative, discipline-based system to one that develops responsibility with positive *remedial action*, all without punishment. We are talking about broader action, not just action in the context of wrongdoing. This same definition speaks to staff, not to the institution qua institution. Also, for me, the word *sensitive*, standing alone, seems less powerful than *responsive*. I suspect the word sensitive is also too touchy-feely for some. For me, *responsiveness* encompasses being informed, sensitive, and action oriented. Reflect again on diabetes. Using the trauma term *trauma sensitive* is like naming diabetes, being aware that insulin is a needed medication, and then being sensitive to the difficulty of lifelong self-injection and the family and work implications of having a chronic illness. These are all important steps to take. Sensitivity will help people with diabetes feel less stigmatized and may ease the self-administration of injections. But that's not enough.

Trauma responsive. Being trauma responsive is to reach the "highest state" achievable with respect to trauma. "Becoming trauma-responsive means looking at every aspect of an organization's programming, environment, language, and values and involving all staff in better serving clients who have experienced trauma."[24] Start by substituting *students* for *clients*. Then substitute *schools* or *educational institutions* for *organizations*. With these adjustments, this description of being trauma responsive has many plusses. First, it speaks to organizations and individual educators. Both need to be trauma responsive. Institutions do speak and message.[25] Second, it speaks to values as well as programming, the macro and the micro changes referenced earlier in this chapter. Nevertheless, this description is sorely lacking, because it uses the word *looking* as the main activity, and surely we can agree that we intend to do more than look at the problem of trauma. This book isn't about observing the problem of trauma; it is about action to take toward it in our educational system.

Using the diabetes analogy yet again, *trauma responsive* would involve naming diabetes, developing an understanding of its significance and treatments, appreciating the need for and difficulties of self-administered insulin, and then helping a patient develop new strategies for dealing with the insulin injections: new needles, the possibility of installing a pump, changes in diet to lessen the number of injections, and better and less invasive methods of detecting blood sugar levels.

All these trauma terms and their differing meanings lead me to a new formulation for the goals of this book, centered on the term *trauma responsive*. With this new definition, the overriding goal is to create trauma-responsive schools:

> Becoming or being trauma responsive means educational institutions and those who work in and engage with them becoming aware of, informed about, sensitive to, and responsive to the effect and impact that trauma has on students across the educational pipeline and includes the implementation of value-driven policies and practices to ameliorate trauma's impact.

That leaves out one term: *lastic ready*. In a sense, any school that meets the just-created definition of *trauma responsive* will, a fortiori, be lastic ready. As noted earlier, lasticity cannot be robustly achieved unless trauma is dealt with first. If we address trauma effectively, students can enter the world of lasticity and benefit from it. Linking *Breakaway Learners* with the present book, our goal here is to create lastic-ready students. For success in this, students must be enrolled in trauma-responsive schools from early childhood on.

Change Doesn't Have to Be Uniform

In making change, we typically look for replicable and scalable models beginning with a pilot, and if the results are good, the pilot is applied more widely. In this method, there is a replicable model that will work for all locations, in all situations, for all individuals. In the context of trauma in education, however, homogeneity is not a solution. Rather, we need deeply personal and contextualized approaches. What matters is that certain core values be replicated. Value replication is not the same as program replication; programs can take many forms and should. What remains constant are the values that undergird all the programs, values we identify in Chapter 7 as the five *S*s.

Reflect on the effort to improve completion rates for the Free Application for Federal Student Aid (FAFSA) form through nudges to students in a position to file these complicated documents. For these students, FAFSA is the gateway to financing postsecondary education. Small-scale efforts used personalized emails to students, and the results were positive—more students completed FAFSA forms when they were nudged in this way.[26] However, when the effort was scaled, the results were different. Students did not feel the personalization, the driver behind the original nudges.[27] Mass emails from unknown parties just went unnoticed or unattended to, as the sense of caring inherent in the small-scale projects was not experienced.

In addressing trauma, we do not need identical solutions across the nation; we need personalized solutions that fit the communities where they are implemented. What is needed in one region of the nation is not the same as in another; cultural heritage, gender, and historical context all matter. A program in El Paso needs to be different from one in Dayton, Boston, or Chicago. One on an Indian reservation needs to be different from one in rural Vermont.

Change Won't Be Easy

A concrete example: I met with a remarkable teacher of students, many of whom had failed at many other high schools. She suggested that my trauma-responsive campaign, with its five core values, including changes to punishment and disciplinary approaches, missed the boat. She described this scenario: She had a student experiencing a full-fledged outsize response. He was throwing tables. He was swearing. He was talking about drug deals and sex. He was disrupting others in the class. He could not be calmed down. The teacher suggested sending him out of the class, out of the school even. With 20 other students, she could not devote her time to this one student.[28] She had to banish him, so she could get to the job of teaching the other students.

I listened. I heard her lament that the school lacked resources and she was stretched thin with daily behavioral issues among her many traumatized students. There were too many state mandates and too much paperwork. After a pause, and thankfully we were away from the school grounds and in a calm setting, I said I actually understood. I, too, had been in classes where students disrupted learning for others. Not only was the incident bad for the student experiencing the trauma; it was bad for all the other students.

But what if we did processing in place? What if she could have contacted a member of the administration? What if she contacted the school psychologist (assuming one existed)? What if that person came to the classroom instead of sending the student out of it? I was advocating for an approach called processing in place, increasingly being used for classroom management and students who act out or have the potential to do so.[29]

"Wait," the teacher responded, "You want the principal to come into my class?" Yes, was my reply, and his or her job was to work with the student melting down or acting up. The principal could use trauma-sensitive approaches, and if his or her presence and actions were not enough, the student and principal could go into the hall or some central place created for handling just such situations—not the principal's office. Her tart response was, "You haven't met my principal."

Picture how this works with a principal who has been bought in. Instead of sending the student out, the teacher asks for someone to be sent in. Might that change alone message? Whoa. If you act out, you don't get to leave; you are pushed to stay. If the principal is well trained in trauma, he or she will not be a threatening presence to the students or the teacher but instead a connection, someone who focuses attention on the student in need. This wouldn't be like being sent to the principal for acting badly. No, this would be the teacher recognizing that she needed help to control this student's outburst and leadership that would engage in the solution. Imagine how this would message to the other students.

We need to shift how we think about and handle trauma symptomology in schools at the micro and macro levels. Traumatized students should not be punished or disciplined, as negative events are the genesis of their behavior.[30] Of course, they can learn that their behavior is intolerable in the classroom and they must regulate it. They can learn what their triggers are and how to pause. And they can be helped if their school employs macro and micro approaches to trauma.

Trauma Matters

We now turn to the nine factors that suggest for me that a change can happen in how we view and handle trauma in education. Readers may not agree on all nine; indeed, they may not agree with most of them. But it is not the individual factors that matter; it is the overall gestalt, the messaging, delivered by these nine factors. Also, these nine factors lead us to the justification for the generation naming developed in Part III of this book. The name Generation T—with *T* for *trauma*—has its roots, then, in Part II.

CHAPTER 7

Change on the Horizon

Cultural change is not usually initially apparent, but indicators often emerge, in a confluence of context, current events, the engagement of high-profile individuals, and pressing need. Despite this time of extraordinary partisanship, enabling trauma-responsive educational systems is not, in and of itself, a political issue, although debates on gun control may tinge the discussion.

Lessons from Smoking and Civil Rights

Two cultural shifts are precursors to an altered outlook toward addressing trauma in education. The first is the public's widespread rejection of tobacco use, inspired by the Surgeon General's reports on smoking. At one time, smoking was commonplace in the United States. Despite the efforts of the tobacco industry to fend them off, it was confronting smoking opponents, including President John F. Kennedy. A ban on cigarette advertising on television further reduced smoking, which came to be seen as a public health issue and a costly one.[1]

The second cultural shift was the civil rights movement, with catalyzing events and remarkable leaders demanding equality. Legislation and legal decisions pushed the movement forward, as did speeches that ring in our ears today.[2] Student protests led to arrest, injury, and even death, as discrimination in educational settings propelled the move toward civil rights, particularly in the 1950s. Segregation in education and harm to children galvanized many.

In both these instances, progress forward was not easy or fully successful. Discrimination continues and vaping has become popular. Cultural change is progressive and advances by stages. In *The Tipping Point*, Malcolm Gladwell notes that cultural change occurs when a tipping point approaches and there's a confluence of the right people, the right time, and the right context; such a tipping point does not require "big" events.[3] In the education system, addressing trauma is at a tipping point, and once the tipping occurs, the speed of change in institutions will increase substantially.[4]

As with smoking and the denial of civil rights, something negative is affecting lots of individuals we care about, and we need to do something now to improve their situation. People are dying from the effects of trauma.

It is hurting infants, young children, youth, and adults. When the tipping point occurs with trauma, cultural change in our educational system will be dramatic and rapid; we will be positioned to view and then address trauma's impact for the benefit of all students.

Context Counts

The times we live in facilitate a fresh look at addressing trauma. First, the events of September 11, 2001, changed the nation, altering our perceptions of safety. Subsequent violent attacks only heightened our fears. Security increased; we became concerned about large gatherings, transportation systems, shopping malls, cinemas, and places of worship. Concerns about opportunities for terrorists persist. Laws have become stricter, with loss of personal freedom.[5] And vigilance is promoted by the Department of Homeland Security imperative: "If you see something, say something" (www.dhs.gov/see-something-say-something). Our culture is now suspicious and painfully aware of risks in locations previously considered safe. Adding to the aftereffects of 9/11, not only did approximately 3,000 people die in the terrorist attacks, but more than 3,000 children under age 18 were left behind, and pregnant survivors have passed down post-traumatic stress (PTS) to their children.[6]

Consider the articles noting the number of children of firefighters who died on 9/11 who have become firefighters.[7] The most recent class of firefighter recruits in New York had 13 children of firefighters who died on, or from causes related to, 9/11.[8] The stories accompanying these new recruits are replete with ongoing concerns about the safety of the next generation. And given trauma's propensity to be retriggered, one can only assume that these new firefighters triggered trauma memories (along with some positive memories and pride, to be sure) in their families.

Second, the United States has been at war for the past 18 years, the longest continuous period of war in our history. Many soldiers have died in Iraq and Afghanistan (among other locations abroad), and many have been injured. Military families have experienced one or both parents being in a war zone for years.[9] All these factors trigger trauma and post-traumatic stress (PTS). Awareness of the PTS suffered by many veterans and active members of the military is now common, and people are conscious of the more than 20 daily suicides of veterans.[10] Trauma isn't new to any of us, whether we are in the military or not. It is omnipresent.

Nine Factors Toward a Tipping Point

Nine factors push us to a tipping point in addressing trauma in education. These encompass the three steps proposed by Gladwell: right people, right time, and right context.

Prevalence of natural disasters. Natural disasters have increased over 7% annually. Social media increases awareness of disasters near and far and of how we often fail to get help to the affected areas quickly, as effects linger and death tolls rise. In 2018, Hurricane Florence killed 39 people and caused $14 billion in property damage in North Carolina. Hurricane Michael killed 39 people and cost $16 billion in Florida. Maria's impact on Puerto Rico was devastating.[11] Now we've got COVID-19.

When such disasters strike, what happens to children and their schools? Who helps the children in the United States, let alone the larger global community?[12] We do not have educators on disaster relief teams, so trauma-trained teachers could assist students in shelters, something that could be accomplished with relative ease. How do we reopen schools in ways that are trauma responsive?[13] Whenever and wherever those students return to school or college, they carry their trauma, and many educators are also personally devastated, straining their capacity to handle their students' distress.

School shootings. The rising incidence of school shootings affects students, their families, and educators in the affected schools and in other schools. Social media conveys to the larger public what has happened. Unfortunately, we haven't yet been able to pre-identify those headed to schools to kill classmates.[14]

Historically, we were accustomed to seeing schools as places of safety. However, since the shooting at Columbine in 1999, there have been at least 11 mass school shootings with fatalities and numerous injuries.[15] In 2019, at this writing, there have been 64 incidents of gunfire in schools with 11 deaths (including suicides) and 41 injuries.[16] On college campuses, 190 shootings occurred between 2001 and 2015, injuring over 400.[17]

What happens to the affected students at these schools? Whether it was a mass shooting, a suicide, or the shooting of a parent at the school, these events likely traumatize virtually every person in that school. When we close the schools, we add another stressor, the elimination of processing in place and as a community (see Chapter 8). Educational personnel and families are affected, as is the wider community, including other schools nearby.[18] With subsequent shootings, the trauma can be reactivated, or retriggered.

Trauma's tentacles. As devastating as trauma is, we tend to hope that its effects are short term. The event happens, we provide some interventions, and then all is well. Nothing could be further from the truth. Three examples poignantly bring home this point. The Sandy Hook Elementary School shooting occurred in 2012. There were 27 deaths. Periodically, we see newspaper accounts on anniversaries of the shooting that demonstrate its lasting effect on survivors.[19] One year after the Stoneman Douglas High School shooting, two students who had survived committed suicide. Several days later, the father of a victim of Sandy Hook did so.[20] Trauma's effects have long tentacles, and its symptomology lingers even when one gets help and works to recover. It isn't enough that 17 people were shot at Parkland. Now two more people died related to that shooting, devastating the community yet again and retriggering the trauma that had occurred the year before.[21] Indeed, the motto "17+2" has appeared in posters in the Florida community.

Trauma as an equal opportunity offender. In a flood or a mass shooting, harm often afflicts individuals across the socioeconomic spectrum. Fires, hurricanes, and school shooters don't ask to see your tax returns before they do their harm. In the United States, we do better solving problems that do not call for political or class divisions; we allocate more attention and money to problems when we aren't forced to address our belief systems in terms of social services provided by government or even the private sector. When we can say that a problem is not "just a poor people" problem, we are more willing to act. For our purposes here, when all children can experience trauma and its symptomology, the willingness to solve the problem with some immediacy increases.

An example of this unfortunate reality is the opioid crisis, which has garnered considerable attention and efforts to remediate its harms.[22] That is, at least in part, because the victims are not all poor.[23] Addiction can afflict all socioeconomic classes, and vastly different approaches were taken to the crack epidemic.[24] We look at opioid-addicted individuals as needing help for their illness, although as a factual matter the opioid crisis affects the poor and people of color with much greater force than other populations.[25] Opioids are generally obtained legally through prescriptions from legitimate physicians, encouraging a willingness to eschew criminalization, the approach taken toward crack.

Trauma's ability to affect you on your own doorstep. Trauma affects not only the children and adults enrolled in educational programs but also those working with them. This fosters a wider and more accepting audience for trauma remediation. If educators see and feel the effects of trauma, in themselves, their schools, and perhaps their families, they become a constituency that can add considerable leverage to the effort to make needed change. There is nothing like something being one's own issue to make it relevant.

Data show we are more willing to work on problems that affect us personally (self-interested vs. selfish) but only those where the benefits are shorter term, too.[26] When problems affect others or the benefits are way down the road, we can more easily distance ourselves. But when a problem lands at our door and teachers, professors, and others in schools are affected by trauma's reach, we have added motivation to open the door and act. The point is not to address how to change motivation and reflect on human behavior but to suggest that our self-interestedness can help the push to make trauma a topic to address in our schools.

Legislation and legislators. Among local, state, and federal legislators, a remarkable push has urged more attention to and more funding for programs designed to ameliorate[27] trauma affecting children. I attended the first federal hearing on trauma and the importance of programs to help children survive traumatic events, particularly family traumas as reflected in high ACEs.[28] The following words from a Government Accountability Office study were referenced: "Trauma is a widespread, harmful, and costly public health problem, and is especially detrimental to children."[29] The hearing saw trauma as a public health crisis that was damaging our children.[30]

In July 2019, three federal legislators introduced a bill, the Trauma-Informed Schools Act of 2019. Similar legislation was introduced in 2018, suggesting that traction was not strong then. While there is plenty to quibble about in the legislation, the effort to create macro and micro changes in schools, including in punishment and discipline, and the recognition of teacher training are notable.[31] This followed introduction of the Resilience Investment, Support, and Expansion (RISE) from Trauma Act, authorizing funding for initiatives on trauma that affects children, including increasing public awareness, coordination among organizations, pilot projects, hospital-based programs, creation of arts opportunities, and ensuring that the youngest children get trauma interventions.[32] I have concerns about substance, but there are many positives in this bill, and it shows considerable awareness of the issues.[33]

On the state and local level, California's Surgeon General, Nadine Burke Harris, discusses a newly updated ACE test being administered by pediatricians to the parents of young children in her book *The Deepest Well*. Her agenda in office centers on children and reducing toxic stress,[34] as well as compensating specially trained health providers who administer the ACE test to their patient population.[35] As an immigrant, female, person of color serving as the first surgeon general in her state, she has not been reluctant to speak out on the impact of trauma, toxic stress, and race on children.[36] Vermont recognized the importance of ACEs early on and pushed pediatricians to administer the ACE test to parents of young children as part of Vermont's Blueprint for Health and offered initiatives to curb high rates of ACEs in Vermont youth. In Walla Walla, Washington, a community came together to help its traumatized students, and it all started with recognizing the importance of ACEs.[37] The documentary *Paper Tiger* showcases the challenges the town faced and its success (kpjrfilms.co/paper-tigers/). The town has been lauded nationwide for its efforts.[38]

The human voice heard. As important as federal, state, and local legislative efforts are in addressing childhood trauma, the most powerful element in effecting change is voices.[39] The voices of those within and outside power are compelling and, like a positive virus, catching. In the 1960s, powerful voices spoke and sang about discrimination, war, equality, and peace. Hope, not cynicism, ruled the day. I see that again today, not to emphasize my rose-colored glasses. We are hearing powerful voices.

At the House Oversight Hearing held in July, even more impressive than the testimony of witnesses were the words of the committee members when they poignantly shared their own stories of trauma, including the words of recently deceased Representative Elijah Cummings from Baltimore, who referenced his being placed in a "special" school for those considered "slow." I am not sure these legislators had planned that degree of personal disclosure, based on the expressions of their staff members. They divulged having a parent die, getting cancer, and being discriminated against with a startling authenticity rarely felt in the chambers of Congress. The stories were heart wrenching. Something touched a chord.

These voices added to the voices of youth in the movement March for Our Lives, which was started by the survivors of the Parkland shooting. With 200 chapters in the United States so far, this movement organizes school walkouts[40] and gives students a platform to speak out about gun control and the importance of voting.[41] Focus for a moment on the Parkland students who joined the anniversary march for the school shootings at Columbine.[42] Some people wondered why they were marching for something that had happened before they were born. Just think about that. For the Parkland students and their families, legislators, community, and schools, the time for silence had passed. In these youth, we can see a tipping point being reached.

Imagine: global youth voices consistently being heard. Voice is at least one pathway for how attention to trauma will gain traction—through those who have experienced it and are increasingly unable to keep quiet.

Large-scale trauma caused by powerful people. There have been enough bad actors in positions of power who have abused others and caused trauma that we can't turn away and say that trauma is not abundant. What passed for acceptable no longer is, and the #MeToo movement has been a powerful response. Victims are speaking out, among them the gymnast Simone Biles, who spoke about her abuse by the team doctor, Larry Nassar.[43] Many affected young people are still in school, their trauma carried into the educational environment.

We can thank Jeffrey Epstein, whose behavior in life and whose death attracted wide attention, for changing attitudes.[44] He traumatized many women, and even up to the moment of his death, he was gaming the system to the detriment of others, with the help of his enablers.[45] Epstein's reach extended to education; he donated to universities, academic programs, and labs, including those designed to be secret.[46] The recent conviction and sentencing of former movie mogul Harvey Weinstein, accused by many women of sexual assault over decades, is but another example, and some of his victims have since shared how this outcome enabled them finally to find their voices.[47]

Amalgamation and associations. A number of associations and other organizations are now addressing the impact of trauma on education. They focus on specific segments of education—higher education and early childhood are less prevalent—and appear not to be fully coordinated, but their existence bodes well for making progress if we can get these groups to work together and forego autonomy in exchange for vast change and engagement. Here is a sampling of just some of the entities: the National Child Traumatic Stress Network (which also has a network, www.nctsn.org/about-us/strategic-partnerships), Trauma and Learning Policy Initiatives (traumasensitiveschools.org/), the ACEs Connection Resources Center (www.acesconnection.com), the Center for Youth Wellness (centerforyouthwellness.org/), Project 180 (project180ga.org), and the National Center on Safe Supportive Learning Environments (safesupportivelearning.ed.gov).

If you take the nine factors listed above, view them as a group, and reflect on the growing number of organizations working on changing the educational system so it becomes more cognizant of trauma, the opportunity for emerging change becomes evident.

Pivoting Right

In *Breakaway Learners*, one pillar of lasticity is *pivoting right*, that is, moving in the right direction. Traumatized students have many choices to make along their pathway through education. They can make poor choices or can be guided to make better ones. One of the indicators of success for students is the capacity to make wise choices.

Think about the concept of pivoting right in the context of education. Can we get our educational institutions, just as we ask our students, to pivot right, namely, to adopt macro and micro strategies to create trauma-responsive schools? I think we now have the right choice architecture in place based on the factors described in this chapter. And to repeat an old adage: If not now, when?

There is one further issue to face as we turn to specific macro and micro changes, that of responsibility. Who is responsible for changing the way our education landscape works? Is that the job of educators? Legislators? Parents? Children? We can't discuss how changes can occur and be implemented if we don't know who will be making those changes and how they will be made.

Who Isn't Responsible?

Once we recognize that we need immediate trauma-responsive educational institutions across the educational landscape, we can name any number of people and institutions that should step forward to make these changes happen. The question of responsibility rests on whether the changes are macro or micro (see Chapter 6). Different responsibilities can be allocated, depending on whether the changes are cultural (macro changes) or what occurs in educational institutions and with educators as they engage with students daily (micro changes).

Even before that, we can answer this critical inverse question: Who is *not responsible* for creating trauma-responsive schools? The answer is: students. While traumatized individuals can work to ameliorate some of their trauma history by engaging with other individuals and institutions adept at responding to trauma, those who are traumatized did not cause their own trauma. Whatever big *E* event occurred (see Chapter 1), the trauma and its symptomology is what happened *to* them. It is not what they did.

In helping to heal trauma, we cannot, then, operate off a deficit model, a point also emphasized in *Breakaway Learners*, where we pour help onto and into traumatized individuals as if they could then cure themselves. Telling a student to become more resilient or develop a better mindset or deploy grit or get tougher and not so "snowflakey" will not ameliorate trauma. Nope, these efforts won't work. Even a teacher's aide working with a child is not enough, unless that person is trauma trained. Naming doesn't work either. You can't tell a traumatized person, You're traumatized; now move on. Naming trauma for an affected individual does have benefits, to be sure. Perhaps it enables someone to self-identify his or her triggers in situations where the autonomic nervous system allows some reprieve and cognition can be employed. But naming is not a cure-all. It's like the base hit described in Chapter 6. It doesn't get you across home plate.

Indeed, in my own life, a close relative said about the trauma I suffered that kept being retriggered by my husband, who was in the throes of dementia, "Just get over it. We've all experienced trauma. It's not our fault you had a bad childhood. Deal." Basically, the relative was saying, "Snap out of it. Act like a wife and mother now." I couldn't, and the person shouldn't have asked me to perform as if nothing had happened in my past. The relative was asking the impossible, and obviously didn't "get" what being traumatized means.

We need a model that is the responsibility of others to deploy to assist those affected by trauma. When trauma is retriggered, other individuals need to be able to understand what is happening and respond in ways that are, at a minimum, trauma informed, trauma sensitive, or ideally, trauma responsive. The autonomic nervous system prevents the person experiencing trauma from being responsible for identifying and then dealing with trauma all alone.

This is a paradigm shift; we assume that if we have individuals resolve their own issues (more tutoring, more effort, more attentiveness, more focus) and we punish or discipline them negatively when they fail in this effort, that we have done our part. No, we haven't. No amount of work grounded in a deficit model will aid those who have been traumatized. That's because these individuals aren't deficient. Do we say with a straight face that those with diabetes are deficient? Those with cancer? Those who have suffered brain damage in war? No. There is no reason to have different rules and approaches for trauma. Once one has experienced trauma, it is part of who one is forever; the younger one is when exposed to trauma, the harder it is to deal and heal.

Who Is Responsible?

At the macro level—policy and culture change—there are a number of candidates for responsibility. Obvious stakeholders are medical providers, especially of children and families; local, state, and federal legislators tasked with improving the well-being of their communities; boards of education, boards of governors, and boards of trustees, charged with overseeing institutions; and leaders who run school systems and colleges. We can add employers who complain about a lack of qualified workers; they can and should participate in improving educational outcomes and creating workplaces that meet the needs of employees. Therapists, school counselors, and social workers can and should assist in making macro changes. Religious and community leaders can and should play a role as well. However, here's the catch. It has two pieces: Those with responsibility need to develop a trauma lens and then work together with each other with a shared recognition of what is needed.

Finding the Trauma Lens

Those responsible for helping to ameliorate trauma in an educational setting need to have a trauma lens (trauma perspective) in front of them at all times. The best way to conceptualize this lens is to think about a book series, *Poemotion*, by Takahiro Kurashima. His books contain black-and-white or color drawings of lines and squiggles and shapes. These images are almost three-dimensional but not quite. Then, in each book, there is a single sheet of plastic that one places over the images and *voilà*: The images start to move and come alive. While every page has a different image, they are all animated by the single sheet of plastic laid over them. Without the sheet of plastic, the images are almost inanimate. They are not engaging. With the plastic sheet, you see things you did not see without it. You see movement and shapes appearing out of nowhere (Figure 7.1).

Figure 7.1. Animating Seeing

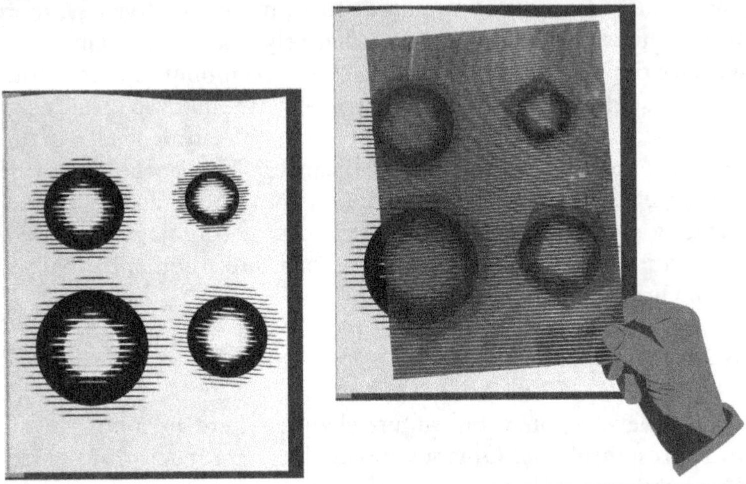

With a trauma perspective, everyone will see students differently. They will perceive different "shapes" the student takes and are better able to engage with the student because they can "see" what the student may be feeling or expressing without the student's even recognizing the origins of what is happening within them.

Finding a trauma lens is not as easy as putting a piece of plastic on a drawing. First, as has been addressed, people experiencing trauma or its retriggering are often unaware of what is happening to them and why their reactions to seemingly normal events are outsized. We often, as noted, cannot name what is happening to us; we need others who can see and name the traumatic symptomology. And in the midst of trauma retriggering, individuals are not thinking clearly or thinking at all; their autonomic nervous system is blocking important brain functions. Add to this that witnesses to the outsized behavior often do not default to a trauma explanation for what they see. They may see behavior that seems out of order, exaggerated, or ridiculous, but don't see that it is the result of trauma. What would even encourage someone to come up with a trauma explanation for behavior? Neither the traumatized person nor the witness can explain what just occurred.

Trauma is slippery this way. It hides from the person experiencing it and is not in the repertoire of experiences of those witnessing it. Capturing trauma—putting it into focus—is tough work. I know this from experience. I can be writing about trauma and its symptomology and yet not recognize the retriggering in myself when I have an outsized reaction, including to what I am writing. One would think that I could do better: I know what trauma does. But that's the point. I know because I can think it through. When events are personal, my cognition is impaired by an active autonomic nervous system.

Collaboration?

Having a trauma lens is not enough. Those with responsibility need to get out of their silos and work in unison on shared initiatives. Egos need to be submerged, and the greater good needs to take precedence. Early childhood educators need to work with professors; middle school principals need to work with high school principals. Colleges and universities need to work with each other and with other educational institutions. Effective trauma-responsive institutions are of a piece, one fabric that enables students to succeed.

A change in the corporate world has given me hope in our capacity to work together. Typically, the prime obligation of corporations and their boards is shareholder interests. Increased shareholder wealth *über alles* is the motto. There has been, however, a critical shift, advocated for decades, toward a belief that corporations also owe a duty to the larger community. The Business Roundtable, a group of almost 200 of the most prominent businesses in the United States, issued a statement about the role of corporations that expands their obligations: "While each of our individual companies serves its own corporate purpose, we share a fundamental commitment to all of our stakeholders. . . . We commit to deliver value to all of them, for the future success of our companies, our communities and our country."[48] The argument has this guiding principle: What is good for communities is good for shareholders. Taking care of larger interests, above and beyond money, has economic value. That's a wow statement and a paradigm shift for sure.

Macro Change

Key to macro change is recognizing our obligations to more than self-interested and fiscally measured rewards. We will all do better as a society if we act responsibly toward the larger needs of our community. In the context of children, perhaps that is a more possible, realistic take: We need for the next generation to be in good hands if we want the United States and its corporations to survive and thrive. To ensure that the next generation succeeds, we need to address their trauma, which the members of this generation continue to encounter. If we do that in our schools, we contribute meaningfully to our economy, our larger community, and our democracy.

Do we care enough about the next generation to work to help the current generation overcome trauma? Robert Putnam suggests that we don't care enough about all our children; we only care about the children who are like our children.[49] I am less pessimistic. The current state of education and the failures of so many children suggest, as Chapter 6 describes, that we are on the cusp of change.

To that end, I am inspired by the hope found in the last chapter of *Destroying Sanctuary*.[50] The authors assert: "We have not written this book with the purpose of leaving our readers dejected. . . . The process of [change from existing approaches to a Sanctuary Model] begins with getting everyone on the same page—surfacing, sharing, arguing about, and finally agreeing on the basic values, beliefs, guiding principles and philosophical principles."

Micro Change

Micro changes need to occur throughout schools—in hallways, offices, the nurse's station, the health center, the gymnasium, the playground, and on the athletic fields. For teachers, professors, coaches, school nurses, administrators, counselors, maintenance and food service workers, and security staff to introduce micro changes in support of trauma-responsive schools, they need training. Those entering these fields need educational opportunities as part of their preparation.

Sadly, such learning opportunities are not widely or consistently available, except among school psychologists (although even some of them are not trauma trained). Schools of education may offer only the occasional seminar or course or part of a course on trauma-responsive approaches, and coaches and school nurses are unlikely to be trauma trained as part of their education and certification. Trauma training is ad hoc. We can try to get schools of education to introduce programs for current students and graduates. We can try to increase nursing students' knowledge of trauma in schools by improving their curricula (relevant for the growing health care field of trauma-informed care), and we can educate existing school nurses. We can create trauma courses, including online, that lead to certification. We can try to adjust the requirements of certifications and recertifications for all professionals who work in education. This last is a long and cumbersome process, especially with each state controlling the criteria for certification. In fact, none of these changes will be quick, and we want to ensure quality course offerings.

Add to all this the difficulty of developing trauma responsiveness in postsecondary education. Professors, coaches, student life personnel, librarians, deans, and other leaders and support personnel are, generally speaking, all hard sells. Many already bemoan their workload; their added responsibilities; the plethora of requirements set by institutions, accreditors, or the government. Consider ad hoc implementation of micro approaches: We can message that promotions and extra pay (assuming monies are available) will be available to those who engage in trauma-responsive efforts. We can offer free courses and time off to take them (also a cost). We can develop quality online efforts that are cost free to those employed in the educational pipeline. Some or all of these might be effective.

Here's another approach. Educators struggle because of the trauma their students exhibit, impeding learning and student success. The educators themselves struggle with primary, secondary, and vicarious trauma. Might their own self-care and self-interest push them to further training? Self-interest can be a motivator. Ask this question: If not the professionals within educational institutions acting to introduce trauma responsiveness, then who? The students aren't an option. Neither are parents, including because some of them caused the trauma or are traumatized themselves.

When I once discussed training individuals within community organizations, a psychiatrist responded, "That is not their skill. They have too much to do. The medical community is charged with addressing the psychological impact of trauma. Community workers can only focus on wellness, not trauma." In other words, he was saying: "Don't tread on my psychiatric turf." Micro changes in education are not substitutes for therapy or psychiatric intervention. But seeing that the autonomic nervous system is on high alert and then working to lower it does not require a psychiatrist. Trauma responsiveness in many settings will enable individuals to engage more effectively, learn more effectively, and progress through life more effectively. Isn't that worth it? And educators are in a position to implement these concrete strategies, detailed in Chapter 11.

This is too important to toss in the proverbial towel or to leave the action to only those with medical degrees or intensive health-related education.

The Six *Ts* and *Breakaway Learners*

Creating a trauma-responsive environment is not self-activating. It rests on the animation of the five *S*s (stability, structure, safety, subtlety, and someone[s]); these are the central values at the core of trauma-responsive programs and environments that have already been referenced several times in this book and that are described in even greater detail in the next chapter. Animating lasticity, the central concept in *Breakaway Learners*, also requires, in addition to its five fundamental pillars (elasticity, plasticity, pivoting right, reciprocity, and belief in self), the six *T*s (trust, transparency, tranquility, tolerance, temperance, and teachers and teaching.) Not surprisingly, these latter six *T*s match up closely with the five *S*s needed to create trauma responsiveness.

For lasticity to take hold, *trust* is key, and it is not automatic; breakaway learners are not naturally trusting, since trust has been violated so often in their past. Honesty and disclosing truth—*transparency*—are essential, too; breakaway learners aren't fans of phoniness. They have seen that too often, trying to pass for authentic conversation and engagement.

Predictability and consistency, or *tranquility*, are key because breakaway learners often have experienced the opposite in their personal lives. That students act out because of what has happened to them requires *tolerance*, not punishment or negative discipline. Developing thoughtful decisionmaking—deliberating, not just impulsively reacting—is key to success too, and can be labeled *temperance*. Finally, *teachers and teaching* are central, and seeing everyone engaged in schools as educators goes a long way toward creating a culture of success.

In the context of this book and trauma responsiveness, the value of *stability* encompasses tranquility and teachers and teaching. *Structure* includes temperance and transparency. *Safety* is reflected in trust and at least a modicum of tolerance as a student learns to value kindness, care, and respect. *Subtlety* is reflected in transparency and temperance as well as teachers and teaching. And *someone(s)* is explicitly in the category of teachers and teaching, broadly defined. What these overlaps demonstrate, importantly, is that if students can learn in a trauma-responsive environment—with the five *S* values firmly in place—they will be predisposed and ready to be lastic. Lastic students in lastic educational environments can succeed.

There is hope, then, that we can move toward a trauma-responsive educational system—one that incorporates the five *S*s, which coincide with the values undergirding lasticity. The next few chapters start the process of considering the kinds of macro programs and approaches we can institute and the types of micro changes that will improve the experiences of traumatized students. They embody the five *S*s. The key is not that these programs and changes be replicated; it is that the values described through the five *S*s be embedded in the programs. It is the replication of *values*, not programs and changes, that matter.

CHAPTER 8

The Trauma-Responsive School

The five *S*s mentioned in Chapter 7 and explained in greater detail in this chapter can be deployed in concrete ways by educational institutions to enable them to move toward becoming trauma responsive. This chapter posits one model of an ideal trauma-responsive school, one that includes a set of changes incorporating the five *S*s. The model addresses changes related to, among other things, space, experience of place, pedagogy, content, curriculum, and discipline. In formulating the ideal school, we will deconstruct the ideal to identify initiatives and approaches that can realistically be employed in the near term across the educational landscape. These deconstructions lead to identifying and explaining the macro and micro suggestions that appear in Chapter 9 and 10, respectively. Before turning to this exercise in deconstruction (which is actually *construction*, in that we are designing a trauma-responsive educational system), one caveat helps set the stage for what follows.

A Caveat

As noted previously, no single approach to becoming trauma responsive works for all educational institutions in all locations for all students. Context matters. Culture matters. Place matters. Becoming trauma responsive can differ from location to location. That is not only to be expected but also wise. It recognizes the vast differences between educational settings, teachers and students, and communities. As long as the five *S*s—the key values undergirding a trauma-responsive school—are present, the form and nature of the responsiveness to trauma are neither critical nor required. The model of an ideal institution is an exemplar, one of many that could be created.

A good measure of whether an educational institution's culture is trauma responsive is how students feel, behave, and learn in that institution. Students who have been traumatized will know intuitively, especially given their hypervigilance, whether the institution's culture is responsive to their needs, and then they will behave responsively to that. They may not know the phrase *trauma responsive* or even that they have experienced trauma that affects their learning. In a sense, this is similar to creating the idea of a "safe space," discussed later. No single physical space is required; instead, what occupies space is an institutional aura of responsiveness, which is a different way of conceptualizing space by focusing on the "air," not the "walls."

Harvard professor Anthony Abraham Jack notes in a remarkable essay that the elite college he attended didn't "get" students like him and failed to understand their life histories and ongoing family and community obligations; the college lacked trauma responsiveness. Neither he nor they knew they were so lacking in understanding. He wrote:

> But the full weight of my responsibilities, even the most quotidian ones, was often as invisible to me as it was to my adviser and financial-aid officer. And sometimes students like me continue to carry the weight of home long after we graduate and in ways we still aren't aware of. I got a text from home days before my 32nd birthday—after I'd gone to college, earned my doctorate and secured my position as a professor—asking me to "call DirectTV and take your name off the bill." I had to ask: "My name on the bill? Since when?" The response: "Since we been living here."[1]

For the record, that period of residency referenced in the last line was almost 20 years. And the description: Accurate. Poignant. Revelatory. Emblematic. Note, too, that in this quote and in Jack's entire essay, the word *trauma* is absent. Its absence speaks volumes about the importance of naming, both the naming of trauma and of those who experience it. It speaks to the need to name Generation T, described in Part III. It is what will enable institutions and those within them to change their culture to respond to the students in their midst.

Why Deconstructing the Ideal Is Key

In a perfect world with abundant financial resources for education, we would rethink every aspect of schools and colleges to facilitate student success academically and psychosocially. On the level of theory and practice, we know that educational space speaks and signals; we know that bad space is harmful to learning and healing.[2] We can imagine, too, changes to what is taught when and how. We can consider changes to school calendars and length of class periods and student engagement with one another and with adults. But given the economic realities in educational arenas, a common reaction to this approach is that focusing on the ideal is a waste of time; what we need to do is develop strategies that do not require a dismantling of everything we now do. We need, instead, solutions to our existing structures, physical structures, and internal institutional structures, that message powerfully that the place and those working in it are trauma responsive. The individuals working in these institutions need skills—trauma skills—so they can become trauma responsive.

This type of pragmatic response leads to employing the usual approach: lists. Here, this would encompass a listing of possible macro and micro changes that are doable and incorporate the five *S*s. The list to be sure would be incomplete, although it would be designed to be representative of types of changes. Then readers could pick and choose from and adopt and adapt those changes that fit their own institutional culture. This is the approach I used in *Breakaway Learners* and also when I described strategies for reopening schools following a natural or human-caused disaster.[3]

Lists of suggestions are the common approach taken to demonstrate change. In many circumstances it is not a bad route; educators, when presented with ideas—new ones together with ones that they have thought about in the past—can usually see how the items on the list can be used in their institutions. They can both think and talk through how these changes would work in practice and in context. Then the goal is to take these concrete lists to their institutions and implement what changes they can, assuming there is a recognition of the importance of what appears on the lists.

The list approach is something I considered using here to identify possible macro and micro changes, but it seemed too disengaged from the way this book is structured and how trauma responsiveness works. Readers could just read down the list and select items they could relate to, in a somewhat passive task mode. I have opted for another way of offering solutions for creating a trauma-responsive educational institution, to engage readers differently. It begins by describing in detail what an ideal trauma-responsive school would look like—physically and functionally.

As readers reflect on the described trauma-responsive institution, they can identify for themselves the abundant trauma-responsive aspects that appear in different contexts: what the building looks like, outside and inside; what happens in the school spaces; how teachers, staff, and administrators engage with students. Stated differently, readers will see the five *S*s in action but the *S*s will not initially be labeled. Readers are placed in the position of finding the five *S*s—stability, structure, safety, subtlety and someone(s)—in every aspect of the ideal institution described, kind of like intellectual and emotional hide-and-seek but with a clear aim of encouraging new ways of seeing and experiencing education that is responsive to trauma. Thereafter, the five *S*s are explored and "matched."

The approach does not stop with descriptions. After describing one model of an ideal trauma-responsive educational institution, we probe the whys and hows for the many aspects described, including outside the ideal.[4] How would the ideal school operate? What would its central features be? How would it engage students, and how would it address teaching and teachers?

The hope, too, is that readers would have their own sense from reading the ideal about why the school would function as expected (or not) and which of its pieces could be employed in their own institutions effectively, even absent the ideal. It is also hoped that feeling and reactions will occur when readers reflect on the ideal school. Some aspects may not feel comfortable or right; some may feel too radical or unfeasible; still others may feel just right, the kind of idea one has been searching for for years but could not find or identify, let alone implement.

There is one added feature to approaching change through an ideal model. Readers will see that parts of the model reflect what is being done now in some educational institutions, perhaps even their own. These familiar features, however, do not have the label *trauma responsive*. Indeed, there are many good things we already do in educational settings without knowing that they are hugely beneficial to students showing trauma symptomology.[5] To be sure, we also do things that are the antithesis to trauma responsiveness, again without knowing that our actions are adversely affecting many students.

The presence of elements already in existence adds to my hope, described in Chapter 7, that change can happen. If we are already doing things in schools that are trauma responsive and we can give a name to these items or activities or behaviors, we can see that the distance from the ideal to real is not as great as we thought.

The Ideal Trauma-Responsive School

Figure 8.1 shows an educational institution for children ages 6–12, although it could be adapted for younger or older students.[6] Remember, there is no one ideal.

Building, furniture, and fixtures. The institution is a single pie-shaped building. For larger institutions, there could be multiple linked pies vertically or horizontally. Assume there are seven pie pieces (large rooms) in the pie, each dedicated to one discipline. The choice of disciplines can vary depending on the age level and approaches of a school. Assume here—and the choice will be surprising to some, as the topics may not seem "academic" and "learning" based—that the pie pieces are filled with these seven topics: art, music, athletics, reading and writing, math and statistics, science, and social studies. The outside border of the pie slices would be glass and enable access to the outside and continuous light inside. The ceilings should be high, 10 to 12 feet—for children this will feel quite high. The roof, if there is only one building or several horizontal buildings in larger schools and no stacking of pies, could have different degrees of slant, and those could message respect for culture and cultural diversity. Picture a roof in a pie school located on an Indian reservation where the room slopes upward from each slice to create a peak; the ideal school would resemble a tepee, a critically important symbol in Native American culture. As mentioned earlier, a tepee was constructed on the campus of Heritage University and is a place where

Figure 8.1. An Ideal School

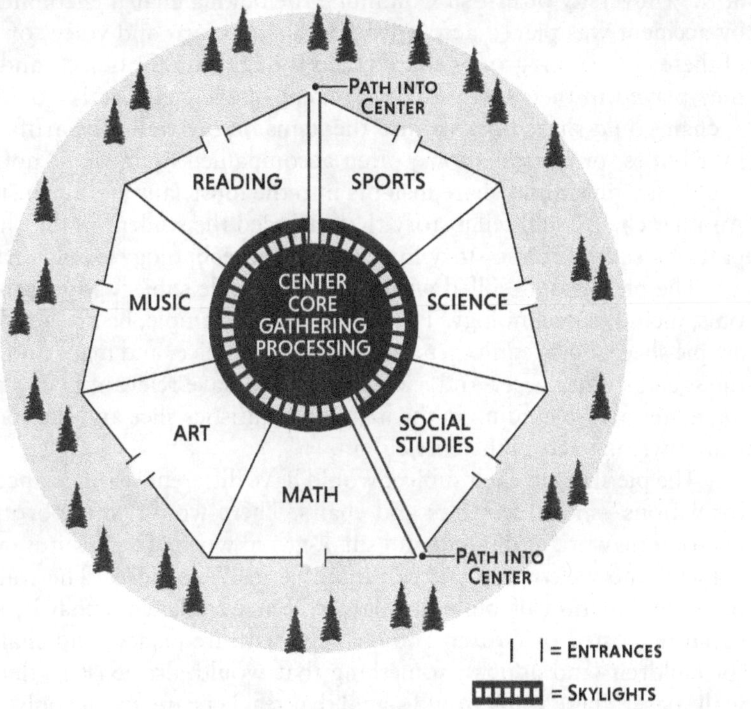

all students can go to find peace and comfort. The roof could take other shapes too, resembling a ship or a tower, depending on its location. The roof is about cultural sensitivity and diversity, and the building messages about acceptance of cultural differences.

The center of the pie has a hole large enough to be a space where students can eat and gather in small groups with each other or with adults. The space, called, say, the Center, can also be used for presentations and for individual students to meet with teachers or outside professionals, to enable processing in place. The Center is intended to be in constant use; it is not decorative or ceremonial space that sits asking to be admired.

If the space is at the top level, the ceiling would be glass, open to light and enabling observation of weather changes. In the Center would be tables with comfy chairs; on the tables would be tactile objects—LEGOs®, squishy balls, colorful modeling clay, fidget gadgets, bendable creatures like Gumby, paper, crayons, markers, and an abacus or two. Also in the space would be "talking chairs," positioned to face items on walls to which the chairs had a connection, because these chairs would speak to students about what is on the wall.[7]

My first experience with such chairs was in the Museum of Anthropology at the University of British Columbia; the talking chair I encountered quite by accident was placed across from indigenous art, and voices of members of these indigenous groups shared their thoughts on the objects and the roles they played in their culture. The content of the chairs' talk could change. A chair could share insights into the items on the wall, say, artifacts, dinosaur bones, or constellations, often accompanied by music. Another chair could play music and share insights into the musicians and the instruments. Another chair could tell a story that included the student in the chair being part of a self-affirming story line, something technology would enable.

The pie slices are filled with easily accessible subject-appropriate materials, including technology. There would, for example, be art supplies in the art pie slice, sports equipment in the sports pie slice, and maps and globes in the social studies slice. And each slice would have relevant books and writing materials—including in the math and statistics slice and the sports slice. Call it writing across the curriculum.

The pie slices in each subject would have different seating capacities and formations—movable tables and chairs. There would be opportunities for one-on-one work and large- and small-group work. The furniture would be colorful and welcoming and not infantile in size or look. The walls would be a combination of bulletin board–like material; whiteboards, so things could be posted or written and changed with frequency; and chalkboards, for children (and adults), something that would also exist in the Center's wall space. These walls would signal that teachers are not the only ones who can fill them or use them. Everyone in the slice can fill the walls.

Concentrated learning. Each student would be required to spend time in four institutionally identified slices: (1) Art or Music, (2) English or Social Studies, (3) Science or Math, and (4) Sports. The students would select which particular four slices to include in their schedule and in which order. For the balance of the school year, they could add in new slices or repeat slices. Everyone (well, almost everyone) would be in a slice for a month. This would bring students of different ages into the same slices, so students would be working together across age groups and at their own level. There would be multiple teachers in each slice, working with each of the students. Assume each slice would have between 20 and 30 students at any one time. Note the student role in selection and timing, another aspect of empowerment and moving the locus of control from an externality to an internality, a valuable step for anyone traumatized. Note also a college corollary to this: students choosing majors in colleges, a difficult hurdle for many. And perhaps we can rethink, based on this ideal school, whether "majors" at any level make sense any longer, something Hampshire College is addressing in its reconfiguration where majors are eliminated and students focus on solving central issues of our time.

Notice too that this approach eliminates short bursts of learning in prescribed 30-, 45-, or 60-minute slots, whereby the time to get engaged, do the work, and then get work for the next session means the actual learning time is too short in many instances. Also, for some students, changing subjects is jarring, and it's hard to do if there are subjects in which one excels and in which one feels like a failure. Daily reminders of failure are problematic. So are transitions.

In some ways, this approach resembles that taken at some colleges where students concentrate on one course or a small number of courses to enable them to focus and engage deeply.[8] While trauma responsiveness is surely not the underlying rationale, a trauma-responsive approach would recognize the value of students not going from class to class and adjusting and readjusting each time. There is no reason why jumping from class to class works any better for younger students, and with more nontraditional students entering postsecondary education and often balancing family, work, and school, concentrated learning (done well) is beneficial.

One more related point: Just because students focus on one subject does not mean that they are doing the same activities every day and boredom will set in. Efforts to engage students include field trips and movies as well as kinesthetic, visual, and auditory learning. Students can engage with each other and the outside world, including conducting interviews and surveys. Working on a subject does not have to be pedagogically simple. When educators share teaching a subject, they have the challenge of making it engaging for an entire concentrated period while incorporating all the needed learning. Learning is not just content, as we know. Learning is also about problem-solving, analysis, effective communication, quality engagement, asking and responding to good questions, and opening doors to new and creative approaches and solutions.

Problem-solving and interdisciplinary engagement. There would be considerable engagement between slices. In some months, there would be a shared problem designed by the teachers or administrators on which every slice would work independently within its discipline. At the end of the designated month, each slice would present its findings in the Center, learning how other slices addressed the same problem. Students would be sharing their expertise with other students, who had their own expertise.

Suppose the problem was how to create cleaner water in the local community. The Art slice could design posters or paint a mural notifying local community members of the issue and even displaying their work outside the school. Science students could study the water, gathering samples, learning why it wasn't clean, and reflecting on solutions. English students could write press releases on the water problem and present them to local government officials or write up proposed regulations, reflecting on how rules work and whether they needed to be specific or general. Other students could conduct surveys and collect and manage key data.

Now consider this assignment for all the slices: Contemplate the use of triangles in the discipline of a particular slice. In Math, there could be lessons in geometry with different kinds of triangles. In Art, there could be a study of artists, such as Miro or Calder, who used triangles in their work. In Music, students could play triangles and look at music for the triangle. A song could be composed. In Sports, the participants could design triangular plays in basketball, test them out, and adjust aspects of the plays to work more effectively (smaller triangles, different types of triangles, different players in different parts of the triangle). All this work would be shared with other slices in the Center.

There could be opportunities for the students, as a collective, to suggest a topic to cover in the slices. This would enable students to control some aspect of their learning but only if there was enough student interest and power in the idea and a sense from both teachers and administrators that the selected topic would have enough academic and psychosocial heft. Suppose students collectively wanted to study a particular cartoonist or actor or wanted to learn about fashion and current and future trends or wanted to explore gaming and game design or chose to focus on Harry Potter. All very doable.

Being in the moment. As and when critical new events occurred in the news, particularly those related to trauma (a hurricane or fire or plane crash or school shooting or a virus), this event could be dealt with directly and promptly in the slices. This approach is akin to pop-up courses, described later in more detail, in which all the slices would participate. These events will be in the minds of many students, aided of course by social media, but they have not had a place to process and share what has occurred. The goal is to create a new pop-up course to allow immediate processing. The content and approaches of such courses would differ depending on the age of the students.

Consider this example. Tyler Skaggs, the popular Los Angeles Angels pitcher, died during the season in a hotel room while his team was on the road. He had pitched 2 days before. His autopsy revealed that he had ingested fentanyl, oxycodone, oxymorphone, and alcohol. In the school, this situation would be addressed in each slice, to get at the nature of the drugs taken, the risks of combining substances, the sudden loss of life, and how to memorialize a player and whether that changes after the autopsy results. Questions could be asked about how a professional athlete acquired all these drugs and whether there was team knowledge or participation or silent acquiescence. All the slices could share this information in the Center. Assume this pop-up topic was addressed over a period of 2 or 3 days, long enough to process and short enough to be able to return to whatever was being covered that month in the slice.

To elaborate, in the Science slice, there could be an investigation of the types of drugs taken and their effects on the body, alone and together. There could be an effort to explain why certain combinations of drugs are risky. In the Social Studies slice, students could look at drug addiction in the United States, including among athletes, asking whether there are other athletes who have died from drugs. For some, this topic might be a trigger; indeed, the whole subject in every slice could retrigger trauma but the point is that the retriggering is understood, expected, and under the watch of trauma-skilled educators. The Art slice could design a memorial to the player, deciding how to celebrate his life.

And, with the even more recent death of Kobe Bryant and his daughter Gigi, there could be a concentrated effort to understand what happened and why and how to memorialize these two individuals and the others who passed away. Consider topics like the safety of helicopters (compared to planes or cars), how navigating flights in bad weather occurs and could be optimized through technology or training, and how we deal with sudden untimely deaths of iconic figures. The point is to use the ideal school to process current issues in ways that enable understanding and demonstrate trauma sensitivity and responsiveness.

Rovers and roving. In this model, teachers stay in the slices, with the students moving in and out. Imagine that specialized teachers rove, meaning they go from slice to slice to add in specialized knowledge from their own discipline. They could also work with students one-on-one in the slice into which they are roving. The rovers, while moving between classes, would be regular faculty members, so if someone from a particular slice left or was ill or on leave, the rover could step in. Think about a rover with expertise in economics or finance. The rover would add this perspective to the problem being studied. Suppose the rover spoke several foreign languages and understood foreign cultural norms. He or she could bring another language and culture into the slices. A rover would spend about a week in each slice.

There would also be several student rovers, for whom the selection described above was not working effectively. They were too antsy to choose where to go or could not make a final decision. For these students, roving is their option in addition to spending time in the Center. These students could latch onto a slice or move from slice to slice. Since both students and teachers would know there are a handful of roving students, they would be prepared to help these students engage in the activities on which those in the slice were working. Roving students would be participating with the other students, not just sitting at the side of a slice.

The Center as center. If particular students were struggling on a given day, teachers would know that the Center was a space where the students could go—not as punishment but where they could re-center themselves. In extreme cases, a teacher in the slice could call for a teacher or counselor in the Center to come into the slice to help a child or group of children. Disruptive behavior is hard on other students and the teacher. The Center would become a cool-down place for students, where the message is that the exhibited behavior is not acceptable in a class but there is a place to process. Today, many struggling students are sent away—sent home or to professionals outside the school. Some are given drugs to calm their behaviors. Because privacy is protected in the Center, there are opportunities to bring professionals in and enable processing in place, right there in the school.

Instead of traditional fire or earthquake drills that appear as if out of nowhere, as addressed in Part I, students could design drills together, with help from police and firefighters in the community. Together they could construct an ideal drill and then test it out collectively in a planned way. Psychologists and counselors could participate in the planning and debriefing, too.[9]

Besides student involvement, which shifts the sense of control from an externality to an internality, the ideal school has traditions. For starters, there are presentations by all the slices in the Center. Then there are activity tables in the Center that remain available every day; you know you can go to a certain table and find LEGOs. Then there are rovers who consistently appear. And there are outsiders who cease to be outsiders because they enter the ideal school regularly and engage with students in the Center.

Opening doors. How comfortable would family members be when entering these schools? Would they feel the same disquiet they commonly feel entering traditional schools? Suppose there was a special space in the Center for parents and guardians. They would be welcomed, and sometimes invited, into this space to work with teachers or psychologists/counselors and their own child during the day. Access to the Center could be possible early in the morning or after school for parents who worked different shifts. Since there are many teachers in a slice, one teacher could step into the Center to work with parents on given days for specialized issues or problems. Maybe there could be labels for where parents could sit.

Another key aspect of the ideal school is how it treats the start and end of the school day and the return to school after it's been closed. Suppose each student entered into his or her slice at the start of the day—like entering a traditional homeroom. (The slices would all have access doors in the glass at the back of the slice.) Students would have a space with their name, a place to put their things, and teachers and students who recognized them. If they wanted to wander into the Center to get food, they could do that. Suppose on days that followed weekends and vacations there were special activities, all designed to enable students to engage more fully, activities that were sensory based and not related to their content areas. Students would know that following a weekend or vacation, there would be opportunities for a slower ramp-up, giving them time before the work in the slices began. In particular slices with particular students, these sensory activities could be used to begin every school day.

There would be plentiful opportunities for teachers in slices to plan, meet, and work together, until they moved their students to a different room for a different learning opportunity, like library or a sports team. That would help teachers who felt that they had to deal with all the issues on their own. There would also be opportunities for all the teachers across all the slices to meet and work together. Some of that work would involve sensory activities and discussion of how they were managing not only their slices but also their class preparation, their engagement with students who were struggling, and their own sense of well-being and health. The administration could assist with these meetings or step back and let the educators engage in, plan, and control what was effective for them. These would all be opportunities for a student case management system where the issues of struggling students could be addressed by the collective; there could be a multidisciplinary case management approach, again making coordination easier and easing the burden on an individual teacher. And there could be assurance that in these meetings each student would have at least one adult from within the ideal school with whom they had a meaningful connection.

What would the principal and other administrators do in this ideal school? Where would they have their offices? How and where would they engage with parents and students and teachers? Looking at the architecture of the school pie, it is clear that there is no walled-off office space where administrators would sit and where students would be sent. Indeed, the administrators would be in the Center, perhaps in a segment of it. The bulk of their day would be spent engaging with others in the Center and going into the slices, even if only for a few minutes. And if there was an issue with a student in a slice, these leaders, with or without a counselor, could help with processing in place. And what about paperwork, forms, payroll, and other administrative duties? If schools were all working together, these functions could be shared and coordinated. Shared services among schools and colleges are possible if entities are willing to forgo autonomy in exchange for well-designed coordinated systems. These could be located off-site, reachable via text, phone, Skype, or some other medium.

Students younger and older than those attending would be able to visit and engage in the ideal school. College professors could come in as rovers. High school teachers, too. Older students could visit slices for a day as part of their education. Younger students could engage in activities in the Center. The point here is to create engagement across institutions and the individuals in them. The school would have activity that was both internally and externally generated. The ideal school would welcome outsiders in to share their work.

The Five Ss

In Part I, we saw that in the context of trauma, the traditional approach of replicable and scalable pilots wouldn't work. Instead, given the importance of context and culture, a set of foundational values should be incorporated into all programs. A checklist could ensure that these foundational elements were applied and interpreted to reflect communities' needs, cultural norms, and traditions. When these values are incorporated, we change culture; we can become trauma responsive. The ideal school just described incorporates all five Ss.

The five *Ss* are, as noted in the previous chapter, the animators of trauma-responsive programs, and all five are necessary for success. As also noted in the prior chapter, there is inevitable overlay with the six *T*s of *Breakaway Learners* that animate lasticity: transparency, tranquility, temperance, tolerance, trust, and teachers and teaching. Both need factors that push the issues forward and facilitate the adoption of something new. These activators are not easy to understand and adopt. The five activators for trauma responsiveness, like the six activators for lasticity, recognize the deeper structures needed to enable lasting change and reflect an understanding of trauma and its impact on the students enrolled in our schools. The five *S*s can be described in greater detail as follows:

Stability. A major aftereffect of trauma is destabilization. The world as one knew it is fundamentally changed, disrupting all aspects of one's being. If a parent dies or is imprisoned, if one's home is demolished by a tornado, if a friend is shot right before one's eyes, the world is turned over. A viral pandemic can do the same thing: overturn our world as we know it. Key to improving conditions in any environment that is the locus of trauma is reestablishing stability. This can occur in many ways, all of which are situation and community specific. One is for schools to have consistent workforces, with minimal turnover. The same teachers, the same principal, the same nurse, the same coaches, and the same guidance counselors are essential. The larger world may have shifts, but the school personnel stay consistent.

This is a challenge in many locations, where teacher turnover is commonplace, even in the middle of an academic year. High-poverty schools, where stability is most needed, experience the greatest turnover.[10] Only about one-quarter of teachers in Teach for America stay for 5 years, and many who do stay change schools. Just as children become attached, their favorite teacher leaves.[11] How well do we address this loss of teachers? Do we have thoughtful ways of enabling affected students to process the changes, or do we just announce that so-and-so has not returned? Worse yet, are we silent, as if not speaking about the missing faculty will make us unaware of their absence?

For a college's student athletes, the departure of a favorite coach can be debilitating. A change in college leadership is destabilizing for faculty and staff and often trickles down to students. In smaller institutions, presidential change can directly affect students if the president has been meaningfully engaged with students. The same is true for the departure of a principal. Leadership changes in educational institutions put educators on edge: Will I be accepted? Will I be liked? Will expectations change? Will my workload shift? My responsibilities? A way to maintain stability is to have low educator turnover.

Another is to promote school traditions, such as school songs, flags, and colors. Other school traditions might be that every Tuesday is breakfast for lunch or every Wednesday has an all-school assembly. In higher education, there is a plethora of traditions, from minor to major. And their absence is noticed if they disappear. Smith College has Mountain Day, when classes are canceled and students are supposed to head outside and enjoy nature. At Southern Vermont College, where I was president, there was cookie delivery, when the dean of students and the president delivered home-baked cookies to every residential student in the first week of a semester. In some institutions, the older students help the younger students one afternoon a week, reading and coloring with them, which many younger students enjoy. In others, students in a particular grade give a speech to an assembly; these short speeches are widely anticipated by students, who know they may have a chance to present one. On college campuses, there are repeated events such as convocation, homecoming, and Spring Fling. At exam time, there are milk and cookies in the dining hall and faculty and staff doing midnight breakfast for students.

Whatever the tradition, it creates stability, and stability ameliorates the chaos of trauma. So whatever programs or initiatives we introduce to deal with trauma and its symptomology need to promote stability.

Structure. The word *structure* has many meanings,[12] in law, architecture, and science. In education, structure can mean many things: the building where education takes place; the approach to learning that is organized and developmentally constructed, starting with foundational knowledge; or constraints that limit freedom of student movement and activity to establish order. For our purposes, I am not referring to a physical structure, although the concept of building has relevance, as does what is on the walls and in the halls, explored in the ideal school and subsequent chapters. I am also not referring to hierarchy, rigid rules, and order that inhibits individuality and creativity. I am referring instead to structure that facilitates learning, creates a sense of comfort, and recognizes the individuality of students. Think of it like sentence structure. We don't want jumbled sentences where meaning is confusing or unclear. Structure doesn't dictate meaning or produce identical sentences; rather, it creates opportunities for sentences that have a backbone—architecture—that allows them to be constructed and understood.

Consider these examples of structure that will benefit traumatized students: Homework assignments are always placed on the left corner of a chalkboard or whiteboard (or through other means for students with different learning styles). Desks are arranged not in straight lines but in configurations that facilitate learning, and each student has his or her name on a desk (in high schools or colleges where students change rooms, it could be a name card). Desks are arranged where no student is in the back, unnoticed. And perhaps there isn't a front, especially not for students placed there to aid their concentration. Think circles and squares and U shapes. True, this is difficult in learning environments where chairs, desks, or tables cannot be moved, but a teacher can always move, and teachers can come in from different locations. Paper, pens, books, chalk, or markers are always in the same place, so you know where to find them.

When and after trauma occurs, things feel disorganized. People feel out of place or as if they have no place. Regularly used items have been destroyed or cannot be found because they have moved or one cannot remember where they were because of trauma's impact on memory. Think about school supplies always being in the same baskets or buckets. On a college campus, think about books always being on the same shelves in a library, where access is consistent and welcoming.

Structure—not rigidity or hierarchy—helps calm trauma symptomology and diminishes anxiety, because it facilitates functionality.

Safety. Given the amount of violence that has entered schools, it seems almost oxymoronic to suggest that all schools must be safe. In this book, I am not using the word *safety* in this sense. I am not referencing security guards, metal detectors, bomb-sniffing dogs, or gates, making schools feel like prisons. Interventions to ensure physical safety for students in all educational institutions are beyond the scope of this book.

As used in this book, safety refers to protection from teasing, harassment, bullying, and other behaviors that make students feel unwanted, unappreciated, and targeted at school. Traumatized students can feel singled out. They are hypervigilant and can quickly sense or anticipate teasing or harassment. Sadly, many students, of all ages, feel unsafe in school as a result of the behavior of other students, and the school environment itself feels unsafe.[13] Imagine how unsafe it feels if such a student has experienced trauma, the symptomology of which already predisposes him or her to heightened emotions or to isolation. For students to feel safe—free of threatening behavior in school—educators need to be more aware of what is being said to whom, by whom. This is a new role for some educators, who see their function as limited to content distribution and classroom learning. They do not see themselves as listeners during recess or at athletic events or in hallways. They are not used to calling out students for what may be viewed as good-natured jesting or developmentally appropriate teasing. There are those who think bullying and teasing toughens us up and prepares us for the real world. I beg to differ. The fact that many of us were teased and harassed in school and no one protected us and we turned out okay is not a justification for allowing that behavior.

Students who are teased and harassed need to feel that there are safe ways of getting help and that asking for help is not a sign of weakness. Unfortunately, often students who are teased and harassed do not know how to report the incidents safely.[14] Consider a collective effort to create a community of caring, kindness, and respect in all educational institutions, making them values that matter. Students themselves can help design such programs, deciding on steps for reporting problems, activities to message the negative impact of harassment and teasing, and what can be put on hallway walls to communicate the institution's commitment to being a welcoming community. Student involvement moves the locus of control from an externality (what is being done to a student, akin to trauma) to an internality (where students feel they can have some impact on what is occurring). Shared efforts among schools from early childhood through adulthood that foster a culture of care, kindness, and respect could be used.

There is no one pathway to facilitate institutions that exude care, kindness, and respect. But consider activities that allow schools to engage with others outside their walls to see the positive impact of these variables. Consider a day where students deliver random acts of kindness in their communities and report back on how it felt. Empathy can be fostered and mirror neurons can be activated.[15] Educators can also role model care, kindness, and respect, with each other, with students, and with guests in their classrooms. Coaches are key personnel who can do this, too.

In a trauma-responsive community where educators are trauma skilled, the students will feel safer. In some ways, this *safe space* concept is similar to the signs put on faculty and staff offices and community rooms in colleges, creating places where students who experience difference through their sexual orientation or gender and feel discrimination and absence of comfort of like-minded individuals can go.[16] They are often designated by signs, indicating, You are safe here. While controversial and criticized as fostering difference, these safe spaces are connected to trigger warnings (also criticized), preparing students for threatening situations so they can remove themselves from them, as noted in the introduction to this book.[17] Safe spaces designate places you can go, while trigger warnings signal places to leave.

Subtlety. At first blush, it may seem odd to add the value of subtlety to programs designed to encourage trauma responsiveness. Think about subtlety as paying attention to small things that are important and worthy of attention and recognizing the differences between individuals, including those of the same age or gender. Think about the word as reflecting the need to walk softly, to recognize that we don't always need a hammer to get what is wanted and needed. Think about the word as meaning the capacity to recognize things that are not obvious.

Reflecting on the value of aging, Frank Bruni observed that older individuals could afford to be "awake to individuality and alert to subtlety."[18] Recognizing individuality and subtlety has value in creating trauma-responsive programs. Trauma-responsive programs beg us to avoid blunt instruments while being highly attentive to students. As Christina Bethell observes, in discussing how to assist children who have been traumatized and what protective factors can be adopted, "Every moment matters. Every interaction with a child has a reaction in that child."[19]

Suppose that after a summer vacation an educator starts the new semester by asking students, "What amazing fun things did you and your family do this summer?" For some students, there was no fun that summer but only family illness; having to work; or not even having a family, as one parent is absent and the other has problems with addiction. This seemingly innocent question was loaded with assumptions that may have fit many students but certainly not all.[20] What if the educator focused on individuality and subtlety and asked instead, "What did you do this summer that had an impact on you?" Different approach and likely different answers. As Bethell noted, every encounter counts.

Suppose an educator wants students in a class of 25 to form groups of four or five for a project. There are clear benefits to small groups that can work together for one or more projects both in and outside class.[21] But here's the tricky part: How will the groups be selected?[22] Suppose the educator lets the students select their own groups. Will some students who are new in the school or experiencing trauma not be asked to join a group? What if the groups become cliques? What if the groups reveal efforts to keep some students out, those who are too serious, live far away and commute, or have no money to buy snacks for the get-togethers? Students who know and like each other may work comfortably together, making learning easier. Self-selection, however, is not the only possible approach. An educator could create the groups based on his or her knowledge of the students' skills, or members of the groups could be randomly selected from names placed in a hat. Or an educator could use different approaches over the course of a semester.

As noted, trauma can take many forms, as can its symptomology. Our brains differ and so do our responses. So we need to think through how a group-selection process will affect individuals and whether, unintentionally, educators are not helping or are even causing harm. We need to look at the subtle aspects of groupings and consider their effect on students.

I am reminded of the children's game musical chairs, in which there is one less chair than the number of children. Music plays and when it stops, the children rush to get a seat and one child is left without a chair. Then another chair is taken away, the music starts and stops, and another child is left without a chair. With increasingly fewer chairs, fewer children are playing and many children are on the sidelines. I'm sure I'm not the only one who dislikes this game and the lessons it teaches.

This game is totally without sensitivity or responsiveness to trauma. What child who had issues with attachment through family dysfunction (and high ACEs) wants to be left out? And who needs the anxiety that accompanies each round as children try to get a seat when the number of seats is too few? If one's autonomic nervous system is already on alert, why put it into added alert based on a fear of being left out when the music stops? What kind of game discourages friendship and kindness by having students compete for a seat? Certainly, we can come up with better games that engage children, are fun to do, and encourage camaraderie and group participation. Before one complains that sports do just this—some people get to play and others don't—we need to recognize the positives of team sports, a topic to which we will return in Chapter 10.

Someone(s). Any trauma-responsive program has to incorporate the concept of reciprocity: Everyone affected by trauma needs someone to whom to attach. This person gives a traumatized individual a sense of caring and stability, someone on whom to rely. Call this positive-relationship creation.[23]

The importance of human connection is tied to an understanding of how trauma symptoms are expressed. Traumatized people can feel alone and that no one understands their situation; they can feel embarrassed or guilty; they can feel detached or disassociated. Attachment is hard for many traumatized people, as their trust in others or in the safety of the world has been threatened. That is why traumatized students need someone in the educational institution to attach to, and the job of attaching is on the educator, not the student.[24] Educators need to be on the lookout for students who need someone, and if they are the right fit, they need to become that person and if not, find a person who is a better fit. This applies to all students, regardless of age. Toddlers and adults both need positive role models to whom they can attach.[25] For those without such positive adult presences, it is hard to remain stable, to learn, to engage, to process, to succeed.

Part of the difficulty of this piece of the trauma-responsive picture is that educators and others in the educational system do not see their role as attaching or being active role models for their students outside the classroom. For educational institutions to be trauma responsive, the role of educators has to expand. One's role is not limited, if you are a teacher, to the classroom and the delivery of content. If you are a professor, your role is not limited to teaching and open office hours. If you work in the kitchen, your role extends beyond making food, and if you are a security guard, your role is not just to identify wrongdoers.

As expressed poignantly by the teacher Jesse Lahey, "I've had to switch up my priorities and expectations, not to mention my acronyms. Today, I'm less concerned with boosting my students' A.P. (Advanced Placement) scores than I am with mitigating the consequences of their high ACE (Adverse Childhood Experiences) scores."[26] Brava. How many teachers have so willingly and easily seen their changing roles and accepted the importance of these roles to learning and student success?

There is one more critical aspect to the *someone(s)* engagement with traumatized students. Studies have shown that positive childhood experiences (PCEs) can offset ACEs, discussed earlier.[27] PCEs include but are not limited to quality experiences with adults, such as specifically identified teachers.[28] Thus, besides preventing ACEs, we can create PCEs, and there is a test that measures these positives. Research in this area is still in the early stages, but the findings suggest that trauma-responsive schools can provide PCEs.

Values

While there is no one model for a trauma-responsive school, we've noted that certain values embedded in schools at the macro and micro levels encourage traumatized students to engage more fully and succeed. Those working with highly traumatized students will find increased fulfillment and personal well-being in trauma-responsive schools. The ideal school described here, with the five *S*s deeply embedded, may not be replicated precisely but can be expanded and explored as long as the values stay in place. Chapters 9 and 10 identify strategies in the model that can be applied in current institutions. The goal is to embark right away on creating trauma-responsive schools. We now turn to these strategies, which I hope will transform existing institutions starting today.

CHAPTER 9

Deconstruction I: Macro Changes

Deconstructing the model of the ideal school is essential in moving from naming trauma to taming trauma. The suggestions culled from the ideal school model can be used in educational institutions, remembering that macro changes, to be described in this chapter, can take many forms and shapes, as long as the five *S*s are present. The ideal school encompasses features from existing educational efforts that, as good as they are, often go unlabeled, unnamed. When we can rename these efforts as trauma responsive, we see these activities through a different lens. That shift in lens makes change possible, through an added level of understanding of what we do, perhaps instinctively.

The model of the ideal school includes the behaviors of students, educators, and families, behaviors that may not conform to what is seen in educational institutions readers may be familiar with. That does not mean the behaviors are uncommon. Educators may not have been able to see them, so they perceive them as nonexistent, particularly if they involve themselves. Further, some behaviors are culturally constructed, and information is needed to understand the outlook of cultures toward education.

As we dedicate two chapters to deconstructing the ideal, there are two things to keep in mind. First, not every aspect of the ideal model will appear in the two chapters and not because what is left out is unimportant. It has everything to do with prioritizing. And there may be features of a trauma-responsive school that are not in the ideal model, features that may have real value.[1] That said, omissions in this and the next chapter open the door for added examples, explanations, and perspectives. These two chapters are like conversations, ones that we can and should consider continuing.

We begin with the six central features of the ideal school model.

Space and Place

Our educational institutions message through their space, and it is critical that the space where education happens be trauma responsive. That means what is on the walls and in the halls message that students are welcomed, that there will be acceptance and not punishment, and that there are opportunities for engagement.

Reflect on what is currently on the walls and in the stairwells in existing schools. Consider the colors of the walls. Ask if there is any central congregating space. Are there opportunities for self-expression on the walls that can change from week to week or even day-to-day? While the ideal school has numerous opportunities for posting and writing on walls (bulletin boards, whiteboards, chalkboards), these can be created in any existing educational structure, as can opportunities for using chalk. Consider places to use chalk through replacing flooring materials (often a washable, durable surface) with cement. Buckets of chalk and erasers can be hung on nearby walls. There has to be institutional buy-in; otherwise, things placed on the walls will be taken down or erased or removed. Some institutions have strict rules about who can post what where. The ideal school empowers students to post in many ways.

Light is another central feature of the ideal school. Light from doors and windows and light from above. Consider installing skylights or light pathways in ceilings and walls. Even old buildings made of concrete or brick can be modified to provide more light. The purposes are many. We want light because it lifts the mood and reduces the divide between the inside and outside; learning and play can be in both places.

The furniture in the ideal school gives signals too, from the colorful movable desks and chairs to the talking chairs that provide insight and calm. These items certainly must be paid for, but one can change existing furniture by rearranging it in different formations (unless it cannot be moved). Or what if comfortable beanbag chairs were placed throughout a school? What if soft furniture were added to a central space like the library? And talking chairs can be created but museum-quality talking chairs are not required.

An additional point pertains to high school and college: Existing furniture may not fit the students. As people become heavier and bigger and with more learning materials in classes, we need to increase chair sizes and use writing surfaces that detach from the chairs. Think of veterans returning to school who are sitting in narrow chairs where they can barely slide in between the chair and the affixed table arm. Consider the difficulty of beanbag chairs for some older adults returning to college after decades. Adult students may not be comfortable plopping down in chairs low to the ground; perhaps they would prefer a sofa or large reading chair.

A striking feature of the ideal school is its pie shape. The pie slices, with their opportunities for engagement, can be replicated by combining some classrooms in existing schools to create bigger spaces with more teachers. That will not create chaos; rather, it will foster opportunity and freedom. Taking down walls (yes, assuming they are not weight-bearing walls) in existing schools will message openness and present real chances for students and educators to work together. Many leaders wall themselves into their office areas—at one institution I was at, the leader hid behind the walls of his office suite. When a new leader arrived, the wood paneling was replaced with glass, signaling openness in the new regime. As a leader, I had an open door accessible by anyone, even folks without an appointment (something changed by my successor, unfortunately). Sure, I had an assistant who welcomed people in an adjacent room, but my office door was open and the office had a porch with doors open to the outside. "Come in" was the message. I even had a piece of art outside the door that said "SPEAK."

I have been in schools that look like prisons. I have been in schools within other schools. I have been in schools that use trailers because of overcrowding. I have been in schools made of concrete. I have been in schools where additions have been made to create something that resembles a maze. I have been in schools that are so clean you could do a medical operation in the hallways. I have been in schools where classrooms could be reached only through the library. I have been in schools with foreboding seminar rooms lined with dark paneling and moldings that took years to carve, with walls filled with photos or portraits of white men (former board chairs and leaders). I have been in schools where the best space is largely unused on a regular basis, akin to grandmothers' living rooms where the furniture is covered in plastic.

I get the difficulty of changing space and place, particularly when money is short (let alone when will or buy-in is short). I get compliance with the Americans with Disabilities Act and fire codes. I get disruption, too. But suppose we made changes that enabled different signals. This is *good* disruption. Create glass doors. Remove the mazelike feel by putting drawn feet to follow on the floor or creating maps. Change the flooring to something colorful. Add color. Move the entrances if feasible, which it likely will be, given all the doors a school has. All the better if these changes can be done as an activity involving students, families, and community members. And while one's at it, create a vegetable garden inside or outside and share the food grown.

One more critical observation: In the pie model, the Center (see Chapter 8) is in the center and as such messages its centrality. However, in an existing school, the Center could be located elsewhere. The concept of a Center where form and function are in perfect harmony is an ideal. A Center could be "off center" in a school while still enabling students and educators to, among other things, find their center.

A Center could be created in existing space by taking down walls in some central location. For example, at the top of stairs, two or three classrooms could be eliminated and replaced with a Center. (Yes, classrooms are often at a premium, but if we change what occurs in classrooms and how teaching is done, we can combine classrooms and thereby better meet space needs.) Many reading this may reflect on existing student centers as possible Centers. In many instances, these are freestanding buildings to which students have to walk. For the Center concept to work, it has to be within the space where classes occur and ideally where at least some faculty have offices. Otherwise, the ease of getting to and the purpose of the Center is eliminated. Consider the possibility on larger campuses of several Centers, each located in a key building where classes are held and faculty have offices. Today, some centers do exist, although the types of activity within them may not mirror what occurs in the ideal model. In other words, we could already have centers, but we are not wearing our trauma lens in reflecting on what occurs or could occur within them.

Play Table

In the ideal school, including one or more play tables is of much greater importance than may appear at first blush. For deeply traumatized children, the capacity to play can be inhibited. These children need to learn to play, and one of the first signs of emerging from their trauma is their growing capacity to play.[2] Play therapy is not just the interpretation of play (slamming a doll or bashing a house or drawing a house on fire or a prison), although to be sure, that has relevance. For some children that is the second phase. The first phase is actually learning to play. Then they can move to playing to learn.

And while on play, we can reflect on humor and laughter, something to treat with sensitivity and without guilt in a trauma-responsive environment. Being trauma responsive does not mean never indulging in laughter or joy or fun. A trauma does not forever eradicate pleasure, although pleasure may be hard to find and to enjoy for months or years afterward.

Indeed, learning how to laugh and have joy and fun without guilt is part of what needs to be achieved in a trauma-responsive school. While we have focused on trauma symptomology, it is also important to address preventative factors that ameliorate symptomology. We noted engagement with others, described in Chapter 8 under the heading "Someone(s)," as a protective factor. Humor, laughter, and fun are protective too, when and where they are appropriate. The play table is a place where this type of learning can occur: It is all about fun and is in a school, signaling that learning and fun are not mutually exclusive. Indeed, one can laugh to learn, an observation that has led me to use the phrase "laugh2learn" in my work with children and adults.[3]

Traumatized students pay a price for the absence of play (children and adults alike). In one group of charter schools, academic rigor is paramount. When a student finished his or her work in whatever subject, they were to read. Indeed, reading a book was the "reward" for completing tasks ahead of time. This meant students did a lot of reading, which of course has many benefits. For some students, however, this made reading feel like a burden. Reading was no longer for pleasure, because for these students it felt required. What a sad, unintended outcome. The joy, fun, and pleasure of reading were gone. Such loss has had an impact as students from these charter schools have entered higher education, where copious reading is required.

When it comes to postsecondary education, the idea exists that higher education is too important for play, and fun is wrong or happens elsewhere. We divide learning from play—learning happens in classrooms and play happens in residential halls or on athletic fields. We do that in the workplace too—work is where serious things happen. This division is artificial. Learning happens in many places and spaces of which the classroom is but one. We can combine learning with humor and laughter. A trauma-responsive school is not devoid of humor and fun—it is a place where one learns about and engages in both.

For traumatized postsecondary students, learning to play may still be needed, particularly if they did not attend a trauma-responsive institution for their early education. Part of the problem is age related. If one plays at an early age, it is largely risk free. But if one plays hard at an older age, there are real dangers: overuse of substances, sexual promiscuity, activities that put one at risk like cliff jumping or motorcycling or driving at high speeds. For students in their 50s and 60s, learning to play without guilt is difficult, and play may be hard to do in ways that are comfortable and not fraught with danger.

Children can play physical games (with real learning from a coach about one's body and the rules of the game). Adults cannot suddenly play professional baseball or tennis, even if they are physically fit. Adults can spend time with strangers, and if they do it just for fun or kicks, there are real risks, of hurting others or hurting themselves by landing in dangerous situations, contracting sexually transmitted diseases, or being abused. Adult play requires some serious reflection. "Play time" can be gained by watching others play; mirror neurons let us do that. Watching athletic events in person or on television does engage the viewer. As scientists have noted, many couch potatoes are not actually lazy loungers. They are watching sports and actually getting pleasure and some physical activity (stomping, waving, jumping up and down) from the viewing. Another avenue for adults is playing with their children. Indeed, building in time for play between adults and children could help both. As an adult, one may not want to color in coloring books (despite its growing popularity as a form of relieving tension), but one can color with children. And as an adult, one can surely color outside the lines.

The Role of the Educator and Secondary or Vicarious Trauma

Historically, we have had a somewhat narrow definition of what it means to be an educator, particularly in postsecondary education, where content rules. Indeed, many teachers are hired not because they teach well but because of their particular expertise. Think of nursing or physics professors one might have met. They may be brilliant at their profession, but they cannot communicate effectively with their students. Early childhood and elementary teachers are often better at teaching, although some remain rigidly glued to a prescribed curriculum. Some of that rigidity is encouraged by the tests students must take and by accrediting and licensing requirements. Add to that the pressure created when teachers are evaluated based on student test scores.

I recollect one early childhood center on an Indian reservation where group work was discouraged because the licensing organization required that there be alternative initiatives for children who did not want to participate. This idea of multiple activities available to children makes sense if one has sufficient staffing. Without that, it is impossible to do two or three different activities that require oversight. And if one brings in an outsider like me, the inability to do a group activity because of regulations has a negative impact. And if several children want to be alone or do their own things, that is fine too and does not eliminate the value of a group activity.

The ideal school posits a way more flexible approach, with educators having broader responsibilities. They have an increased role in engaging with students, being those *someone(s)*. For some educators, this is not a comfortable position. They may have mastered their content areas but are not expert at interpersonal skills. Some of these added skills can be taught, although for most noneducation professors, if they learned about pedagogy in graduate school, it was by trial and error. For those going into teaching, schools of education could offer courses on trauma responsiveness, which could also be offered to existing educators, including online.

The reality of education today must be acknowledged. It is not really a choice whether an educator wants to be trauma sensitive because absent this quality, learning is harmed. Although not all educators will be adept at being sensitive, if they connect with students in some fashion (including through academics if appropriate), the latter can overcome high ACEs. Learning will not be effective if we stick to what we are doing. Inequities will persist.

Trauma has costs. Childhood trauma survivors suffer economic deprivations as they age: They may have more and costly illnesses, and truncated educations lower their incomes. Their difficulties in forming quality relationships hamper the development of a stable family life, potentially causing further economic instability. A study attempting to quantify the annual costs of high ACEs found that even without allowing for the toll of natural disasters, the estimated annual cost in the United States of ACEs is $748 billion (with a *b*).[4] Thus, the sooner we succeed in reducing ACEs, the more economic savings we will have. Call this added incentive to act now. And some of those savings can be redirected to creating trauma-responsive schools that will enable savings.

The ideal school model recognizes that community is vital for educators, many of whom may themselves have experienced trauma, including in a school shooting or a hurricane. In addition, when they deal with the trauma the students have experienced, they are affected by secondary trauma. In their effort to help the students, they may not take sufficiently good care of themselves, making it harder for them to do their jobs or to continue in them. As previously noted, when educators leave, whether from secondary or vicarious trauma, it is disruptive for the students they serve.

As addressed in a poignant article on mental health workers in New Orleans following Hurricane Katrina, the article observes that in an environment of trauma, it is hard for caregivers to take care of themselves.[5] They are too busy to maintain their own, preexisting caregiver community. For adults encountering trauma for the first time, the manifestation of symptoms may not be immediate. They can take several years to appear, and they never fully heal. Adults need to reconstitute themselves, as they are forever changed.

These findings and some of the observations and terms used fit the context of an educational crisis. Mental health professionals left New Orleans, many because of mandatory evacuation. Consider the impact of this void on individuals who were in therapy before the hurricane, not to mention those needing therapy after it. In education, reflect on students whose schools are closed and whose teachers disappear, something occurring in the context of COVID-19. For already traumatized students, the absence of a place to go and of known teachers is further traumatizing.

Why do we have no educators on disaster relief teams? Wouldn't it make sense to have people trained to help children, especially if the educators are trauma trained? Why aren't we trying to enable students and educators to get together, even if not at a school? True, that may not be as productive, but it will allow engagement. It will help educators too, because besides seeing students, they will see their own peers.

A significant observation of one of the Katrina therapists was that the therapy she did after the hurricane did not resemble the therapy she did before. She reported, "I . . . worried that some of the things I was doing during a therapy hour did not resemble the therapy I was accustomed to doing. In many obvious ways, the therapeutic stance was abandoned and familiar boundaries seemed insignificant. It was not uncommon to share information about community resources or activities."[6] This therapist was "traditional," keeping to the therapeutic hour and the clear boundaries that prevent therapists from divulging their own experiences or feelings in the therapeutic setting (which has been challenged of late).[7] The hurricane, however, changed her role.

And so it is with educators. The traditional classroom learning period and the focus on content are all altered in the ideal model of a trauma-responsive school. In the face of trauma, traditional roles get upended, and educators (and therapists) are often on unfamiliar turf, carrying out their professional responsibilities differently. That may not be easy, but it is surely necessary. Context and knowing one's students force a change on educators who want to help their students more effectively.

Recognizing her changed role, the therapist quoted above who was dealing with the Katrina aftermath explored what she gained; what she observed is also applicable to educators: "I have at once been humbled and enriched by this experience. I think that I appreciate the complexities, the textures of life's experiences differently than I have before now. Having shared the intimate experience of trauma with so many people makes room for a kind of connection I had only sampled and not quite captured before Katrina."[8] Think about the way educators engage with students in the ideal school. They learn more about who their students are and their experiences; they see and respond to a student's trauma. They engage with students outside the classroom. They connect more fully, becoming the someone(s) for many traumatized students. They might even share their own traumas to establish authenticity. While these moving boundaries and changed relationships are outside the traditional role of educator, they benefit not just the student but also the educator. To return to the essay excerpt in Chapter 6 from Professor Jack, he too might have had a more personalized, nuanced experience had the institution he attended had trauma-responsive professors and administrators, some of whom had experienced trauma and changed as a result.

In short, trauma in our students and in ourselves changes who we are and what we do. And it isn't easy—for anyone.

Antifragmentation

We justify and encourage interdisciplinary approaches in today's educational system for many reasons, including that the real world is not carrying subject labels and those in the workforce need to move across and between disciplines. But there is another way to reflect on interdisciplinarity: It encourages the parts of our brain to work together. It messages psychic openness. It enables thoughts and feelings to emerge once the autonomic nervous system is quieted.

In the ideal school, interdisciplinarity abounds. First, the pie slices work together. The educational institution focuses on disciplines, but then there is a sharing of outcomes, allowing students to see unanticipated connections, including in areas where they might not expect intersectionality, like math and music. Roving teachers add to an interdisciplinary approach, injecting a different discipline into the preexisting discipline in the pie slice.[9]

Another antifragmentation approach engages students in activities that lower their autonomic nervous system responses; such responses fragment the brain, disabling function in parts of it. If the nervous system responses can be lowered, pathways can be opened and cognition augmented. The focus on a single subject for a month is also designed to limit fragmentation. When students move from class to class in educational institutions, they are fragmented; for traumatized students, time is lost settling into each new class and then preparing for the next class. Deeper engagement in a single location with consistent teachers and non-movement works against fragmentation.

In some ways, this suggested approach resembles the approach at some colleges where students concentrate on one course or fewer courses to allow them to focus and engage deeply.[10] While trauma responsiveness is surely not the underlying rationale, a trauma-responsive approach would recognize the value of students not going from class to class and adjusting and readjusting each time. Moreover, there is no reason why jumping from class to class works any better for younger students, and with growing numbers of nontraditional students entering postsecondary education and often balancing family and work and school, concentrated learning (done well) is beneficial.[11] Concentrated learning also allows consistent development of psychosocial skills, encompassing working with others, and improves work products with time to make changes and improvements to them and assignments that continue without being easily forgotten.

The ideal school also fosters student choice. Currently, administrators and teachers make many choices for students. Course selection in lower grades is severely limited, and in postsecondary education, the door opens but often ends up closing because of the requirements of core courses and of a major. Empowering choice, particularly when educators can assist with making them, diminishes fragmentation. Students choose courses, limiting the control (not advice) of educators and administrators. That lessens fragmentation. And the number of choices in the ideal institution is limited, as too many choices can lead to a kind of paralysis. Importantly, trauma can freeze individuals' choice mechanism and impairs their capacity for full thinking. Traumatized individuals may feel guilty as they choose courses they want, rather than what their teachers, families, or friends might prefer or even mandate culturally. Quality choice helps build quality choice architecture, which may be lacking in traumatized individuals. *Breakaway Learners* discusses helping students pivot right—make good choices and reject the many bad choices they could make. Traumatized students face many choices; why not create structures to optimize their choices?

Punishment and Discipline

Many current approaches to student punishment and discipline operate off the principle of removing the student. In the ideal school, the approach to trauma is vastly different; instead of students being sent away or out, they either process in place or go to the Center.

Our current system of punishment in many educational institutions focuses on the bad behavior, not its causes.[12] A student acts out (an outsized response) and the educator doesn't ask why but instead tries to solve the problem by punishing the student, taking what can be characterized as the easy way out. In a different approach, many educators try to punish the offending behavior instead of the student, an improvement but not good enough as an outcome. Just for starters, traumatized students have trouble distinguishing between punishing behaviors and punishing individuals.

As Chapters 3 and 4 on trauma symptomology describe, traumatized students may have challenging behaviors. They can overreact and be disruptive, shout, dramatize, and throw things. They can have trouble concentrating. They may push others away, sometimes literally. For educators who are not trauma trained, it is hard to know what is causing the offending behavior. We often connect the behavior to the offender—the behavior is bad and this is a "bad" kid. The same holds true in higher education when students act out and are punished. The student senses that both the acts and the person doing them are bad; the student is "bad."

I appreciate the need for consistency in punishment and negative discipline. For many deans, consistency becomes the hallmark of fairness: All students misbehaving the same way need to be treated the same; we cannot be seen as favoring one student over another. Otherwise, as the argument goes, students will learn about the imbalances in how bad acts are treated and complain about the inconsistency, perhaps raising the specter of discrimination. Colleges write codes of conduct, hold disciplinary hearings, and mete out punishment based on preset standards. This echoes criminal law, where we have sentencing guidelines to ensure that lenient judges do not let criminals run loose and that harsh judges do not overpunish. And, it enables us to avoid discriminatory behaviors, whether recognized or not.

I think our approach to student behavior operates off faulty premises. First, it assumes that students have acted with intent. Second, it assumes that students could control their behavior. Third, it assumes that students behave badly, knowing what they are doing is bad. Fourth, it places a premium on consistency, in the name of justice but also of convenience. If you have standardized approaches, the burden on those charged with carrying out the punishment is lessened. The potential for discriminatory behavior is arguably narrowed.

Instead, we should ask students why they did what they did. It is worth discussing the behavior and its effect on the students themselves and others. When one actually listens, the reasons for "bad acts" are not consistent. Yes, there is responsibility at one level for one's actions, but how to punish or discipline is hugely personal and situation specific. We seem to be so stuck on consistency that we fail to recognize that the causes of the behavior are not consistent. By not looking beneath the surface, we homogenize wrongdoing students. We avoid the complexities of human behavior and the root causes for why students act (or fail to act) as they do.

The ideal school looks at punishment through a trauma lens, examining why each student behaved as he or she did. The punishment or discipline is developed after learning the *why*. Moreover, one punishment eliminated from the repertoire except in rare instances is removal from school or a campus. Punishing students who skip school by removing them from campus is counterproductive: The punishment gives the offending students exactly what they want: absence from their educational institution. Sending a college student off campus with no place to stay if they are far from home is torturous and deprives someone of a "home," which could be one of the very reasons they are acting out. I have always been struck, too, by the assumption that students are beyond understanding why different students might be punished differently. Assuming race and ethnic discrimination are not at work, students—particularly those who are traumatized—can see differences in student behavior that may be invisible to administrators. For starters, fellow students may know more about a student's personal life than the educators meting out the punishment.

Directing students to the Center is a form of rehabilitation, allowing them to process with the help of adults what they did and why. And what about empowering students to make suggestions about their own punishment? It might just be that they will develop better approaches than those charged with punishing them. Context matters and students get context. Younger students can be guided toward understanding context. Sadly, traumatized students get arbitrariness too; they have often lived with that for years in their childhood.

Take this example, drawn from my experience on the campus where I was president. Two students called 911 when a fellow student was ill from overdrinking and the students who were with him got worried about his well-being. When the town police (rather than campus police) arrived, the two reporting students were arrested for underage drinking, and yes, the ill student was transported to the local hospital. When I heard the story, I thought the two students who were drinking deserved praise, not punishment. Sure, they were drinking underage, but they did absolutely the right thing: They got help for the student in trouble, regardless of the consequences to themselves. They did what we want students to do: care for one another. To return to choice architecture and pivoting right, they did pivot right and make the right choice when it really mattered.

Because the police were involved, the legal system was activated, the school's disciplinary code was evoked, and a disciplinary hearing was scheduled. Where, I kept asking the dean, was the positive feedback for the accused students? She kept mentioning consistency and standard approaches and potential leniency for first-time offenders. Wait, I kept saying, when do you tell these students they did the right thing—the most important right thing—they cared for another human being?

Finding no solace in the dean's approach and not yet being willing to overhaul that whole system (which would have included firing the existing dean and hiring a new dean), I happened upon the students in the hallway and asked them to join me in my office. From the looks on their faces, I think they thought they were being expelled. Let's just say they did not anticipate anything good would come from being in my office. Once they arrived, I shared that I wanted them to know that they had done the right thing—they had looked out for another student. That is precisely the behavior we want in students and in our larger society. I mentioned that they needed to be careful about overdrinking. I indicated that I would try to get the legal system to curb its standard practices. And I thanked them for caring. I told them they had made an excellent decision.

I have no idea whether these two students had a history of trauma. But I know this much: If they had, they would have appreciated the effort to respond to them on a personal basis. And if they were traumatized, punishment would seem to reinforce their lack of belief in self and their sense of inadequacy, which accompany trauma. If their trauma symptomology was to isolate themselves, the fact that they reported the illness of a fellow student—despite putting themselves at risk—was remarkable. They engaged to help someone. Can't ask for much more than that.

The Center and Truth

One value that emerges from the Center in particular and the ideal school in general is authenticity.[13] Because traumatized individuals are often hypervigilant, authenticity is crucial. They can detect when people are not being honest in their beliefs, whether that is evidenced by the latter's actions or inactions.

Authenticity emerges from combining the five *S*s. The ideal school, with its educators deeply engaged with students and each other, showcases the difficulties of trauma and its impact. Authenticity is revealed by the well-being of the students and their educators. Schools filled with students with trauma could lead to chaos in classrooms and an absence of learning. But the ideal school, with the five *S*s working together, presents the opposite. Through its commitment to stability, structure, safety, subtlety, and someone(s), students whom many perceived as doomed emerge. And if working well, the educators do not leave the ideal school in droves; they stay and are professionally fulfilled.

Messaging to students and families needs to be authentic too. The subsection "Opening Door" has examples elucidating the requirements of authenticity, although that word is not specifically mentioned. You cannot have glass doors surrounding administrators if you aren't willing to be seen doing your work. You cannot engage with families in the Center, where others are present, if you cannot be open and honest with the families, reflecting a heartfelt willingness to work with them to help the children in their care. And yes, of course, privacy should not be breached; that's part of feeling safe.

When you have walls, halls, and floors on which anything can be written or posted, you need to believe in the central values embedded in the ideal school, including the values of subtlety and safety. And the presence of pop-up courses that address current events, in an effort to get the students to process what is occurring in the here and now, produces authenticity. You can't deal with current events in the here and now to enable real processing unless authenticity is present. And the larger concept of processing in place requires the presence of truth in real time.

One example of the absence of authenticity at a university showcases what occurs when trauma responsiveness is lacking. The fallout from the lack of authenticity will surely be felt. Here's the story. At the University of Pennsylvania, the newly hired head of student mental health services, Gregory Eells, jumped to his death from the 17th floor of his building. The suicide was shocking at many levels. Eells was highly regarded. The prior decade, he was at Cornell University, a place with no shortage of student suicides. He was deeply committed to student wellness and arrived at Penn knowing that suicide prevention was a central aspect of his work. Indeed, student mental health is an issue on many campuses.[14] Eells left no suicide note.

Since Penn's Counseling and Psychological Services was committed to improving its operations following Eells's arrival, the university's approach after the suicide was shocking by any measure, including taking into account needs for privacy and personal desires. Its response started with an email from administrators sent to undergraduate students announcing Eells's death. The email never mentioned suicide. It noted the availability of mental health professionals 24/7 and provided contact information. The email stated, and I quote: "It is with sadness that we share the news of the *sudden* death of Dr. Gregory Eells, Executive Director of Counseling and Psychological Services (CAPS). Dr. Eells died this morning in Philadelphia" (emphasis added).[15] Others have noted the absence of any reference to death by suicide.[16] The email was sent the same day as the suicide.

Perhaps the thought was that the cause of death was not confirmed or there was a legal prohibition on characterizing the death before the state disclosed its finding. Perhaps his widow wanted the truth omitted. Perhaps the institution thought using the word "suicide" would be too triggering. But surely the writers (the vice-provost for university life and the chief wellness officer) knew that suicide would immediately be suspected; in our world, and with our speed of communication, a suicide like that would not be hidden. Not to be too blunt, but people had seen the body splayed on the ground.

There are many ways the email could have messaged that suicide was the likely cause of death if confirmation did not exist. "Sudden" is not sufficient. If it was known that the death was a confirmed suicide at the time the note was sent, it is hard to believe that the university would have avoided the word *suicide*. It is probable that the two writers consulted others from the mental health services office about the email, and it is hard to imagine that suicide was not discussed. We know from studies that mentioning suicide does not cause it, and asking someone who is depressed, "Are you thinking about killing yourself?" is not hurtful and does not encourage suicide. It may help prevent it. Transparency matters.[17]

There appears to have been no follow-up from the email writers in the days that followed. Equally if not more shocking, did they think the issues would disappear? Generic email notices were sent to students that their mental health appointments the day following the death would be handled by Student Health Services, but apparently with no explanation. Picture a student reaction to this mass, impersonal email and redirection to a new mental health setting. One supposes CAPS (the campuses mental health facility that also allowed walk-ins) was closed.[18] Closed? Seriously? After the suicide of its head, the place for solace was closed? The suicide was on Monday. The first official statement from CAPS came on Friday.

What happened between Monday and Friday that enabled the silence, when silence was the last thing needed? The text of that communication on Friday has not been made public. One has to wonder if it mentioned suicide. Seriously, who permitted that silence, especially among mental health professionals? I get that the mental health professionals were devastated by the suicide of a colleague, but the response was remarkably antitherapeutic. Ironically, the students on campuses acted by placing sticky notes on the campus "LOVE" sculpture. I ask again: Where were the adults?

In short, the Penn emails and approach were inauthentic, the antithesis of what is needed in the context of suicide. There could not be a more blatant example, sadly, of an institution not being trauma responsive.

Macro Changes and the Brain

In a sense, the ideal school replicates the brain. The ideal model has brain-like features such as interdisciplinarity and the presence of feelings as well as thought. The ideal school sees the mind-body connection. The efforts to prevent fragmentation are like activation or regrowth of the neural pathways. Recognition of the autonomic nervous system's impact on thought is evident, including through exercises designed to lower autonomic nervous system symptoms. The ideal school has an architecture, but it is open and enables the development of myriad ideas and solutions.

The macro change suggestions in this chapter assume full brain function. In Chapter 10, we turn to micro changes, some of which are ways to lift the inhibitors of thought. Indeed, embedded in the ideal school are both macro and micro features that produce trauma responsiveness, as evidenced in Figure 6.1. In the real world, we would want both macro and micro changes. However, even micro changes produce benefits, as noted in Part I, by lifting the allostatic load carried by traumatized individuals. As we leave macro changes, we should note that they do not need to be implemented as a whole to have beneficial effects. Indeed, even partial implementation of macro changes moving an institution toward being trauma responsive has benefits. Keep that in mind to prevent becoming discouraged as we now deconstruct micro changes in the ideal model school.

For encouragement as we proceed, consider this possibility: If the educational institutions we create are trauma responsive, they may accomplish more than we anticipate. These institutions might be deemed positive childhood experiences (PCEs) or positive adult experiences (PAEs), mitigating even further the effects of trauma measured by ACEs. We return to this possibility in the last chapter of this book.

Deconstruction II: Micro Changes

Deconstructing the ideal school to identify micro changes (and why to make them) is the next essential step in moving from naming trauma to taming trauma. Indeed, taming comes from combining the macro and micro changes and their adoption.

The micro change suggestions culled from the ideal school model described in Part II can be used in educational institutions across the landscape, adapted for the ages and stages of the students. Because they are micro changes, each one does not need to contain all five of the *S*s needed for macro changes. Just as we have five categories of macro changes, there are five types of micro changes: *transitions*, *use of the senses*, *materials on the walls*, *rovers and pop-ups*, and *teams and teamwork*. While in a perfect world they work together, micro changes have benefits even in the absence of massive macro change. We need to be accepting of partial change, given the difficulty of any change in educational settings.

Transitions

We are notoriously bad at transitions generally, not just in education. We do not recognize their complexity and challenges.[1] They are particularly difficult for traumatized individuals, in part because any trauma is a transition from what one was to something different and unerasable. A rape survivor is forever changed. A child who witnesses a parent being shot leaves a childhood without trauma and enters one with trauma. Subsequent transitions then retrigger the autonomic nervous system, making new changes feel unsafe, even when they are not. For some traumatized people, even leaving their home to go someplace positive can retrigger the autonomic nervous system. They get ready to leave then, before locking the door, they go back to check the stove five times to make sure it is off. Were they not leaving and just staying at home, they would not be checking the stove with frequency.

In the educational system, there are numerous transitions, small and large. Students transition from home to school and then back home. They transition from class to class during the school day; they transition from one school to another at a certain grade level or they move geographically. For traumatized students, all these transitions can trigger their autonomic nervous system, and these individuals struggle to find their balance, their center. Yet despite the high numbers of traumatized students in our educational system, we give short shrift to the impact of the repeated transitions built and baked into the system.

When students move through the educational pipeline, changing schools, we assume that a single orientation is enough. Whether the orientation is for a couple of hours or a couple of days, we assume that once students are "oriented," that is sufficient. Nothing could be further from the truth. At orientations, students do not hear or connect to what is being said. They are focused on the new space, finding the bathroom, how to get from class to the cafeteria, getting their ID, and searching for familiar faces. Their autonomic nervous system is on high alert, making cognition difficult. It matters how we welcome new and existing students each day. Many students come to school with their autonomic nervous systems on high alert, yet we start classes right away and launch into substantive material as if everyone were ready to engage. We do the same thing following holiday breaks and summer vacation. We forget or ignore that for some students summers may have involved a shooting; a hurricane; involvement with the criminal justice system; immigration problems; or a virus or another illness, their own or a family member's.[2] In the summer of 2019 alone, 53 people died in mass shootings, Hurricane Dorian appeared, and migrant families were threatened with indefinite detention. What if we tried some exercises each day, to calm students' autonomic nervous systems, for all or the most difficult transitions in the educational system? What if we started a new semester or a return after a break with an autonomic nervous system–lowering activity?

Consider a greeting to students from administrators, teachers, or professors at the institution's entrance as students come into the building—wouldn't a personal welcome make a difference? Even better if it is a welcoming committee. If students entered through a pie slice in the ideal school, their teachers could be at the doorway welcoming them. Many schools already do this in the lower grades (although it is rarely labeled as a trauma response), but this approach ceases as students age, based on the belief that they are better adjusted. That assumes they leave their trauma behind or that it is tamed, whereas trauma lingers and is retriggered. Transitions don't stop being hard because we keep doing them. Our invisible trauma backpack doesn't disappear.

Further, educators need to know students' names—which they do in the early grades but less so in colleges and universities. Most people will feel anonymous if they are not referred to by name—and "You in the Red Shirt" is not quality identification. Moreover, students' names should be pronounced correctly; at times teachers may need help with this, given increasing diversity in our schools, and may need to ask students how to pronounce their name. Mispronunciation indicates disrespect and a disregard for cultural identity.[3] For a traumatized student, the outcome can be retriggered symptomology.

I still vividly remember that at my son's high school graduation, the class dean was charged with calling each student to the stage to receive his or her diploma. This dean was a woman of mixed heritage and was fluent in several languages. A student named Ricky Rodriquez approached the stage and the dean referred to him as "Ricky Ricardo," the name of the character who was Lucille Ball's husband on their television show. It may have been an easy slip for some to make, but it was highly embarrassing for the student, the dean, the student's family, and everyone else at the event. There were gasps and then silence. The student was one of few students of color enrolled and was on scholarship. The misstatement has endured in many memories, I am sure.

Consider the questions with which we start a semester: Where did you travel to this summer? What did you do for your vacation? Did you have a fun weekend? What did you get as a gift over the winter holidays? Such questions, as noted earlier, assume that students had a wonderful experience while not in school. They traveled and had fun. They received gifts. They had celebrations. For some, particularly traumatized students, however, these assumptions are false. Fun vacations and gifts may not be possible for many students and their families, not only because of cost but also because the family is not together. What if instead of the standard questions, teachers and professors started with "Welcome," or "Welcome back"; "I'm so glad to see you and have you as my students this year. I think there's a lot we can accomplish together and look forward to many successes."[4] What if educators said, "Write down or draw, for yourselves or to share if you want, one thing that had meaning for you this summer—something, someone, or someplace that affected you." Younger students can share this in private conversations; some students may not be open to sharing their thoughts publicly. But this approach allows for personalization, evidence of subtlety.

Wouldn't that kind of question open the door to many answers and later conversations? Might it help educators learn more about their students and the lives they lived outside school? Might the answers enable self-reflection and a calming of the autonomic nervous system? The questions lead to naming what actually happened, not mislabeling a summer as one that resembles a Hallmark card. Through this practice, an educator role models a critical skill: asking good questions. Often the quality of a question is more important than an answer. A quality question can reflect a deep understanding of a person or subject area or a sensitivity to context and the person being asked. There is no better way to learn to ask good questions than to be asked them. Law students know this and often try out the questions they are asked daily on friends and family.[5] Post-pandemic, this matters too.

A shared activity that brings students together gets them to focus on school and not on whatever they brought into school in their trauma suitcase.

What if a teacher put on music and asked students to drum softly to the rhythm? What if the teacher handed out feathers and asked students to trace the outline of their hands with them? The point is to break the autonomic nervous system's alert system so students can be better positioned to learn.

We often do not reflect enough on new educator transitions. We have new members of our educational community sign paperwork galore. We allocate them a computer and get them an ID and some keys. We show them their classroom. We show them where to find the copier. We take them to the teachers' lounge. But when do we orient faculty and staff to the mission of the institution? When do we talk about what the institution stands for? We assume students are comfortable and ready to engage, but we don't share the most important information with them: the values and approaches of the institution and why they matter. We just assume they can absorb this critical information or have done so through interviews. By not doing the educator transition more effectively, we lose an opportunity to message—and the message we do deliver may run counter to what matters most to us: quality engagement. We need to incorporate new personnel in a manner that better messages the values of the institution.

I have often reflected on students' curiosity about their new instructors. Instead of sharing information, we keep a strict dividing line between what happens within the school and outside its doors. It reminds me of the traditional dividing line between therapist and patient. The therapist knows a lot about the patient, but the patient knows almost nothing about the therapist. The patient may wonder, Is the therapist married? Does the therapist have children? Does the therapist like music or dance? Has the therapist ever encountered his or her own trauma? Was his or her pathway to success a straight line forward? Similarly, students wonder about their educators. Are they married? Are they in their profession because they love it or they just landed there? Did they get good grades at school? Did they ever mess up along the educational pipeline? I think many of my graduate students thought I slept with my books, and that's why I brought my son to class at least once a semester—so they could get a glimpse of the life I lived outside the classroom.

I think we can do better. I have tried the following approach, with success. Near the beginning of a school year or semester (certainly *not* the first month), the educator tells students to close their laptops or books. Then he or she says, "This is Ask Me Anything Day." The instructor tells the students that he or she will answer honestly any questions, as long as they are not indecent, they may have about life, professional or academic pathways, or other topics.

I was always struck by the initial silence that followed this invitation. Students did not raise their hands. Later on, reactions did improve when students knew this was a tradition in my classes, but even so, the questions were slow to come. Usually, I'd have to prod: "Come on. Ask me anything.

You must be curious about something." Then once the ball got rolling, the questions were wonderful. I disclosed that my career pathway had taken many unexpected turns. I shared going back to work after I had a child and how on my first day back after maternity leave, I was sent on a plane to another city to handle a court hearing. I shared getting bad grades on a paper or a test. Those stories were always viewed with an uncertain glance as if they were saying: Could have fooled me; I thought professors only got As as students.

Here's the point: We need to humanize education, and that involves understanding who our students are. Further, students need to understand who their educators are and why they are there, rather than in some other school or university or some other job, outside education. And sadly, there is that old adage "those who can, do; those who can't, teach," not exactly an affirmation of the choice of individuals to teach. It matters for traumatized students that individuals in their school are committed to their success and have made complicated choices in their own lives so they understand life's ups and downs. Personalization is a two-way street, and while educators traditionally disclose little, there are benefits to disclosing more. Think again of the Dr. Jack story in Chapter 6. The faculty and administrators did not know the student, and the student did not know them (or himself).

When I was a college president, I often invited students, faculty, and staff into our home, and it happened so often that our home was almost like another campus building. I remember two particular reactions. When coming up the path to the front door, invited to dinner, a student was speaking to her mother on her cellphone. I heard her say, "No, I didn't do anything wrong. That's not why I'm going to the president's house." Another time, a group of students refused to come to my house, and their reasons were something like "Why would I want to go to a White woman's house so she can show off all her possessions?" My assistants finally convinced a few of them to give it a try—they might be surprised by the experience. Once welcomed into my home and brought into conversations and, yes, shown interesting art on the walls, these students started to feel more comfortable. True, the dog helped. True, good humor and other students and faculty helped. But the point was that they could get comfortable in a new setting if they were overtly welcomed.

Much of the discussion on transitions here has been about arriving at and settling into a new space, but there can also be difficulties in departing. Students heading off to college often fight with their families in the weeks before departing in an effort to make leaving easier. Some parents cling to their children as they transition away, the parents seeking to maintain ties by remaining in constant contact as if they could partake in their children's experiences. Post-pandemic, departures will have new meaning.

Then there are issues at the other end of the spectrum: leaving college. At Southern Vermont College, we introduced a unique program to help low-income, Pell Grant–eligible students succeed in higher education. We had the contours of the problems they faced in place. We had a remarkable leader overseeing the project. We had strategies that resembled the foundational elements of lasticity described in *Breakaway Learners*; indeed, lasticity was born from the work with these students. We were building our wings while flying.

Late in February, when the first class of these breakaway learners was set to graduate, which they would do in May, at a rate that far exceeded all predictions (84% compared with a projected rate under 10%), something happened. Members of this first class encountered a set of hurdles. Several became pregnant, several got (very) bad grades, and several dropped out. Now remember, this is 3-plus years in college with abundant stellar work to help them find success and then this occurred.

What happened? At that moment, I recalled for the first time a student whom I knew well who every semester or so as he approached graduation would flunk a course. That way, he would get to stay in school and not have to enter the "real" world. He had found a safe home in the college and did not want to leave. I invited him into my office and shared that I thought he was intentionally or subconsciously flunking. I said I believed in him, he was ready to graduate, we would still be here to support and engage with him, and the college would still be his home after he left. He listened. He was quiet. He then said softly, "I think you're right." He then spent the next two semesters finishing all his courses with excellent grades. He went on to get a graduate degree and has been a success working on civic change and the empowerment of young people. I am in touch with him and his family—still.

What we had missed in February was that we had not prepared our breakaway learners for the world beyond college. We had so focused on graduation as the endpoint that we failed to see and appreciate that the transition out of college into a new situation would be difficult—so difficult it might not be worth trying. In building the wings of the program, we had not anticipated the challenges of graduation. We fixed the problem but did lose some students in the process—students who I still hope will return to college at some point in their lives to graduate. They are at most four or five courses short, and they could complete their education at any number of institutions and get a degree.

On a related note, sometimes students who lose athletic eligibility fail to graduate because they leave when they are no longer playing. There is one such student whose failure to graduate—he was one course short—haunts me still. He said he couldn't finish; it was too expensive; it was too far from home; it was too late to come back as all his friends had graduated. He was "beyond" college; he was working. I kept and still keep thinking: one course, just one course. But for this student, the effort to return was too high a hurdle; and yes, he had been traumatized and suffered from PTS, and transitioning back as a nonathlete would be hard. But a part of me still wants to visit him at his home and encourage him to take some course somewhere to graduate. Perhaps I am doing this for my own sake, because we failed him as an institution. We couldn't help him transition back.

Transitions are hard for students who have experienced trauma, and we can do lots on the micro level not only to make these transitions easier but also to use such opportunities to optimize the experiences of students and message a welcoming environment.

Use of the Senses

In Part I, we identified the wide range of trauma symptomology that traumatized students bring with them to their schools and universities. We noted the autonomic responses over which students have no control: fight, flight, and freeze (and fainting and flocking). Unless these responses are lowered, learning cannot happen, because the autonomic responses cut off higher brain functions. Autonomic responses also can be retriggered with further events, meaning that some students are in a constant state of high alert. If this continues, additional symptomology appears—triphasic symptoms, whereby students act out, separate themselves, over-perform, or some of all three.

Educators must do more than merely recognize symptoms. They need to take actions that lower the autonomic responses. That is the distinction between trauma *informed* and trauma *responsive*, terms defined in Part I. The best way to lower autonomic responses immediately is to focus on the senses. For our purposes, I identify six senses: touch, smell, taste, sight, hearing, and balance. Consider these examples.

At the beginning of class, ask students to stand on one foot, the nondominant one, for 30 seconds without holding on to anything. This is not easy. You really need to concentrate to get your balance. Through this exercise, the autonomic lock on students' brains loosens up and learning pathways open. The activity has another meaning: Students need to find their balance, their center, to learn and engage.

An exercise for students that readers can try themselves or with a group of colleagues is as follows: Put your dominant hand on an 8-by-11-inch sheet of plain paper. Start by tracing it with a feather, just to get the sensory feel, and feathers in particular feel wonderful as they touch a person's skin. Indeed, the feather can then move across the hand and the wrist, to further activate the senses. Piles of feathers are a good thing to have, generally speaking; they are tactile and soft and appealing.

Then with a pen, pencil, or crayon, trace a line around that hand with your nondominant hand. This won't be that easy unless you are ambidextrous. Then fill in the outline of your traced hand with whatever you choose—letters, lines, designs, shapes—using your nondominant hand (see

Figure 10.1. A Real Traced Hand of an Educator

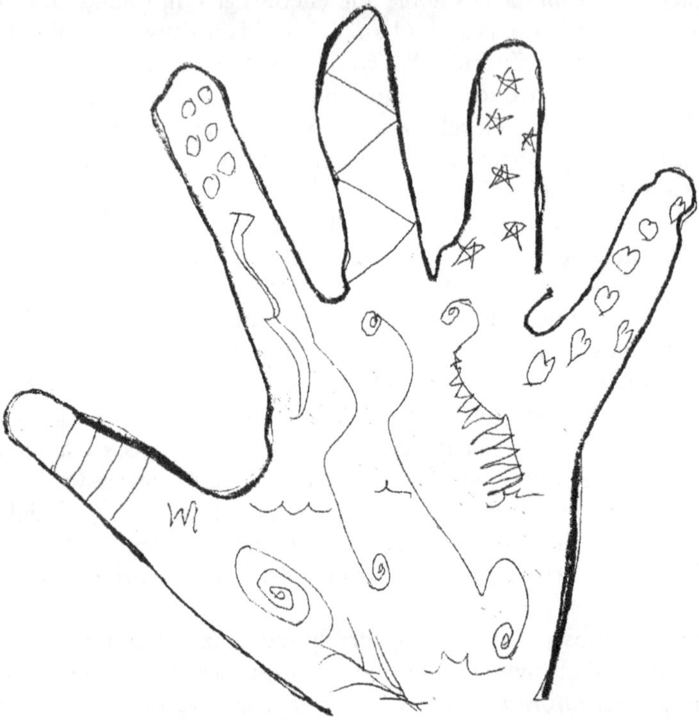

Figure 10.1). One can ask students to write words on the paper too, only with their nondominant hand.

This activity uses the senses of touch and sight and effectively breaks the cycle of the autonomic nervous system by releasing the "lock" put on the brain and then opening up neural pathways. The exercise, then, creates an opportunity for someone whose autonomic nervous system is on high alert to find a pathway into his or her calmer self. If teachers or professors started classes with such exercises, many more students would be open to learning in these classrooms.

Try this other exercise. Give every student a paper towel and an ice cube. The student puts the ice cube in the center of the paper, which is held by its four corners. Have students watch the ice cube melt and share what they are seeing and feeling as it melts. If different students have different-size cubes, some more porous than others, the exercise will have more diversity.

Other types of sensory activities can be deployed. Think about taste. If a professor is covering particularly difficult material, why not bring in food for the students and acknowledge the difficult material being addressed?

When I was teaching the most difficult materials in law school, and students knew when units were particularly tough sledding, I'd have cookies, coffee, and tea for all 100 students in the class. I'd say, "I know this material is hard. So take some food and we'll work through it together. I've taught this material to hundreds of students in the past, and I know you can do it. So just hang in there with me." Or think about hearing. Play music to start the class period. For smell, light candles with calming scents and see if students can recognize them. For touch, have students use stress balls or other tactile items.

Reflect on having animals in classrooms. Sure, they teach responsibility and enable students to care for another creature, but petting an animal or watching a fish swim also uses the senses and calms the autonomic nervous system. On a trip to Okinawa, I saw tropical fish tanks in places where travelers might get tense: airports, car rental lots, restaurants. Yes, the aquariums had visual appeal and the fish were stunning and perhaps no one realized their benefits on the autonomic nervous system. However, for those who were anxious traveling, driving on a different side of the road, or eating strange food, the fish were calming. Better than the sign at some check-in counters at airports that reads: "We know travel is hard; don't take it out on our staff." Consider how many schools and colleges have used pets following a campus tragedy. I brought our sheepdog to our college after 9/11 for the first few classes after the school reopened, as noted earlier. He'd meander up and down the aisles, with students frequently petting him. (For the record, sheepdogs are hypoallergenic, which eliminates a host of risks.)

Ponder schools and universities that grow vegetables or flowers. Students get their hands in the dirt, and the flowers they grow can decorate classrooms; the visual effects and the fragrances are beneficial. In schools where food is grown and then taken home by students, the sensory benefits are prolonged, extended into a student's home. All the sensory activities proposed here break the autonomic nervous cycle and open brain pathways.

Materials on the Walls

Opportunities exist for educators to reflect very differently about what is on the walls of their classrooms, a topic also addressed at the macro level that has micro possibilities too. Even in the absence of macro changes and institutional buy-in, there are ways to change what appears on walls, especially those in classrooms. In many lower grades, teachers post students' work—collages, pages of coloring, or handwritten poems or stories—all over the walls and sometimes in the halls. The walls in the ideal school are designed for posting a wide assortment of materials.

Now reflect on what is on the walls in high schools and colleges. It is as if we decided that what appears on walls in the early grades is elementary in every sense of the word and that such efforts do not belong in the higher grades or in college. That misses the role of imagery in affecting how we feel and how we process information and in determining whether we feel included or excluded. Can anyone remember anything on the walls in their college or graduate school classrooms?

Further, as noted earlier, many institutions display portraits of old White men who have held positions of power. These aren't welcoming images for students who are diverse or female or have felt White oppression. For students, the portraits raise questions like, "Do I fit? Where do I fit? When will I fit? Can I ever fit?" Walls in some elite institutions are covered with expensive works by non-alumni/ae artists who are well known (at least to some). Plaques honor wealthy donors (some of whom are alums) or famous award winners who are alumni/ae. These raise those same questions for current students. They ponder: "My name will never be on a wall; I can barely afford to be here. I can't win a prize if I can't even get through a course with a passing grade."

For traumatized students, many of whom already feel they do not fit at home (if they have one) or in their family (if they have one) or in their community (where diversity may not exist or the community may have been destroyed), educational institutions need to be places where they can feel they fit. One way to create environments where students fit in is to change what is on the walls. Students' art has value. If we move away from famous art by famous artists and focus instead on artwork done by students, this messages.

Further, I wonder why we don't include art by the adults in the educational community. Yes, there is often art by the art professors, but what about art done by other members of the community? Photographs by a nursing faculty member. Paintings by a history professor. Pottery by the financial officer. The point is to maximize the ways art can add to students' sense of comfort, easing their allostatic load. Seeing yourself in a space is key to opening the doors to learning. Ponder the possibility of art and writing exhibits in all our educational institutions. Students will feel pride when their work is placed on walls (although some may shy away from this, which needs to be respected). One of the downsides of trauma is that it makes those affected feel inadequate. If you lose your belief in self or have had it pounded out of you, and if you are not acknowledged for your positive strengths, learning is diminished. Fear of failure can take over. Why not put success on the walls? So, even if we can't take down the more alienating items on walls, we can add to what is there.

I have been struck to the core by what is on the walls of many schools where there is recognition of trauma's impact. Some schools have powerful posters in the hallways messaging pathways to success. There are posters about belief in self and about community. What if students could take some of these posters and hang them in their homes, where they may feel uneasy? They could then carry the feeling of the school and its welcoming environment into a space that may feel alien, uncomfortable, or unsafe. Consider the words on a poster I saw in one school, ostensibly quoting Oscar Wilde: "Be yourself; everyone else is already taken." Suppose you see that on many walls. Suppose one has smaller versions of the poster that one can place on one's desk. Suppose there are magnets with quotes one can take to where one lives or hang on a key chain. Imagine discussing what the quote actually means. Have students find other quotes they want posted that have meaning for them. In my own high school yearbook, I had this quote, surely reflective of the difficulties of my childhood and the abundant family dysfunction that was too vast to remedy: "Life is Not a Problem to be Solved but a Reality to be Experienced" (Soren Kierkegaard).

Protest art, available at no or low cost or that students can create themselves, can also be deeply appealing to students. We the People distributes art posters for free that message about equality (www.amplifier.org). Many of their posters were at the 2017 Women's March.[6] For a donation, they offer stickers that have power, too. Indeed, consider the possibility of a pop-up course on protest art.

And let's not forget the value of three-dimensional art such as pottery and sculpture. I have often been struck by the installations of Cristo and Jeanne-Claude (I have a piece of cloth from the Central Park exhibit *The Gates* [christojeanneclaude.net/projects/the-gates], with its rows of orange fabric flowing through space). They wrap structures in different materials and then nature affects the works, through wind, rain, sun, and water. For another example, consider the remarkably stunning work of African sculptor El Anatsui (/elanatsui.art/); he drapes buildings with sculptures (that resemble fabric) constructed from discarded alcohol bottle caps, tops, and rims.

Why don't we mimic their efforts in schools to activate the senses and create group projects where the slide or swings are wrapped? This uses so many senses—touch, sight, smell, hearing, and balance. Recycled materials could be used. In sum, we can use our walls, halls, stairwells, and the roof and other outdoor space to lower the autonomic nervous system.

Rovers and Pop-Ups

Rovers and pop-up courses were described in Chapter 9 as macro changes in the ideal school; however, these can also be micro changes. An entire school's using rovers on a regular basis or incorporating pop-up courses in the curriculum requires buy-in on a large scale, within and across institutions. Nevertheless, there are small ways to implement rovers and pop-ups that are not systemic but still have value. Consider these examples.

A professor or teacher could invite a guest (who would appear more than once), or *rover*, into class who could discuss his or her discipline and how it relates to the material being covered. A lawyer rover could enter an

English class and talk about copyright, come into a class on innovation and talk about patents, or participate in a class on marketing and talk about trademarks. An outside expert, or better yet one from the institution, can enrich our understanding of material and integrate subject matter, for example, English and law. The process speaks to the larger issues of fragmentation that occur in the minds of traumatized individuals.

I have been struck by graduate school professors not going into undergraduate classes in their institution. Why, apart from snobbery and time, would a professor in a medical school avoid undergraduate courses on the political process or equity and equality, sharing how these topics affect their fields? Surely health care is impacted by politics (and laws) and inequalities of both treatment and outcome. Sadly, we get stuck in our silos and fail to see the many benefits that come from crossing disciplines. And, by the by, the professor from the medical school coming into an undergraduate class may learn a lot (including from preparing for the class), and the experience could be enriching in unanticipated ways, creating a true win-win. Might this message, too, about the possibility of graduate education?

Turning to pop-up courses, they can be used across an institution to explore current events, particularly troubling events. A localized version of pop-ups can take place in particular classes when an educator decides to step away from the curriculum and provide materials related to a particular current event on students' minds. This approach can be used when a disaster occurs in a student's own community or in another and has been used in the context of the coronavirus as noted earlier.

Referring back to my experiences of 9/11, mentioned in Part I, when we restarted classes, I worried about just picking up where we left off. I reflected on what material in the subject I was teaching, contract law, would be relevant to the issues raised by 9/11, and I found a relevant topic. In contracts, existing legal doctrines cover what happens when a contract cannot be fulfilled because of materially changed circumstances. A singer cannot sing in a concert hall if it has burned down. A tenant cannot live in a building if it no longer exists. A contract for services can't continue if the person involved has died. The legal doctrines known as impossibility, impracticability, and excuse are invoked. In the aftermath of 9/11, these legal doctrines would come into play often. Why not teach those? Wouldn't they make more sense contextually if they were taught immediately upon reopening?

Teachers could similarly change up the subject they teach to align it more directly to a current event. I get that with subject matter testing, as in Advanced Placement (AP) or statewide tests, deviation from the standard curricula is problematic. But surely, dealing with student trauma, enabling processing, and lowering autonomic nervous system responses are more important than getting a score of 4 on an AP test.[7] Take how Hurricane Dorian devastated the Bahamas. Students with family there care about this topic. For students who experienced earlier hurricanes, Dorian retriggered their trauma. Trauma from other past natural disasters such as fires or explosions can also be retriggered by the images of the Bahamas destruction. Consider a pop-up course on what causes hurricanes or on the relief offered by nations and nonprofit organizations following disasters. Consider a pop-up course on how the news and social media treat hurricanes or on the health consequences of a hurricane when medical facilities are destroyed and doctors are evacuated.

The point is not necessarily to ask students to confront their own trauma publicly but to offer a pathway into that trauma through a discussion of a topic led by a teacher. Key to pop-ups is having existing faculty teach the courses as opposed to bringing in outsiders (which can be done with rovers, although not ideal there either). This messages that educators care about and can help students process such difficult topics in place. Even without a Center (see Chapters 8 and 9) or an institutional commitment to pop-ups, there are ways to get at the concept of incorporating current material. Teachers often may mention a current event and then move on. That is not what pop-ups do; rather, they enable in-depth analysis, even over several days. The idea is to recognize the importance of an event by spending time thinking through at least some aspect of it.[8]

I harbor hope that if pop-ups work effectively, students will share what they learn in the pop-ups with other students and perhaps with people outside the educational institution. Sharing will be made easier because they will have content that they have discussed in the pop-up and processed. They can go well beyond saying, "Hurricanes are dangerous." Students could speak to the *why* and *how* questions: Why is the number of hurricanes increasing? How is relief delivered and distributed to disaster sites? How is medical care provided when hospitals are destroyed and people relocated without their medical records? Aren't these questions we want students to ponder as they prepare to enter the workforce and enter communities?

We do not need to be wed to a single teacher with specific expertise in pop-up content, a topic described next; teachers can learn along with students. A trauma-responsive institution could be nimble and flexible enough to adjust as a semester progresses through the decisions of both teachers and students, studying what matters, and learning in an interdisciplinary way. Consider this in a sense a call to the "current" studying of what is (and how it came to be). And since trauma appears and reappears when "current' events happen, this is a way of enabling processing that combines relevant content with a trauma-responsive approach. COVID-19 offers many pop-up options.

Teams and Teamwork

The ideal school model offers many opportunities for teamwork, a way of helping traumatized students interact with each other and with educators. We know that problem solving in teams can improve learning, as students may be more willing to engage in small groups and share ideas, as seen in Montessori education.[9] In addition, having small groups with faculty involvement develops relationships between students and educators, and faculty learn more about students and their learning strengths and can focus on these, not on the weaknesses, within the group. Small-group work can be helpful even if done in only several classes.

The ideal school puts a premium on faculty teamwork also, creating opportunities for faculty to work together daily in the slices, through cross-disciplinary engagement, and in the Center. These opportunities discourage secondary and vicarious trauma by giving teachers a sense of community. In a perfect world, this is an institutional effort—including across institutions, but any faculty teamwork will help, even if done at the micro level. Teachers can meet, no matter if that is not the overarching culture of their institution. They can meet for dinner or gather in the late afternoon. They can do things together outside school confines.

All these micro activities will be beneficial, even without macro engagement.

A totally different form of teamwork is exercised in the ideal school's Sports pie slice. Abundant criticism of high school and college sports has been heard about high cost, excessive time commitment, lack of compensation, frequent injuries, and outlandish behavior by coaches. The National Collegiate Athletic Association (NCAA) has not exactly been a paradigm of excellence in its handling of college sports. Meanwhile, many sports programs in the lower grades have been eliminated because of tight budgets. Nevertheless, plenty of learning is achieved through sports, assuming there is good coaching. Students learn about rules—every sport has rules. They learn about abiding by the findings of referees and other officials, even when they disagree with them. They learn about winning and losing. They learn about working together, where the collective matters, as in soccer, baseball, and basketball. I am reminded of a line found on sports T-shirts: "There is no I in team." For many students, teams provide comfort, even in losing seasons. Teams are a family. They eat and travel together. They cheer each other on. They practice. They sacrifice. They laugh and cry together.

An emerging literature addresses the value of sports for traumatized students.[10] Several factors are beneficial: (1) Students can use their bodies, which improves physical and mental health; (2) They can connect with adults, specifically coaches; (3) Through being with their teammates, they can feel support and guidance, not only while playing their sport but also related to larger life questions; (4) Traumatized students can change their mindsets and lower their autonomic nervous system response; (5) Structure, goals, and deadlines offer students a form of security; (6) Perhaps more controversially, students can be aggressive, allowed to shout and yell at will; and (7) They may excel in this arena, and we are wise to build on strengths a student has as opposed to regularly focusing on weaknesses.

Sports create alternative communities for students who may have no other community with which to engage. Yes, team sports are not right for all students who have been traumatized, but for some students, it is a remarkable way to gain confidence, connections, and community. Teams and teamwork foster community and enable individuals to see that they are not alone and can help each other. And these students may have enormous talent in sports; this enables them to focus on what they can do as opposed to focusing daily on what they cannot do.

Implementing Change

The five types of micro changes examined here demonstrate that we can move toward trauma-responsive schools in increments if we cannot get macro changes in place quickly, or ever. Micro changes will help both students and educators, enabling them to engage more fully and create connections. Such changes are less threatening for some individuals, increasing the likelihood of implementation. The more micro changes, the better, but even if all five types are not implementable, selected items from two or three types will still produce positives. It is worth remembering that the ideas described here are far from exhaustive. Many others will improve the lives of traumatized students. And we can rightly ask whether micro changes are so micro in practice.

To return to James Ryan in *Wait, What?*, doing nothing for traumatized students is no longer an option. That ship has sailed. When approximately half of all students enrolled in our educational system have experienced trauma of one kind or another and exhibit symptomology that affects their teachers, doing nothing is unacceptable if we want to ensure that they and future generations lead productive and successful lives, enjoy physical and mental health, enter the workforce, and participate in their communities.

In recognition that trauma is not disappearing, that change must happen if we want positive outcomes, and that inaction is a decision (an unacceptable one), we now turn to Part III, the final part of this book, to focus on the reasons for and impact of labeling students as Generation T, or Gen T. Regard Part III as continuing the central theme in this book, naming and taming. To this we add the word *framing*. We have named trauma in earlier chapters in Part I and have discussed how to tame it through macro and micro changes in our educational institutions in Part II. We now turn to ways to frame it.

Part III

FRAMING

CHAPTER 11

What Is a Frame?

Part I centers on naming trauma, to understand it and how its complex symptomology manifests in our educational system. Understanding trauma is required for finding solutions at the macro and micro levels. Part II addresses taming the trauma, to benefit both traumatized students and their educators. The macro changes, exemplified by their inclusion of the five *S*s, together with the micro changes, enable educational institutions to become trauma responsive or at least endeavor to become so. Part III is about making trauma-responsive schools the norm, not the exception. The key to that is in the name Generation T, or Gen T.

Parts I and II are, in essence, a painting: a composite image of trauma, its symptomology, and how it can be handled (tamed) in our educational system. Because there is no one approach or solution for transforming traumatized institutions, as emphasized in Part II, the "paintings" we construct will not be identical. Part III demonstrates that by identifying the frame for and the framing of the just-described painting at multiple levels, using the many meanings of the word *frame*, we construct the pathway forward, one that engenders hope, as expressed in Chapter 12. And, for the record, it is authentic, not false, hope.

The heart of this framing is Generation T, or Gen T. The *T* is for *trauma*, although by design the word "trauma" does not appear on the nomenclature. Generation T is the frame we need to build and understand to advance the ideas in Parts I and II. Generation T, which will be defined and ideally frequently used well beyond this book, is about all the permutations of frames and framing. We need to understand the name first and then unwrap how it becomes a frame.

The Definition of Generation T

To appreciate the meaning of a new generational name like Generation T, we need to look at how we define and name generations more generally. Perhaps to the surprise of some, a complex and plentiful literature exists on this subject.[1]

At present in the United States, there are several living generations, each covering approximately 20 birth years: the GI Generation, also called the

Greatest Generation (1901–1926); the Silent Generation (1927–1945); baby boomers (1944–1964); Generation X, or Gen X (1965–1980); Millennials (1980–1996); Generation Z (1997–present); and what is tentatively called Generation Alpha or iGen (2010–2025).[2]

The study of generations aims to accomplish two goals: to identify the common characteristics in a single generation and to distinguish one generation from another.[3] The value of this effort is, it seems, to showcase characteristics of generations as if individuals born within certain years possess identifiable shared beliefs and approaches and attitudes. And because we like some of these attitudes better than others, we are critical of some generations and laudatory of others. For example, it's asserted that Millennials are better educated and more racially diverse than prior generations. Millennial and Gen X women are more likely to be in the workforce. Baby boomers have been characterized by some as selfish and entitled.[4]

We can also think about bigger trends if we characterize generations. Worker behavior, spending, consumption choices, leisure activities, and personal interests can all be measured and compared through data collection mechanisms.[5] We can monetize the findings also, enabling all sorts of entities to profit from correctly characterizing generations. There are even firms that sell their reports on generations on the theory that with generational knowledge, we can make wiser and more lucrative decisions in businesses, education, and society.[6]

There are risks to and criticism of generational research.[7] It homogenizes large groups of people and ascribes beliefs that may not be as pervasive as described or that may have defining limits other than generational birth years. Generational definitions are soft at the margins, and some descriptions of generations show overlapping years, meaning some individuals at the cusp of each generation may have attributes of the prior or next generation. Some have tried to refute characterizations of a generation with countervailing data points, as in Millennials are more narcissistic than the prior two generations.[8] Perhaps one could assert that this trait (narcissism) is a product of age alone—so when we measure younger generations, they get higher scores on being narcissistic, something that will change as they age. The observation that the current generation is more in favor of the military may have less to do with their actual age and more with context, namely the happening of 9/11.

How we name generations is also not clear. One would think there would be a standard procedure or process, but it's simply what names stick; there is no naming committee, and naming can be random and more than a tad arbitrary and capricious.[9] The name Millennials is attributed to William Strauss and Neil Howe because they identified this group as the first to graduate in the new millennium.[10] Some generations are named after the fact—like the Silent Generation—and some are renamed, as was the GI Generation in response to Tom Brokaw's popular book *The Greatest*

Generation.[11] Given their randomness, some wonder why we have names at all.[12] Lots of folks, though, participate in the naming game, among them researchers, historians, journalists, authors, marketers, technologists, and advertisers. Naming generations may be arbitrary, but it does not "negate the reality that growing up during different eras can have a profound effect."[13]

The Meaning of Generation T

It is probable that individuals born within a designated block of years do share characteristics. For our purposes here, however, we are not first defining the birth years of a group of people and then searching for their shared characteristics. Instead, we are focused on identifying the shared characteristics of many of the students enrolled across our educational system. As developed in Part I, such characteristics are exposure to trauma and the experience of trauma symptomology. If trauma is our unifying theme, then birth years are neither the key predictor nor an accurate categorization device. Rather, another definition is needed:

> Generation T is composed of students, at any age and stage, who enrolled in our educational system from 2001 on and have experienced trauma and display trauma symptomology.

The start date is 2001 because our sense of security and safety dramatically shifted following the September 11, 2001, terrorist attacks, and trauma has been prevalent since then. This is not to suggest that there was no trauma before 2001—nothing could be further from the truth—but we now have ways of identifying trauma (naming it) and understanding its symptomology and how it can be handled (taming it). As such, Generation T includes anyone enrolled in any educational establishment since 2001, from infants in early childhood programs, to adults returning for retraining, and everyone in between—students in elementary school, middle school, high school, colleges and universities, and graduate school, and continuing education. This is a different way to define a generation.

The usual approach of dating from a birth year will not work if we are to capture all students along the educational pipeline. Students' ages have changed at both ends of the spectrum, and using birth dates unnecessarily limits members of Generation T. We could limit the range to those enrolled in the educational system through the present (approximately 20 years) to accord with the length used in traditional generational research. But since I suspect trauma is never-ending (the virus confirms that), the end date of Generation T will be some date in the future, when trauma-responsive educational institutions become the norm.

The name Generation T also recognizes that students are far less homogeneous than in prior decades. Today's students come from many cultures, ethnicities, races, and socioeconomic levels. Through immigration, we welcome (though less so now) students from many countries. We also have efforts to integrate schools, though to be sure, we are faltering in this, particularly in private schools and gifted programs. Students now speak multiple languages and practice diverse religions. The home culture of students may reflect profound differences in clothing, dating customs, religious beliefs, and political sensibilities. Despite all this, Generation T can cover all these students if they have experienced trauma and show symptomology. The strict historical view of generations (birth years and homogenization) does not apply when thinking of students in our educational system today who have experienced trauma and its aftermath.

Highlighting this observation, every time I read the Beloit study describing the many shared characteristics and experiences and lack of historic references of their new incoming first-year class (which has now moved to Marist), I cringed.[14] It refers to students from elite colleges in a particular age range (fresh high school graduates through the early 20s). However accurate the descriptors are (such as the new students were born three decades after the Vietnam War started), the inference of this observation is that that war is ancient history to these students. But, at best, that defines a subgroup of today's college students, and they certainly are not representative of students as a whole. Many students had family members who served, were injured or died in that war, and it is very much a part of these students' present, not just ancient history. If we want to focus on trauma and its effects in educational settings, we need to define the generation in question differently.

With this background, we can reflect on why naming a generation in a new way, using a different measurement but respecting decades of generational research, has remarkable benefits. The definition we are creating here of Generation T is intended for a limited context—education. It refers to students who from childhood through postsecondary education have experienced trauma that is revealed through symptomology and impacts our educational institutions. The name is also useful to anyone who works with traumatized students. This encompasses teachers, professors, administrators, school counselors, school nurses, physicians, psychiatrists, and social workers who engage with both adults and children. Generation T is nomenclature that can also be used outside the field of education, and it is possible that the name will catch on more broadly in other fields, such as medicine, social services, economics, and business.

Numerous goals can be met through use of a shared nomenclature for referring to our traumatized students. In naming this group, we are looking for what generational researchers look for, commonalities within the named generation and differences between this generation and prior generations of students. We are asking: What similarities exist among students who experience trauma and show symptomology? Such similarities are plentiful, because trauma does not get cured in any traditional sense; it gets addressed and ameliorated. But we are seeking to do way more than that: Identifying a named generation creates a shared language that people can speak when referring to students. Because the definition covers a wide span of students, it is a way of breaking down silos in our educational system. Through a definition that includes all traumatized students enrolled in education regardless of age or stage, we move away from the fragmentation that views each level of educational institution as a generalizable entity that works only with similar educational institutions serving similarly aged populations.

A new definition based in trauma recognizes that current students in postsecondary education cover a large span of birth years. In addition to high school graduates, we have veteran students, returning students who had dropped out, and older students who had never attended college previously. Many of these formerly labeled "nontrads" are now so numerous that they are becoming known as "trads," a fact furthered by the demographic decline of high school populations given decreased birthrates, particularly in the northeastern part of the United States. A new name like Generation T also messages importance: The people in Generation T, whatever their age, deserve our attention and efforts. If we have no way of referring to all the issues related to trauma and its symptoms across the educational pipeline, we cannot robustly share strategies that can be deployed across the pipeline for the benefit of students as well as educators. We can't make progress if we can't and don't talk to each other with shared definitions, understandings, and commitment. Implementation of the solutions in Part II will be aided by correctly referencing the students, educators, and institutions affected by trauma.

There is an additional feature of naming a generation in the context of trauma. It may serve as a catalyst for positive childhood experience (PCE) or positive adult experience (PAE) if it leads to the creation of more trauma-responsive schools that benefit traumatized students, ameliorating their trauma but also enabling them to become more successful. We return to this topic, also mentioned in Parts I and II, in Chapter 12.

Finally, naming a generation helps those in that generation. Let me explain. Consider an individual who has an ailment that has no diagnosis. This is deeply disquieting for both the patient and physicians because without a definitive diagnosis, it is hard to find an effective cure. Uncertainty is troubling. It is like being on a quest and not finding the end point. Even a diagnosis of something serious is better than no diagnosis at all; it eliminates the feeling of some patients that people think their illness is "in their head." To avoid this whole mess, some physicians have apparently gone so far as to create fake diagnoses, knowing that they are making something up. Once a diagnosis is found, patients express their sense of relief, and some are stimulated to work on efforts to find a cure. They feel better, knowing that they have *something*, something with a name, something others have, something they can share with physicians and friends and families, something that can be researched and efforts made to find a cure. There is comfort in knowing what disease one has even if a cure is not available.

To get at naming from a different angle, in a new book, *Know My Name*, a rape survivor divulges her real name so she can own her story, her past, and her future.[15] Chanel Miller was raped by a swimmer at Stanford University named Brock Turner in a case that received national attention, especially for his lenient sentence.[16] At no time earlier had Miller disclosed her identity; she read a victim's statement while remaining anonymous. Her statement affected many who heard it. With time, she realized she had to be more open. As she expressed in a *New York Times* article published on September 22, 2019, "Before, I wanted the assault to not be a part of my life, and that was the goal. . . . Now it's accepting that it will always be a part of my life, and I just figure out where it lives inside my life." There is power in naming.

Returning to trauma and its symptomology, many students cannot explain their behaviors. They do not know why they act or feel as they do. Their trauma is invisible to them and to others. Educators also often have no way of naming or dealing with what they are seeing in students and miss approaches for alleviating what ails their students because they cannot see or describe the behaviors. Naming what is affecting students would benefit both students and educators. They could own, not disown, their past and make it part of their present and future. Crucially, it would remove self-blame from students, because what troubles them is something that happened to, not was caused by, them.

One added observation. The name selected, "Generation T" or "GenT," is premised on trauma and its symptomology but does not use the actual word *trauma*. Yes, the capital T stands for trauma, but the generation is not called Generation Trauma. That is a recognition that for many who hear the word trauma and perhaps for some who have been "traumatized," the very word has negative, stigmatizing connotations. Although every effort has been made in this book to de-stigmatize trauma (it is something that happens *to* someone, not something caused *by* someone), there is not universal acceptability of the word trauma and it can re-trigger. So, the shortening of trauma to a big T is intentional. For those who want to acknowledge the meaning of the T, which I hope is many people, that naming has power. But for those who are not yet comfortable or are unable to rub up closely to the word trauma, Generation T or GenT is less troubling, less triggering, and less difficult to say and manage and acknowledge in others and in oneself as a member of that generation.

Frames, Framing, and Framed

With this understanding of the name Generation T, we can turn to the concepts of *frames* and *framing*. The multiple definitions of these words are our starting point. As a noun, a frame forms a border around an image, as in a picture frame. It also forms the skeleton of a building, furniture, or other object and describes the various physical characteristics of a person. As a verb, *to frame* is to convince others that someone who is not responsible for an act is guilty of that act. To frame a plan is to create or formulate it. One additional meaning of the verb is to formulate an idea with care, forming the words carefully, as in to frame an idea.

Start with the first definition, frames as borders around something. We know that there can be different types and styles of frames used to create a border around paintings. The same is true for the "paintings" (the stories, macro and micro changes, and the ideal school) generated by Parts I and II. We are, in essence, forming a frame around what it means to be a trauma-responsive educational institution. There is no single goal for framing images in the art world, and to be sure, some paintings are never framed. But when framing occurs, the framing accomplishes several things: It protects the art (especially when behind glass and framed in a way that protects the edges from fraying), and it enhances the visual image and draws attention to what is inside the frame, messaging "Look at me." By framing, one is distinguishing the framed painting from the wall where it is hung, creating a spatial distinction between the painting and the surrounding space that enables a viewer to focus on what is inside the frame without distraction; and it provides a window through which to see the image in all its dimensions.

What Is Trauma's Frame?

First, by framing trauma and its complex symptomology and then identifying the particular students affected by it, we confront head-on the reality that trauma has not been cohesively addressed in the educational system. By naming a generation, we are framing trauma, its symptomology, and the approaches for dealing with it, and that very act of framing focuses our attention on it. The frame (Generation T) makes us look at the trauma painting in all its dimensions; then the frame (the Generation T nomenclature) makes the painting (trauma) stand out as an important issue that we must look at and study from all angles. Then the frame (Generation T) surrounds Parts I and II and places them against the backdrop of education (the wall) and suggests the need to deal with what is on the wall. The frame (Generation T) lets us look inside trauma, its symptomology, and its amelioration.

Add to this that art frames can be constructed out of many materials, natural materials like wood or synthetic materials like plastic or glass, and can be decorative or plain, modern or antique. They can be any number of colors. We can frame a painting by a famous artist or a drawing by a child. We can frame a snapshot of a loved one or a photograph by a professional photographer. We can frame a diploma or a letter that has personal value or the signature of a famous person. Frames are as varied as life's experiences and hold those experiences within them.

We have no way, however, absent a new term, for designing the trauma frame. We know the paintings of trauma and approaches to its amelioration are not identical. But there are shared characteristics, and we have a name now—Generation T—a generation for whom we are trying to find educational improvements that will facilitate their success. In essence, what enables us to see and understand trauma and its impact on education is the naming of a generation.

The name Generation T encompasses students who are different from one another. Some students believe in an internal locus of control (one's ability to control outcomes and destiny), while others believe in external loci of control (God or another higher authority or lot in life or caste status). Some students have an individual concept of self, with responsibility and guilt as part of that perspective; other students have a much more collectivist perspective, where their acts are seen from a family and societal perspective, leading to shame and silencing and diminution of options controlled and dictated by individuals. Other students believe and practice direct communication and are comfortable talking to others outside their sphere; yet others are not comfortable with direct confrontation, viewing it as impolite or intrusive. Some students see their position within American society because of their heritage as "high up" in the echelon, while others see themselves as "low down" based on their own personal perceptions or actual cultural realities.

All these students enroll in our schools, and educators need to recognize how the students' worldview affects their behavior, their forms of engagement, and their response to the trauma they experience. Unlike other generational definitions where we focus on shared characteristics, what Generation T members share are their differences, from age to ethnicity to the experience and symptomology of trauma. Yes, Generation T has shared this: trauma and some form of symptomology. But sharing trauma isn't uniform; indeed, one of trauma's hallmarks is the myriad of ways in which it is experienced.

Other Frames

Several other definitions of *frame* and *framing* have relevance here and enrich our understanding of Generation T. Regard frames as a structure around which things are built. This is very similar to how we create trauma-responsive schools for Generation T. These schools may all be different, but they share the values reflected in the five *S*s: structure, safety, stability, subtlety, and someone(s). An actual frame that is made does differ from another frame, but it has shared features: It is stable; it can be used as a mold from which to build; it enables personalization; it is safe, so what is built will not crumble and it protects those within it; it is done by someone or with someone and then shared with someone. We are building frames for the educational institutions that Generation T will occupy, places that will understand them and enable their success.

There is also a definition of *frame* that is derogatory, one relevant to Generation T, that raises and reinforces approaches used by non-trauma-responsive institutions and that are too often deployed today. Someone can be falsely blamed for something and then will have an uphill battle regaining his or her position, regaining innocence. In a sense, we frame traumatized students when we blame them for their behaviors, their acting out or isolating themselves, their failure to concentrate, their unwillingness to engage, or their lack of memory. And then we punish these students. Such members of Generation T are being framed: As oft-repeated in this book, these students did not do anything—something happened to them. As a group and individually, they are not responsible for their traumas or subsequent behaviors, most of which cannot be controlled in educational institutions without quality educators trained in trauma. The Generation T frame is a reminder that individuals have been framed, and we need to focus on why that framing is so destructive and how trauma responsiveness can shift the approach.

Framing also refers to creating a plan and carefully articulating an idea or argument so others can understand it. Through naming a generation, we recognize the importance of planning approaches to deal with trauma and its effects. The individuals affected in our schools are unlikely to self-resolve what ails them on their own (absent being lastic). Indeed, one of the central features of trauma responsiveness is the presence of someone(s) there to help and engage with the traumatized students. But as the value *subtlety* suggests, one plan will not work for everyone. We need thoughtfully constructed plans that recognize who each student is, the trauma that occurred, and the trauma's context. We need to frame trauma-responsive schools by understanding Generation T, both what happened to the individuals and the symptomology they exhibit as a result. Then we need varied, nuanced strategies to deal with trauma's aftermath. Generation T needs us to know who they are. Part of our job as educators is to understand those who are enrolled across our educational system. To emphasize this point, we need to identify the students we have, not the students we were or we dream about or we want in some mythical sense.

The Generation T Frame

Identifying a generation affected by trauma allows us to frame the problems and solutions. By naming Generation T, we can speak a language that focuses us on what we need to do and for whom. Generation T is the frame around the trauma painting; its members are the ones affected. Its members are the ones often framed for things they did not cause. Its members need us to create solutions deeply responsive to who the traumatized individuals are.

To be sure, we could include in the definition of Generation T all the nonstudents affected directly and indirectly by trauma—families, educators, and communities. However, our goal here is primarily to focus on the trauma's impact on our educational system, and so we limit ourselves to those enrolled in education as the set of folks included in the meaning of Generation T. But here's an idea: Perhaps we need "honorary members" of Generation T, individuals connected to Generation T in one way or another who can also benefit from trauma-responsive educational institutions.

With the naming of a generation, which is at once profound and impactful, we can turn to the final chapter of this book, which addresses why there is hope that we can move the needle and create trauma-responsive educational institutions. At the end of the day, if we cannot move the needle, we will fail not only our students who form Generation T but also the generations to come.

Conclusion: Having Hope

To hope is defined in *Merriam-Webster* as "to want something to happen or to be true." *False hopes*, according to the *Cambridge Dictionary*, are "confident feelings about something that might not be true." Hope is critical for a happy life; it is what motivates us to continue forward despite obstacles.[1] Don Quixote, who lived in a fantasy world, confused dreams with reality and believed that his dreams would always come true. He had false hope. There is something deeply moving about Don Quixote, something that is brought to the surface by the absurdity of his dreams: It is our deeply held desire that the world will be a better place, and we can work productively toward its improvement.[2] We are committed to transforming our ideas (our fantasies) into reality. We work to turn theory into practice.

Here is one thing that I have hope for, something that accounts for this book: I have hope that we can and will introduce trauma-responsive institutions into our educational pipeline in the near term to benefit and enable the success (broadly defined) of Generation T. I have hope, too, that trauma-responsive institutions will benefit the many educators who serve our students, often in difficult situations that affect them personally and professionally.[3]

I don't think this is false hope. It is not quixotic thinking. This chapter explains why.

New Research

A growing body of literature suggests that while ACEs are predictors of long-term negative consequences for individuals, positive experiences can counteract the disadvantages measured by ACEs. Think about that observation and its implications for a moment, particularly as it impacts systemic change.[4]

We have relied, over-relied in some instances, on ACEs to determine educational, health, and interpersonal risks for particular individuals with high scores. ACEs were not created as a personalized diagnostic tool; they better serve as an explanation and a predictor. Remember, too, that ACEs were originally formulated based on a largely White, middle-class, college-educated, and medically insured population to try to understand their behaviors. This suggests that for ethnically and racially diverse low-income individuals who have not uniformly completed postsecondary education, ACEs will be even higher. Remember, too, that the ACE test measures only certain types of trauma. It does not measure, for example, the impact of natural disasters or shootings at schools, churches, and other purportedly safe spaces. It does not measure the impact of school closures or a pandemic. So, when we state that almost half the children in schools and more than two-thirds of adults have at least one point on the ACE scoring scale, we are missing lots of trauma that affects individuals and manifests in our educational system. Trauma abounds.

With all these individuals suffering from trauma, are there positive experiences that can offset high ACEs (and other trauma indicators)? If there are such positive factors, we need to focus on enhancing them, in addition to (not in lieu of) addressing trauma per se. Focusing on addressing trauma and its symptomology doesn't become a less valuable effort if there are positive experiences that offset the negatives. That is because trauma still exists and will persist. Of that we can be sure. If there are positive experiences that counter ACEs, however, we would be well served to develop them ASAP.[5]

Here's the real question that emerges: Can we characterize trauma-responsive institutions, such as the ideal school model advanced here and other models incorporating the five *S*s, as not only ameliorators of trauma, which they most assuredly are for Generation T, but also as positive experiences that simultaneously lower the impact of ACEs on this group? In other words, can trauma-responsive educational institutions serve two masters, namely, dealing with trauma and lowering or eliminating its incidence?

The answer is yes, at least based on current research, which will continue to grow as we move forward. To get to that answer, we need to turn to what constitutes positive experiences that have been measured and shown to counterbalance trauma in existing studies. Once we do that, we can look to see if those positive experiences are housed within trauma-responsive schools. Note that we are looking at the interrelationship between trauma-responsive educational institutions and positive anti-ACEs experiences. If we want to make the further argument that positive experiences of a certain sort ameliorate trauma *not measured* by ACE scores, then we need to extrapolate from the existing studies and identify other indicators of success and happiness that can help us override negative experiences. These last conclusions are, a fortiori, more speculative, as the research on anti-trauma experiences is not yet as advanced as the studies on treating trauma—including post-traumatic stress.

The Powerful Positives

Positive childhood experiences (PCEs), positive adult experiences (PAEs), and health outcomes of positive experiences (HOPE) are all part of the newly expanding field of the science of thriving or the science of hope.[6] We delve into these terms in more detail in this chapter, but this is the key takeaway: There are counterbalances to the devastating effect of ACEs. That means there's *hope*.

PCEs, like ACEs—and providing a kind of counter-ACEs measure—can be scored, via seven categories of experience that assess how much and how often children and adults have encountered identified positive items.[7] There is a cumulative score, the highest being a 7. In using these scores, researchers have put them in categories: 0–2, 3–5, and 6–7, when doing comparisons with other scoring methods of positives and negatives to identify corollaries and comparisons. Note that the ACE test operates off a yes/no answer and then a number score that caps out at 10. So there is not a perfect way to match PCE and ACE scoring, and PCE items were not given to the original subjects of the ACE study on which so many have relied.

That said, there is much to learn from a focus on positive experiences, and researchers have tried to create replicable comparisons that regress for key variables. Now is not the time or place to critique the approaches of researchers, except to note several things: First, more positives exist than the seven identified here, just as more negatives do. Second, additional items appear in some new ACE tests, and if we add to ACEs, then should we not add to PCE? For example, if ACEs include community risks, shouldn't PCEs include community benefits? Third, the research is new and still to be further developed.

The PCE score measures the following seven positive experiences (see: www.psychologytoday.com/us/blog/the-athletes-way/201909/seven-early-experiences-potential-benefits-in-adulthood):

1. felt able to talk to their family about feelings;
2. felt their family stood by them during difficult times;
3. enjoyed participating in community traditions;
4. felt a sense of belonging in high school (not including those who did not attend school or were home schooled);
5. felt supported by friends;
6. had at least two nonparent adults who took genuine interest in them; and
7. felt safe and protected by an adult in their home.

Since I have disclosed that I have an ACE score of 7, it seems fair to divulge my PCE score. As I looked at the seven items, I had to say that reality is not that simple. I had two families, so the definition of home is not clear-cut. And standing by someone is also very subjective. My mother used to say that my father wasn't there for the little stuff but was there for the really big and terrible stuff and would give you the shirt off his back for the latter. I thought then and still think now that little things do matter. So was my father there for a major illness? Yes. Was he there to congratulate me on a good grade? No. Was he there for my dance and theater performances? Yes. Was he there for school-based events? No, except on one occasion where he spoke on Valentine's Day at an assembly on the meaning of our hearts—he was a cardiologist. With those caveats, I have a PCE score of 5. Pretty remarkable actually, considering the high ACE score I have.

Research suggests that the higher the PCE score, the more it reduces the ACE score. Positive experiences can, then, decrease the damage of negative experiences. Thus, we should work to increase PCE scores for the most at-risk students, those with high ACEs. Pushing for improved PCEs could directly involve schools that work with young children in early childhood programs and elementary schools. Educational institutions could focus on parental involvement to augment the PCE score and improve the ratio of PCEs to ACEs. School counselors, teachers, and administrators could add the lens of PCEs.

Further, pregnant women and their partners could be encouraged to build PCEs from the moment of birth. Obstetricians and pediatricians could play a significant role in improving PCEs, as could social service agencies as well as psychologists and psychiatrists working with families within and outside of the educational setting.

I visualize the relationships between ACEs on the one hand and PCEs and positive adult experiences (PAEs, discussed below) on the other as a seesaw. We want to see which side is heavier. Ideally, the end with more PCEs and PAEs will be heavier than that with the ACEs. And there is another seesaw to consider: Trauma-responsive institutions are on one end of the seesaw, and PCEs and PAEs are on the other. If trauma responsiveness is a positive, then this seesaw would be perfectly balanced.

Unanswered Questions

A side question, one not completely answered, is whether timing matters. If you have high ACEs at age 5 but circumstances change and by age 10 you have a PCE score of 6, is there an offset despite the disjuncture in time? Or is the effect lessened if the ACEs and PCEs are not simultaneous? And does the creation of trauma-responsive schools provide opportunities for simultaneity? Does it matter whether the PCEs are family related, and if so, does that create a bigger or better offset?

A related issue. Given that the implementation of trauma-responsive institutions will likely be incremental and a student could move somewhere with or without trauma-responsive schools, how will PCEs affect ACEs? Suppose a student is not initially in a trauma-sensitive institution but later enters one, will the move help offset ACEs? How long is the offset? If a student with high ACEs attends a trauma-sensitive school, then a non-trauma-sensitive school, will the offset endure? Suppose you have an ACE score of 7, as I do, but do not develop the PCEs needed for offset as a child but develop them later, as I did, and have positive adult experiences (PAEs). Will the PAEs offset the ACEs? If one lacked a high PCE score but subsequently had a family with many positives including raising a child, could those PAEs offset a nonexistent or low PCE score?

These are all unanswered questions.

An additional side question arises from research on intense adult-onset trauma and delayed responses in traumatized adults.[8] The question is whether PCEs or new PAEs post-trauma could ameliorate the effects of adult trauma, both immediate and delayed. If the answer is yes, then those treating traumatized adults, in and outside the educational system, could provide PAEs. This matters because PCEs are obviously best effectuated in the K–12 pipeline, with an emphasis ideally on the lower grades. If adult experiences count too, then higher education has a key role in being trauma responsive for not only students traumatized in childhood but also those traumatized in adulthood. Given the increasing ages of and incidence of trauma among postsecondary students, these questions are becoming more important as is the role of higher education institutions.

Think about veterans post-9/11 in our postsecondary institutions. A sizable number of these Veterans probably suffer from post-traumatic stress disorder.[9] Others may have had adverse experiences that feel like trauma after leaving the military and transitioning to civilian life and then entering an educational setting.[10] We know from Chapter 10 that transitions are particularly problematic for traumatized individuals. So can post-secondary institutions improve the educational experiences of veterans, among others, by including more PAEs within their programs? The answer, I suspect, is yes, and perhaps we are already doing some of that without realizing that we are lowering trauma responsiveness as we provide positive opportunities. In a sense, this is akin to institutions being trauma responsive without knowing or labeling what they are doing to help their students progress and succeed.

Consider this additional set of questions. We know that ACEs address only a subcategory of trauma. Do PCEs or PAEs have an ameliorating effect on non-ACE-measured trauma? Given the amount of non-ACE-measured traumatic events in our world, we'd be well served to find positive mediating factors that contribute to tipping the previously referenced seesaw. And, as a caution, we need to keep reminding ourselves that a focus on ACEs, while valuable, is not the be-all-end-all in terms of measuring trauma and its impact on particular individuals; perhaps PCEs and PAEs need a similar qualifier.

PCEs and Trauma-Responsive Institutions

Of the seven PCEs listed above, four *are* directly and positively affected by trauma-responsive institutions. They tip the seesaw. The remaining three items *can be* positively affected by trauma-responsive institutions but only if these reach back and work with their students' families. This may be possible in the lower grades, but it becomes increasingly difficult in the later years or with students in postsecondary education, many of whom are themselves parents. That said, there are initiatives worth considering or adjusting to include parents and that would enhance the likelihood that trauma-responsive institutions address trauma and improve PCEs.

Items 3, 4, 5, and 6 from the above listing of PCEs are positively affected by trauma-responsive institutions and are encouraged by both the macro and micro changes suggested in Part II. The nucleus of the changes—the five *S*s—shows the positivity. Trauma-responsive institutions are stable, safe, structured, subtle, and involve someone(s). Item 3 of the PCE questionnaire addresses participation in community traditions. Assuming—correctly—that a school is part of a community, the exercise of school traditions matters.[11] As discussed in Chapter 8, trauma-responsive institutions can develop wide-ranging traditions from special events on regularly scheduled days to book signings or presentations on set dates.

I am reminded of a debate about a college that had its 1st-year students wear beanies until homecoming. While some might consider this an anachronism, others argued that the hat made students feel part of a tradition and messaged to other students and educators to be available to the beanie wearers if they needed help finding their way, getting an ID, buying books, furnishing a room, or changing classes.[12]

The PCE questionnaire's item 4 relates to whether students felt a sense of belonging at their high school. We know that absent trauma-responsive high schools, many adolescent students struggle to fit in at school.[13] Dropping out of high school is not uncommon, though rates vary dramatically across the country and different student demographics.[14] Trauma-responsive high schools would foster a sense of belonging, as suggested in the ideal school model in Chapter 8. The pie structure of that model encourages engagement within each slice and between the slices, and the Center fosters belonging as well.

One related issue: Item 4 is keyed to belonging in high school. Does belonging in other educational settings before and after high school make a positive difference? For students enrolled in trauma-responsive schools, belonging would begin early and continue into adult education. Merely attending a trauma-responsive educational institution engenders a sense of belonging. The institution is welcoming and makes students feel connected and wanted. As astutely observed by Ghislaine Boulanger, to belong is to feel understood.[15]

Item 5 of the PCE questionnaire looks at whether one felt supported by friends, apparently meaning at or outside school or both. In a trauma-responsive institution, there is explicit building of support among peers, embedded in the vast amount of teamwork practiced, with opportunities for students to work together on lengthy projects. Teamwork is also created through athletics, another piece emphasized in the ideal model. Because of the adult presence in this model, bullying and harassment are decreased, increasing support between students. The nomenclature Generation T should also help students feel supported, not isolated, if they have had negative childhood experiences. Naming is an antidote to isolation and a promoter of supportive behavior.

Item 6 of the PCE questionnaire asks if students had at least two nonparental individuals who took a genuine interest in them. The use of "genuine" is hugely relevant to a trauma-responsive institution, where authenticity is both needed and valued. A trauma-responsive institution is intentionally designed to give students nonparental adults who believe in them and care about them: making connections. At the core of that institution, as at the core of lasticity in *Breakaway Learners*, are reciprocity and the presence of someone(s).

The expanded role of educators, the opportunities for one-on-one work, the presence of the Center, the daily greeting—these are all efforts to give students at least one adult who is genuinely interested in their success. Notice that item 6 is not limited to the educational setting, so the adult nonparental role could be played by other relatives, religious figures, neighbors, or physicians. (And, importantly, some students have no parents at all, a topic not specifically noted in PCEs.) For some traumatized individuals, becoming connected is a learned skill, one that is essential to human beings, and we are not particularly adept at becoming connected.[16] This is because trauma may have created attachment disorders, and the connection to an adult may need to start with the adult. Over time, the student will deepen his or her connectedness. Ultimately, reciprocity is needed, but it doesn't have to be there from the beginning of the relationship.

One additional related point: Genuine interest would seem to encompass listening, because it is key to showing that one cares. Yet listening is not mentioned as a positive in the PCE items. Perhaps it is assumed. The value of listening was emphasized in a conversation I had with Paul Horovitz (brimhallassociates.com/paul-horovitz/), a seasoned, deeply self-reflective educator who has run three independent schools, one in Los Angeles, one in St. Thomas, and one in Massachusetts, all of which had had traumatic events. Addressing the inevitability of traumatic events that affect students, faculty, staff, and families—whether illnesses, deaths, shootings, earthquakes, or hurricanes—he noted that creating listening opportunities was a key strategy he frequently deployed. Different traumas affected different schools, but listening was always critical.[17] Listening allowed everyone connected with the school to process what had occurred. If one listens well, one will learn what steps a leader can take to help students and educators deal with trauma. Trauma-responsive institutions are filled with listening opportunities, and listening is embedded in two of the five *Ss*, subtlety and someone(s).

The remaining three items, 1, 2, and 7, relate to how children engage with their families and whether families were supportive and present in their lives and created a safe environment. Trauma-responsive institutions promote efforts to acknowledge and listen to feelings and deal with difficult subjects. This is accomplished through the senses, the pop-up courses, and the Center, among other components. Safety is engendered through the creation of nonthreatening spaces where students can learn and flourish with their autonomic nervous system not being on high alert. Indeed, safety is identified as one of the five values undergirding trauma-responsive institutions.

But the questions surrounding the positive factors needed are not asking about the school environs but about family and adults not at the school. It is hard to imagine that students with high ACEs will have the types of supportive families that enable them to answer yes to these three questions, except in the context of extended family and siblings. If a child has supportive grandparents or aunts and uncles with whom the child is connected, then the answer could well be yes. If there are siblings that cover a wide age range, not uncommon in blended families, then a yes answer is possible. If there is an adult at home who protects the child, even if not a parent, that will enable a positive answer. Interestingly, in a new study on HOPE, there is an effort to translate all references to parents into a more inclusive definition that encompasses extended families and adoptive and foster parents.[18] That is a twofold recognition. Some children are not raised by their biological parents, and the key here is a broad definition of both family and caregivers.

Trauma-responsive institutions can foster positive answers to Questions 1, 2, and 7 if certain steps are taken. It is possible that in the educational system as a whole, an older student in a trauma-responsive environment can help a sibling in a lower grade. It is possible that by encouraging parents to enter the trauma-responsive school—with their own area in the Center—that messaging of support can occur. Studies have demonstrated that teachers of young children can improve the lives of their students if they visit their homes. Visits also lessen teacher bias, even unrecognized bias.[19]

Other approaches can be taken to engage families. Think about events to which parents and other family members are invited. Would those collaborative events enable better engagement at home? Would parent education at the schools their children attend improve the supportiveness of parents? At the elementary school where I have been an artist-in-residence for more than 3 years, I suggested courses for parents in the morning as they drop off their children, adding that food could be offered and that their workday would not be disrupted if school started early enough. The courses could be certificate or credit bearing and cover topics of interest to the parents, enriching their understanding of the possibilities education provides, which could translate into a deeper willingness to support the children who live with them.

If parents can get more comfortable talking about feelings and are in a safe learning environment where their learning is supported, perhaps they can transfer those experiences into their homes. To be sure, we tend to have disconnects and see things in silos. What happens in one place stays there, a variant of the old joke about Las Vegas. Nevertheless, with encouragement and presence in the schools, perhaps there is an opportunity to lift the barrier and transmit values from the school to families.

Ponder whether parent or family orientation can be given more time and attention. As noted earlier, we are not that successful at transitions, but we could focus added attention there and try to break down the barriers between home and school. Of course, the older the student, the harder this is, because the student may have no relationship with his or parents; may not live with them; or may not be sharing their postsecondary experience with their families for various reasons, not the least of which is the effort to avoid divides based on present and possible future success.

Bottom line: PCEs are embedded at different levels in the trauma-responsive institutions developed in this book. That realization creates hope. Trauma-responsive institutions work both ends of the spectrum: They help traumatized students (and educators), and they provide positive experiences for adults and children that could ameliorate the negative and lifelong impact of high ACEs and other traumatic events. To be sure, the latter point is still somewhat speculative, but recent students suggest that hope is not a far-fetched notion.

The Need for Empiricism

While beyond the scope of this book, we do need to gather data on the effects and effectiveness of trauma-responsive educational institutions and determine whether they measurably improve students' lives. Currently, more than 45 different survey instruments can measure the benefits of implementing trauma-informed approaches.[20] And make no mistake: Empirical assessment is expensive. Acquiring measurement tools and keeping data current to ensure data-informed decisionmaking is costly. However, many items could be measured, from attitudes to academic performance to psychological and physical well-being.[21] We could measure improvements in school culture or look at graduation and dropout rates and at family functioning. The list is endless, and there is no agreement about optimal survey instruments. We cannot, however, just implement trauma-responsive strategies and assume success. We need to measure success, near and long term. Absent such measurements, we will not know if the changes we make are worth the candle.

Rising Tides

Some readers may believe that this book is too tenderhearted, that it creates snowflake-like students who don't just buck up and move forward despite their past. It could be criticized for focusing exclusively on students who have been traumatized, howsoever large that number is and the unlikelihood of it decreasing anytime soon. Further, the book assumes success for most students if they are placed in the right environment, which ignores the reality that some students will never succeed because their life experiences are too devastating. For this group, "A rising tide lifts all boats" will not work; they are stuck on the bottom. Also, what about all the other children, the ones who are not traumatized? Who watches out for them and encourages their growth and success?

Helping others is not about creating snowflakes. It is about creating success. If individual students need help to succeed, why don't we help them? Since when is sink or swim the hallmark of a quality education? Since when is recognizing the needs of those who require assistance offensive, demeaning, or disrespectful toward those who do not? And for the record, even if some students are moored to the bottom and lack a boat because of poverty or other deprivations, we still can lift many of them.[22]

The truth is that trauma-responsive institutions provide quality educational opportunities for traumatized students and the educators who serve them. They also provide quality educational opportunities for the balance of the students. A trauma-responsive school helps all students, not only traumatized students, and the phrase "a rising tide lifts all boats" is apt. It is a learning environment that fosters success and a belief in self.

By naming, taming, and framing trauma, we diminish the tumult in schools and the outsize behavior that can be disruptive of learning for all. By naming, taming, and framing, we enable more students to engage successfully with others, including their peers and educators. We encourage learning in many spaces and places; the classroom is but one. We enable educators to do their job more effectively, helping them deal with their students in ways that enhance learning and make for better professional experiences. By naming, taming, and framing, we grow the success of our families and communities and enhance our physical and mental well-being.

We will all benefit from naming, taming, and framing trauma. When Generation T succeeds, so do we all. A rising tide really does lift most of us most of the time. We can't ask for much more than that, can we?

Endings and Beginnings

There are always topics that are not covered in a book that an author wishes were covered. There are issues addressed in this book that demand further research to prove their veracity. There is additional research needed on many issues involving trauma's repercussions in our education system, particularly positive experiences that can offset trauma's devastating effects on educational progression and success. So in this sense, this book is not the end of the topic of trauma and how to address it in the educational system. It is the beginning of a conversation that needs to happen in earnest now.

I do have one added observation and one wish I want to share before readers close this book. The observation first. I have spoken to many students who have been traumatized and educators who have dealt with the effects of trauma in the institutions they serve. I have been at trauma sites; I have listened to and worked with many who have experienced primary, secondary, and vicarious trauma. I have strong memories of all those conversations, workshops, and opportunities to engage. Generation T has informed the contents of this book; so have educators. In a sense, this book belongs to all of them.

Now my wish. I wish I could interview and report systematically on the responses of even more students to the traumas they have encountered and the efforts others have made, or not made, to help them. I wish I could interview even more educators and report on their responses to the traumas they have had to deal with and the efforts others have made, or not made, to help them. Those interviews, done well, coded and reviewed for common themes and threads, would shed more light on what additional ideas, tools, and skills would have and have had an impact on (whether or not labeled *trauma responsive*) the efforts to enable Generation T to succeed. At the end of the day, it is the voices and experiences of our traumatized students and our educators that inform how we can improve the educational system. Consider this wish my invitation to these individuals to reach out and share. I'd welcome that and look forward to listening to what you have to say.[23]

Notes

Preface

1. Throughout this book, the term used for multiple symptoms is *symptomology*. There is a term "symptomatology," generally used to reference the study of symptoms of diseases. For our purposes, the more informal term "symptomology," which does appear in dictionaries with this spelling, seems apt, as we are not speaking of or referencing the study of diseases.

2. See Alison Kath, "Emotional Dysregulation in Children," Sophia, the St. Catherine University repository website, May 2017, sophia.stkate.edu/cgi/viewcontent.cgi?article=1756&context=msw_papers.

3. For a review of trauma's impact and the skills educators need based on the scientific and educational literature, see John Gailer, Dr. Sandy Addis, and Lynn Dunlap, *Improving School Outcomes for Trauma-Impacted Students*, National Dropout Prevention Center, 2018, dropoutprevention.org/wp-content/uploads/2018/10/Trauma-Skilled-Schools-Model-Final-I.pdf.

4. Daniel J. Siegel and Tina Payne Bryson, *The Whole-Brain Child: 12 Revolutionary Strategies to Nurture Your Child's Developing Mind, Survive Everyday Parenting Struggles, and Help Your Family Thrive* (New York: Random House, 2012), 27.

5. For a compelling account of some of these issues in and outside education, see Mona Delahooke, *Beyond Behaviors* (Eau Claire, WI: PESI, 2019).

6. How educational institutions need to address their traumatized students and how human service organizations serve a traumatized population are similar. Reference will be made in Part II to these parallels, enhanced by the work of Sandra L. Bloom and Brian Farragher in *Destroying Sanctuary: The Crisis of Human Service Delivery Systems* (New York: Oxford University Press, 2011).

7. Karen Gross, *Breakaway Learners* (New York: Teachers College Press, 2017).

8. *Identifying, Preventing, and Treating Childhood Trauma: Pervasive Public Health Issue That Needs Greater Federal Attention,* House Committee on Oversight Reform hearing, July 11, 2019, oversight.house.gov/legislation/hearings/identifying-preventing-and-treating-childhood-trauma-a-pervasive-public-health.

9. Wehmah Jones, Juliette Berg, and David Osher, *Trauma and Learning Policy Initiative (TLPI): Trauma-Sensitive Schools Descriptive Study*, American Institutes for Research, 2018, traumasensitiveschools.org/wp-content/uploads/2019/02/TLPI-Final-Report_Full-Report-002-2.pdf; "Clark, Quigley & Fitzpatrick Introduce Bill to Expand Trauma-Informed Practices in Schools" (press release), Katherine Clark, July 26, 2019, katherineclark.house.gov/2019/7/representatives-clark-quigley-fitzpatrick-introduce-bill-to-expand-trauma-informed-practices-in-schools.

10. Karen Gross, "Proud to Be a Snowflake," Medium, December 22, 2016, medium.com/@KarenGrossEdu/proud-to-be-a-snowflake-e35c810af3b1; "Do 'Trigger Warnings' on School Campuses Help? Counselors and Students Weigh In," *Clinical Mental Health Counseling* (n.d.), counseling.online.wfu.edu/blog/do-trigger-warnings-on-school-campuses-help-counselors-and-students-weigh-in/; National Coalition Against Censorship, *What's All This About Trigger Warnings?* December 2015, ncac.org/wp-content/uploads/2015/11/NCAC-TriggerWarningReport.pdf.

Chapter 1

1. Peter Lattman, "The Origins of Justice Stewart's 'I Know It When I See It,'" *Law Blog*, September 27, 2007, blogs.wsj.com/law/2007/09/27/the-origins-of-justice-stewarts-i-know-it-when-i-see-it/.

2. The interaction between the body and the mind is ably described in Bessel van der Kolk, *The Body Keeps the Score: Brain, Mind, and Body in the Healing of Trauma* (New York: Penguin, 2015).

3. James E. Ryan, *Wait, What? And Life's Other Essential Questions* (New York: HarperOne, 2017).

4. To be sure, those adults who face threats to their life, as in war or the Holocaust, experience profound psychic consequences because they are fully aware of the risks they are confronting and the possibility of imminent death. See Irit Felsen, "Adult-Onset Trauma and Intergenerational Transmission: Integrating Empirical Data and Psychoanalytic Theory," *Psychoanalysis, Self, and Context* 12 (2017): 60–77.

5. Mona Delahooke, *Beyond Behaviors* (Eau Claire, WI: PESI, 2019), 10.

6. Delahooke, *Beyond Behaviors*, 10.

7. Rasheed Malik, "New Data Reveal 250 Preschoolers Are Suspended or Expelled Every Day," Center for American Progress, November 6, 2017, www.americanprogress.org/issues/early-childhood/news/2017/11/06/442280/new-data-reveal-250-preschoolers-suspended-expelled-every-day/; Sara Neufeld, "Expelled in Preschool," *Hechinger Report*, February 22, 2015, hechingerreport.org/expelled-preschool/.

8. Bessel van der Kolk, *The Body Keeps the Score: Brain, Mind, and Body in the Healing of Trauma* (New York: Penguin, 2015).

9. For a chart on neuroplasticity, see "How Does Neuroplasticity Work?" National Institute for the Clinical Application of Behavioral Medicine (n.d.), www.nicabm.com/brain-how-does-neuroplasticity-work/.

10. To be fair and complete in description, there is adult-onset massive trauma, but that is beyond the scope of this book. For a recent book (and review) on this topic, see Elizabeth Hegeman, "Wounded by Reality: Understanding and Treating Adult Onset Trauma (Book Review)," Society for Psychoanalysis and Psychoanalytic Psychology, 2019, www.apadivisions.org/division-39/publications/reviews/wounded.

11. Doreen St. Félix, "The Ford-Kavanaugh Hearing Will Be Remembered as a Grotesque Display of Patriarchal Resentment," *New Yorker*, September 27, 2018, www.newyorker.com/culture/cultural-comment/the-ford-kavanaugh-hearings-will-be-remembered-for-their-grotesque-display-of-patriarchal-resentment.

12. See: Facts about Women and Trauma, www.apa.org/advocacy/interpersonal-violence/women-trauma; Traumatic Stress Changes Brains of Boys, Girls Differently, November 11, 2016, www.stanfordchildrens.org/en/about/news/releases/2016/traumatic-stress-changes-brains-of-boys-girls-differently.

13. We need to be both explicit and honest; there is no benefit trying to hide the truth of a trauma. For a recent example in the context of COVID-19, we have seen efforts to minimize or obfuscate the truth. See: Karen Gross, "I'm Worried: Higher Education Isn't Focused at All on COVID-19's Psychological Toll," New England Board of Higher Education, March 9, 2020, nebhe.org/journal/im-worried-higher-education-isnt-focused-at-all-on-covid-19s-psychological-toll/.

14. "Trauma Center Levels Explained," American Trauma Society (n.d.), www.amtrauma.org/page/traumalevels.

15. For an example of this debate, see Pashtana Usufzy, "Trauma Center Proposals Face Crucial Vote Amid Heated Debate," *Las Vegas Review-Journal*, June 22, 2016, www.reviewjournal.com/life/health/trauma-center-proposals-face-crucial-vote-amid-heated-debate/amp/.

16. For a detailed description of medical trauma centers, see American Trauma Society, "Trauma Center Designations and Levels," Brain Trauma Foundation, January 1, 2000, braintrauma.org/news/article/trauma-center-designations.

17. Anushka Pai, Alina M. Suris, and Carol S. North, "Posttraumatic Stress Disorder in the *DSM-5*: Controversy, Change, and Conceptual Considerations," *Behavioral Sciences* (Basel) 7, no. 1 (2017): 7, www.ncbi.nlm.nih.gov/pmc/articles/PMC5371751/.

18. Renee Fabian, "PTSD and the Difference Between Big 'T' and Little 'T' Traumas," Talk Space (blog), June 27, 2018, www.talkspace.com/blog/ptsd-traumas-difference/.

19. Karen Gross, *Breakaway Learners* (New York: Teachers College Press, 2017), 73. I am reminded of the warning giving many moons ago to new law professors by Professor David Vernon: If you do not disagree with something you wrote as your career progresses, you are not thinking enough.

20. Robyn E. Brickel, "Using 'Big T' and 'Little T' for Trauma Can Be a Big Mistake," Brickel and Associates, May 9, 2019, LLC, brickelandassociates.com/big-t-little-t-trauma/.

21. Brickel, "Using 'Big T' and 'Little T' for Trauma."

22. For an example of the definitional confusion, see Esther Giller, "What Is Psychological Trauma?" Sidran Institute, May 1999, www.sidran.org/wp-content/uploads/2019/04/What-Is-Psychological-Trauma.pdf.

23. "Screening Tools Help in Assessing Trauma," Behavioral Health Evolution (n.d.), www.bhevolution.org/public/trauma_screening.page.

24. Center for Substance Abuse Treatment (U.S.), "Screening and Assessment," Chapter 4 in *Trauma-Informed Care in Behavioral Health Services (Treatment Improvement Protocol [TIP] Series*, no. 57), 2014, www.ncbi.nlm.nih.gov/books/NBK207188/.

25. Karen Hughes, Mark A. Bellis, Katherine A. Hardcastle, Dinesh Sethi, Alexander Butchart, Christopher Mikton, Lisa Jones, and Michael P. Dunne, "The Effect of Multiple Adverse Childhood Experiences on Health: A Systematic Review and Meta-Analysis," *Lancet Public Health* 2, no. 8 (2017): e356–e366, doi.org/10.1016/S2468-2667(17)30118-4; "ACEs Science 101," ACES Too High (n.d.), acestoohigh.com/aces-101/.

26. Christina Bethell, Testimony to the House Committee on Oversight and Reform, July 11, 2019, The Child and Adolescent Health Measurement Initiative, Bloomberg School of Public Health, Johns Hopkins, docs.house.gov/meetings/GO/GO00/20190711/109762/HHRG-116-GO00-Wstate-BethellC-20190711.pdf.

27. "Note to Service Provider," in L. Leitch, Positive and Adverse Childhood Experiences Survey (PACES), 2015: An Alternative to the ACE Survey, Threshold GlobalWorks, March 2017, www.thresholdglobalworks.com/portfolio-items/paces-survey/.

28. Jim Hickman, "Trauma-Informed Care: It Takes More Than a Clipboard and a Questionnaire," *ACEs Connection*, August 26, 2019, www.acesconnection.com/blog/trauma-informed-care-it-takes-more-than-a-clipboard-and-a-questionnaire.

29. Bruce E. Levine, "The Groundbreaking Public Health Study That Should Change U.S. Society—but Won't," *CounterPunch*, July 19, 2019, www.counterpunch.org/2019/07/19/the-groundbreaking-public-health-study-that-should-change-u-s-society-but-wont/; Robert F. Anda, Laura E. Porter, and David W. Brown, "Inside the Adverse Childhood Experience Score: Strengths, Limitations and Misapplications," *AJPM American Journal of Preventative Medicine*, March 25, 2020, https://doi.org/10.1016/j.amepre.2020.01.009.

30. Bethell, "Christina Bethell, Testimony."

Chapter 2

1. Guy Bliesner and Mike Munger, "Fire Drills Are a Waste of Time," *Campus Safety*, March 5, 2014, www.campussafetymagazine.com/safety/fire_drills_are_a_waste_of_time/.

2. "A Look Back at America's Fallout Shelter Fatuation," CBS News, October 7, 2010, www.cbsnews.com/news/a-look-back-at-americas-fallout-shelter-fatuation/.

3. "What Is the Real Ideal Class Length?" Tenney School (n.d.), www.tenneyschool.com/what-is-the-real-ideal-class-length/.

4. "Improving School Communication with a Mass Notification System," *Alert Media*, February 12, 2019, www.alertmedia.com/blog/mass-notification-system-for-schools/.

5. Lulu Garcia-Navarro et al., "Experts Worry Active Shooter Drills in School Could Be Traumatic for Students," November 10, 2019, NPR, www.npr.org/2019/11/10/778015261/experts-worry-active-shooter-drills-in-schools-could-be-traumatic-for-students.

6. If asked, I'd share how a recent alarm at a hotel was mishandled and some 40 people were caught in a courtyard, me included. Had I not known about drills, we would still be there, or had there been a real disaster or shooting, we'd all be dead.

7. Karen Gross, "A Magic Wand in Human Form: A Review of *Step*," Aspen Institute, August 10, 2017, www.aspeninstitute.org/blog-posts/a-magic-wand-in-human-form/.

8. This suggestion comes from a placement project (School House to Your House) run by now retired principal Irwin Adler in Miami, Florida. Although the program was defunded, the ideas remain valuable and can be redeployed in other contexts to engage parents.

9. Some preschools have seen the value of connecting with parents early—with home visits. The value has empirical support and should have some stickiness moving forward in time as the students progress through the educational pipeline. Christina Caron and Katherine Zoepf, "Pre-K Teachers Are Making House Calls. It's Helping Kids Succeed," *NYT Parenting*, August 22, 2019, parenting.nytimes.com/preschooler/preschool-home-visit\.

10. Associated Press, "In Game Honoring Late Pitcher, Angels Throw a No-Hitter," *MPR News*, July 13, 2019, www.mprnews.org/story/2019/07/13/angels-no-hitter-tyler-skaggs.

11. See "May 4, 50th Commemoration," Kent State University, M4Y (n.d.), www.kent.edu/may4kentstate50.

12. New York Law School, *Eight Blocks Away: Memoirs of September 11, 2001*, Tribeca Square Press, 2011, digitalcommons.nyls.edu/tribeca_square_press/3/.

13. Karen Gross, "Portraits of Grief: A Focus on Survivors," New York Law School, March 1, 2003, digitalcommons.nyls.edu/cgi/viewcontent.cgi?referer=https://www.google.com/&httpsredir=1&article=1037&context=fac_articles_chapters.

14. Joseph K. Goodman, Selin A. Malkoc, and Brittney L. Stephenson, "Celebrate or Commemorate? A Material Purchase Advantage When Honoring Special Life Events," *Journal of the Association for Consumer Research* 1, no. 4 (2016): 499, www.journals.uchicago.edu/doi/full/10.1086/688352.

15. "Installation Art: History and Characteristics of Installations—Form of Conceptual Art," *Encyclopedia of Art* (n.d.), www.visual-arts-cork.com/installation-art.htm.

16. www.kimochis.com/. The word "kimochi" derives from the Japanese word for feelings and so one can rightly refer to these as "feeling toys."

17. "Activity Kit for Military Families," Kimochis (n.d.), kimochis9.mybigcommerce.com/activity-kit-for-military-families/.

18. Martha Garcia, "Small Acts of Kindness Can Have a Big Impact," *The Dispatch/The Rock Island Argus*, August 26, 2019, qconline.com/lifestyles/health-med-fit/small-acts-of-kindness-can-have-a-big-impact/article_c5aab2aa-19d9-5a82-8a2a-e9a92164ae10.html.

Chapter 3

1. See Center for Substance Abuse Treatment (U.S.), "Understanding the Impact of Trauma," Chapter 3 in *Trauma-Informed Care in Behavioral Health Services* (*Treatment Improvement Protocol [TIP] Series*, no. 57), 2014, Center for Biotechnical Information, www.ncbi.nlm.nih.gov/books/NBK207191/. Some of the best information describing trauma and its symptomology, including through more recent brain scanning and neurobiology and neurochemistry, are produced by the National Institute for the Clinical Application of Behavioral Medicine (NICABM). Their *Treating Trauma Master Series* covers the neurobiology of trauma, with presentations by Bessel van der Kolk, Peter Levine, and Ruth Buczynski, among other experts. See www.nicabm.com/program/treating-trauma-master/. One of the landmark texts is Judith Herman's *Trauma and Recovery* (New York: Basic Books, 1997).

2. I'd welcome readers' adding to the list of symptomologies provided in this chapter and Chapter 4. A link to where individuals can send their suggestions is provided at the end of the book.

3. Two excellent articles detail the effects of trauma on students. See Caroline Miller, "How Trauma Affects Kids in School," Child Mind Institute (n.d.), childmind.org/article/how-trauma-affects-kids-school/, derived from Jessica Minahan and Nancy Rappaport, *The Behavior Code: A Practical Guide to Understanding*

and Teaching the Most Challenging Students (Cambridge, MA: Harvard Education Press, 2012), and traumasensitiveschools.org/wp-content/uploads/2019/02/TLPI-Final-Report_Full-Report-002-2-1.pdf.

4. The terms *acute symptomology* and *delayed symptomology*, the latter introduced below, are not official, technical terms but are coined for the purposes of this book. The term *symptomology*, referenced in endnote 1 to the preface is an actual term, though an informal one compared to *symptomatology*.

5. New research suggests that microglial brain cells may be doing vastly more "work" than previously recognized in the context of trauma. See Donna Jackson Nakazawa, *The Angel and the Assassin: The Tiny Brain Cell That Changed the Course of Medicine* (New York: Random House, 2020).

6. "Shoes Piled Outside Bar Where 9 Were Killed in Dayton," Fox 8 Cleveland, August 4, 2019, fox8.com/2019/08/04/shoes-piled-outside-bar-where-9-were-killed-in-dayton/.

7. Madeline Holcombe, "Motorcycles Backfiring Mistaken for an Active Shooter in Times Square," CNN, August 7, 2019, www.cnn.com/2019/08/07/us/times-square-gunshot-backfire-stampede-trnd/index.html.

8. Kirsten Weir, "The Lasting Impact of Neglect: Psychologists Are Studying How Early Deprivation Harms Children—and How Best to Help Those Who Have Suffered from Neglect," *Monitor on Psychology* (American Psychological Association) 45, no. 6 (2014): 36, www.apa.org/monitor/2014/06/neglect.

9. Melody Walford, "Trauma and the Nervous System: Stress [*sic*] It's Not in Your Head; It's in Your Nervous System," BodyWise Foundation, August 4, 2017, www.bodywisefoundation.org/blog/bodywisefoundation/nervous-system-trauma.

10. Jeongok G. Logan and Debra J. Barksdale, "Allostasis and Allostatic Load: Expanding the Discourse on Stress and Cardiovascular Disease," *Journal of Nursing and Healthcare of Chronic Illness* in association with *Journal of Clinical Nursing* 17, no. 7B (2008): 201–208, doi:10.1111/j.1365-2702.2008.02347.x.

11. Under the polyvagal theory, the architecture of responses to trauma and stress is somewhat different, although still fitting under the category of autonomic. *Dorsal vagal* refers to what we will term here the parasympathetic nervous system; sympathetic arousal is similar to that described here; the ventral pathway is an "opening"—a pathway that will allow engagement. See Stephen W. Porges, "The Polyvagal Theory: New Insights into Adaptive Reactions of the Autonomic Nervous System," *Cleveland Clinic Journal of Medicine* 76 (suppl. 2) (2009): S86–S90, www.ncbi.nlm.nih.gov/pubmed/19376991.

12. "Your Backup Brain," *Psychology Today*, June 9, 2016, www.psychologytoday.com/us/articles/201111/your-backup-brain.

13. Sophie Leclercq, Paul Forsythe, and John Bienenstock, "Posttraumatic Stress Disorder: Does the Microbiome Hold the Key?" *Canadian Journal of Psychiatry* 61, no. 4 (2016): 204–213, dx.doi.org/10.1177%2F0706743716635535.

14. There are actually more *f*'s than we usually reference, something to which we will return. We can add *faint* and *flag* to the list, something supported by others. See Arielle Schwartz, "The Neurobiology of Trauma—Dr. Arielle Schwartz," October 27, 2016, drarielleschwartz.com/the-neurobiology-of-trauma-dr-arielle-schwartz/#.XWRUsVB7n_Q. I would add *flocking*, although some might see that as delayed symptomology.

15. J. B. MacKinnon, "The Strange Brain of the World's Greatest Solo Climber," *Nautilus*, August 11, 2016, nautil.us/issue/39/sport/the-strange-brain-of-the-worlds-greatest-solo-climber.

16. Matt Bai, "How Gary Hart's Downfall Forever Changed American Politics," *New York Times Magazine*, September 18, 2014, www.nytimes.com/2014/09/21/magazine/how-gary-harts-downfall-forever-changed-american-politics.html.

17. Sabrina Siddiqui, "Kavanaugh's Angry Testimony Raises Doubts over Future Impartiality," *Guardian*, October 3, 2018, www.theguardian.com/us-news/2018/oct/02/kavanaugh-impartial-justice-testimony.

18. Charles J. Sykes, "The Anger of Brett Kavanaugh," *Washington Examiner,* October 2, 2018, www.washingtonexaminer.com/weekly-standard/the-anger-of-brett-kavanaugh.

19. Maria Puente, "Chappa-What? Everything You Should Know About Ted Kennedy and the 'Chappaquiddick' Movie," *USA Today*, April 4, 2018, www.usatoday.com/story/life/2018/04/04/everything-you-should-know-ted-kennedy-mary-jo-kopechne-chappaquiddick/472903002/.

20. Laurel Wamsley, "Wife of U.S. Diplomat Flees U.K. After Fatal Car Crash, Avoiding Police Investigation," *NPR*, October 7, 2019, www.npr.org/2019/10/07/767925703/wife-of-u-s-diplomat-flees-u-k-after-fatal-car-crash-avoiding-police-investigati.

21. Lisa Boothe, "Christine Blasey Ford Has a Credibility Problem," *The Hill*, October 3, 2018, thehill.com/opinion/judiciary/409651-dr-fords-credibility-problem; Jamie Ducharme, "'Indelible in the Hippocampus Is the Laughter'; the Science Behind Christine Blasey Ford's Testimony, *Time,* September 27, 2018, time.com/5408567/christine-blasey-ford-science-of-memory/.

22. There are, to be sure, other choices of color schemes to describe our body's response to trauma. See Mona Delahooke, *Beyond Behaviors* (Eau Claire, WI: PESI, 2019).

23. J. Douglas Bremner, "Traumatic Stress: Effects on the Brain," *Dialogues in Clinical Neuroscience*, December 2006, www.ncbi.nlm.nih.gov/pmc/articles/PMC3181836/; and Viatcheslav Wlassoff, "How Does Post-Traumatic Stress Disorder Change the Brain?," *BrainBlogger,* January 24, 2015, www.brainblogger.com/2015/01/24/how-does-post-traumatic-stress-disorder-change-the-brain/.

Chapter 4

1. J. Douglas Bremner, "Traumatic Stress: Effects on the Brain," *Dialogues in Clinical Neuroscience*, December 2006, www.ncbi.nlm.nih.gov/pmc/articles/PMC3181836/.

2. Sharon Dekel, Tsachi Ein-Dor, Jeffrey B. Rosen, and George A. Bonanno, "Differences in Cortisol Response to Trauma Activation in Individuals with and Without Comorbid PTSD and Depression," *Frontiers in Psychology*, May 18, 2017, doi.org/10.3389/fpsyg.2017.00797.

3. National Scientific Council on the Developing Child, *Excessive Stress Disrupts the Architecture of the Developing Brain*, Center on the Developing Child, Harvard University (n.d.), developingchild.harvard.edu/wp-content/uploads/2005/05/Stress_Disrupts_Architecture_Developing_Brain-1.pdf; "What Happens When Your Immune System Gets Stressed Out?" Cleveland Clinic (n.d.), health.clevelandclinic.org/what-happens-when-your-immune-system-gets-stressed-out/.

4. Grant Hilary Brenner, "New Study Shows Brain Change After Psychological Trauma," *Psychology Today*, December 5, 2018, www.psychologytoday.com/us/blog/experimentations/201812/new-study-shows-brain-change-after-psychological-trauma.

5. "Module 6: What Is the Influence of Culture?" in *Child Welfare Trauma Training Toolkit: Participant Manual*, 1st ed., January 2013, www.mncourts.gov/mncourtsgov/media/scao_library/CJI/2014_Regional_Team_Meeting_-_Trauma_-_The_Influcence_of_Culture_on_Trauma_(NCTSN).pdf; Emily Trepasso-Grullon, "Differences Among Ethnic Groups in Trauma Type and PTSD Symptom Severity," *Graduate Student Journal of Psychology* 14 (2012): 102–112, www.tc.columbia.edu/publications/gsjp/gsjp-volumes-archive/gsjp-volume-14-2012/25235_Trepasso-Grullon_PTSDEthnicity.pdf.

6. "Animal Research Success: Post-Traumatic Stress Disorder," by Emily K. Dilger, BrainFacts.org, March 9, 2012, www.brainfacts.org/archives/2012/animals-post-traumatic-stress-disorder.

7. Bessel A. van der Kolk and Jose Saporta, "The Biological Response to Psychic Trauma: Mechanisms and Treatment of Intrusion and Numbing," *Anxiety Research (UK)* 4 (1991): 199–212, www.cirp.org/library/psych/vanderkolk2/.

8. Denese O. Shervington, *Ending the Epidemic of Childhood Trauma* (n.d.), docs.house.gov/meetings/GO/GO00/20190711/109762/HHRG-116-GO00-Wstate-ShervingtonD-20190711.pdf.

9. There are positives of hypervigilance (and other trauma symptomology) that are described in detail in my *Breakaway Learners*. See Chapter 5, pp. 45–59.

10. *Post-Traumatic Stress Disorder*, National Institute of Mental Health (n.d.), www.nimh.nih.gov/health/publications/post-traumatic-stress-disorder-ptsd/index.shtml; Fabiana Franco, "Dissociation and C-PTSD: The Role of Detachment in Complex Trauma," *GoodTherapy Blog*, November 6, 2017, www.goodtherapy.org/blog/dissociation-c-ptsd-role-of-detachment-in-complex-trauma-1106174.

11. Christine Champagne, "The Moment in the *Glass Castle* Movie That Made Jeannette Walls Cry," *Vanity Fair*, July 31, 2017, www.vanityfair.com/hollywood/2017/07/the-glass-castle-book-movie-jeannette-walls-interview.

12. Rebecca Seligman and Laurence J. Kirmayer, "Dissociative Experience and Cultural Neuroscience: Narrative, Metaphor, and Mechanism," *Culture, Medicine, and Psychiatry* 32, no. 1 (2008): 31–64, doi: 10.1007/s11013-007-9077-8. Complete disassociation (not trauma related) may occur when an individual has multiple personalities, being unaware when they are moving between one and another.

Chapter 5

1. Melinda Smith, Jeanne Segal, Lawrence Robinson, and Robert Segal, "Burnout Prevention and Treatment: Techniques for Dealing with Overwhelming Stress," HelpGuide, June 2019, www.helpguide.org/articles/stress/burnout-prevention-and-recovery.htm.

2. Neal Samudre, "How to Dream Big and Avoid Burnout: Yes, It's Possible, but First, You Need a Reality Check," *Relevant*, May 22, 2013, relevantmagazine.com/life5/how-dream-big-and-avoid-burnout/.

3. Alexandra Michel, "Burnout and the Brain," Association of Psychological Science, February 2016, www.psychologicalscience.org/observer/burnout-and-the-brain.

4. "Did You Know?" Compassion Fatigue Awareness Project (n.d.), www.compassionfatigue.org/.

5. "Defining Vicarious Trauma and Secondary Traumatic Stress," Tend (n.d.), www.tendacademy.ca/resources/defining-vicarious-trauma-and-secondary-traumatic-stress/.

6. "Teachers Are Leaving the Profession at an Alarming Rate," Bored Teachers (n.d.), www.boredteachers.com/news/teachers-are-leaving-the-profession-at-an-alarming-rate; Samantha Hernandez and Max Cohen, "Back to School, Without a Teacher: Inside the Struggle to Keep Teachers at Rural Schools," *USA Today*, September 6, 2019, amp.usatoday.com/amp/2018092001. This article describes a school with no teachers or teachers who quit; that situation certainly makes connections and reciprocity impossible.

7. Lyndsey Layton, "New Analysis Argues That Better Teachers Are Flocking to Better Schools," *Washington Post*, September 1, 2015, www.washingtonpost.com/news/education/wp/2015/09/01/new-analysis-argues-that-better-teachers-are-flocking-to-better-schools/.

8. Brittany Bartkowiak, "Even Teachers Who Work with the Most Traumatized Kids Lack Needed Training," State of Opportunity, April 24, 2015, stateofopportunity.michiganradio.org/post/even-teachers-who-work-most-traumatized-kids-lack-needed-training.

9. See Emelina Minero, "When Students Are Traumatized, Teachers Are Too," Edutopia, October 4, 2017, www.edutopia.org/article/when-students-are-traumatized-teachers-are-too. While this article confuses nomenclature (it uses *vicarious trauma* incorrectly), it is a quality descriptor of what teachers feel and experience in working with traumatized students.

10. One could refer to this as trauma-responsive pedagogy to distinguish it from trauma-responsive institutions and trauma-responsive classrooms. This book focuses on the latter two topics, although trauma-responsive pedagogy is both a worthy topic and one that needs to be explored in vastly greater depth.

11. Karen Gross, *Breakaway Learners* (New York: Teachers College Press, 2017), vii–viii.

12. Gross, *Breakaway Learners*, 13–15.

13. It's noteworthy that this all occurred well before the coronavirus pandemic. And that virus—catching it or the threat of catching it—permeated the news and social media across the globe. Quarantines were instituted; travel was curbed and fear abounded. Sadly, much of our attention was focused on the physical threat of the virus—containment and mitigation. Little attention was being paid to the psychological impact of the actual virus or its threat. That absence meant that people in education were focused on issues like school closures and handwashing; the trauma of the coronavirus or the threat of its attack were not being addressed. I wrote an essay on the topic, and it did not get much attention. I suspect that this is in part because the word "trauma" itself, as noted in Chapter 1, frightens people. And the silencing of the psychological impact of COVID-19 means, at least for me, that we have our work cut out for us in the months and years ahead as students cope with the ramifications of schools' closing and reopening and other similar disruptions. The referenced article, titled "I'm Worried; Higher Education Is Not Focused at All on COVID-19's Psychological Toll," appeared on March 9, 2020, in the *New England Journal of Higher Education* and can be

found at www.nebhe.org/journal/im-worried-higher-education-isnt-focused-at-all-on-covid-19s-psychological-toll/.

14. Karen Gross, "Portraits of Grief: A Focus on Survivors," *New York Law School Law Review* 46 (March 1, 2003): 630–652, digitalcommons.nyls.edu/cgi/viewcontent.cgi?referer=https://www.google.com/&httpsredir=1&article=1037&context=fac_articles_chapters.

15. Karen Gross, "This Isn't Fair to Veterans: The President, Spravato, and False Hope," August 23, 2019, Medium, medium.com/@KarenGrossEdu/this-isnt-fair-to-veterans-the-president-spravato-and-false-hope-b8f2b7531675.

16. Quoted in Karen Gross, "Aging Educators: Still Valuable?" LinkedIn, August 16, 2019, www.linkedin.com/pulse/aging-educators-still-valuable-karen-gross/.

Chapter 6

1. We are not addressing students' trauma that is caused by teachers (and other adults) in schools. Carrie Gaffney, "When Schools Cause Trauma," *Teaching Tolerance*, Summer 2019, www.tolerance.org/magazine/summer-2019/when-schools-cause-trauma/. Instead, we are focused on outside trauma, whether caused by natural or human events that affect children and their success in school. Poor teaching, stereotyping, discrimination (whether overt or subtle), physical or psychological punishment that negatively affect children and retrigger prior trauma are important and not altogether uncommon issues to be sure but beyond the scope of this book. One exception is in the context of establishing the ideal school as a "safe" place, which discussion does reference student-to-student abuse in the form of bullying and is discussed in Chapter 8.

2. Susan E. Craig, *Trauma-Sensitive Schools: Learning Communities Transforming Children's Lives, K–5* (New York: Teachers College Press, 2015); Susan E. Craig, *Trauma-Sensitive Schools for the Adolescent Years: Promoting Resiliency and Healing, Grades 6–12* (New York: Teachers College Press, 2017).

3. Dwyer Gunn, "Can Denver Public Schools Help Kids Experiencing Trauma?" *5280*, September 2019, www.5280.com/2019/08/can-denver-public-schools-help-kids-experiencing-trauma/.

4. Karen Gross, *Breakaway Learners* (New York: Teachers College Press, 2017).

5. Sandra L. Bloom and Farragher, *Destroying Sanctuary: The Crisis in Human Service Delivery Systems* (New York: Oxford University Press, 2011). Through the "Sanctuary Model," with its shared values, there is an effort to get widespread buy-in.

6. In reality, people move over their lifetimes with some frequency from state to state and within a state. Colin Holmes, "The State of the American Mover: Stats and Facts," move.org, April 23, 2018, www.move.org/moving-stats-facts/. And those in the military move with even greater frequency, with many military children attending six or more different schools within their K–12 education. Danielle DeSimone, "5 Things You Need to Know About Military Families," USO, August 15, 2018, www.uso.org/stories/2277-5-things-to-know-about-military-families.

7. "Allostatic Load," Science Direct (n.d.), www.sciencedirect.com/topics/neuroscience/allostatic-load. Tests that measure such effects are invasive and unlikely to be used on children. *Allostatic Load Notebook*, MacArthur Research Network on SES and Health, University of California, San Francisco (n.d.), macses.ucsf.edu/research/allostatic/allostatic.php.

8. Daniel Mauss, Jian Li, Burkhard Schmidt, Peter Angerer, and Marc N. Jarczok, "Measuring Allostatic Load in the Workforce: A Systematic Review," *Industrial Health* 53, no. 1 (2015): 5–20, National Center for Biotechnology Information, US National Library of Medicine, www.ncbi.nlm.nih.gov/pmc/articles/PMC4331190/.

9. N. R. Hamdi, S. C. South, and R. F. Krueger, "Does Education Lower Allostatic Load? A Co-Twin Control Study," *Brain, Behavior, and Immunity* 56 (August 2016): 221–229, National Center for Biotechnology Information, U.S. National Library of Medicine, www.ncbi.nlm.nih.gov/pubmed/26778778.

10. "Agenda," 2019 Fall Trauma Informed School Conference (n.d.), www.cvent.com/events/2019-fall-trauma-informed-school-conference/agenda-140badb1055f4cbe9c2b9401150cfc68.aspx?dvce=1; "Summer Breakaway: A Study of Dr. Karen Gross' Book Breakaway Learners," Eastern Kentucky University Retention and Graduation, July 22, 2018, retentiongraduation.eku.edu/insidelook/summer-breakaway-study-dr-karen-gross-book-breakaway-learners.

11. "Trauma Informed Schools," Oregon School-Based Health Alliance (n.d.), osbha.org/trauma-informed-schools; Jane Ellen Stevens, "Massachusetts, Washington State Lead U.S. Trauma-Sensitive School Movement," *ACES Too High*, May 31, 2012, acestoohigh.com/2012/05/31/massachusetts-washington-state-lead-u-s-trauma-sensitive-school-movement/; "Odessa R-VII School District: Trauma-Informed Schools Initiative," Odessa R-VII (n.d.), www.odessar7.net/vnews/display.v/SEC/District%20Information%7CTrauma-Informed%20Schools%20Initiative; "About Miss Kendra," Miss Kendra, traumainformedschools.org/.

12. "Allostatic and Environmental Load in Toddlers Predicts Anxiety in Preschool and Kindergarten," *Development and Psychopathology* 23, no. 4 (2011): 1069–1087, www.ncbi.nlm.nih.gov/pmc/articles/PMC3202312/.

13. See Gross, *Breakaway Learners*, Chaps. 3, 13, 15, and others.

14. Gross, *Breakaway Learners*, 133–134.

15. Consider how students who are lastic and graduate from college do when they progress to graduate school or the workplace. *Breakaway Learners* addresses some examples, drawing from Southern Vermont College graduates. In their continuing education, SVC graduates have achieved success even in graduate schools that lack lasticity.

16. Benefits will be enjoyed also by the children of those who receive trauma assistance: A growing conviction exists that there is epigenetic transmission of trauma, a topic that, while beyond the scope of this book, is relevant, as it highlights the potential devastating reach of trauma. See Benedict Carey, "Can We Really Inherit Trauma?" *New York Times*, December 10, 2018, www.nytimes.com/2018/12/10/health/mind-epigenetics-genes.html; Olga Khazan, "Inherited Trauma Shapes Your Health," *Atlantic*, October 16, 2018, www.theatlantic.com/health/archive/2018/10/trauma-inherited-generations/573055/.

17. Bloom and Farragher, *Destroying Sanctuary*, 14–15.

18. Bloom and Farragher, *Destroying Sanctuary*, 75–76, 154, 354.

19. Bloom and Farragher, *Destroying Sanctuary*, 272.

20. Daniel Amen, "The Most Important Lesson from 83,000 Brain Scans," TEDxOrangeCoast, YouTube, www.youtube.com/watch?v=esPRsT-lmw8.LK.

21. This broader definition is used in the Missouri Model as the "highest" level of achievement in the move to trauma programs in the state. See Missouri Trauma

Roundtable Through the Department of Mental Health, "Missouri's Comprehensive Public Health Approach for Resilience to Mitigate the Impact of Trauma," January 2018, dmh.mo.gov/media/pdf/missouris-comprehensive-public-health-approach-resilience-mitigate-impact-trauma.

22. "The Solution: Trauma Sensitive Schools: 3. Trauma-Sensitive Schools Help Children Feel Safe to Learn," Helping Traumatized Children Learn (n.d.), traumasensitiveschools.org/trauma-and-learning/the-solution-trauma-sensitive-schools/; "What's a Trauma-Sensitive School?" www.truthedconsulting.com/trauma-sensitive-schools-1.

23. "Trauma-Sensitive Schools," National Association of School Psychologists (n.d.), www.nasponline.org/resources-and-publications/resources-and-podcasts/mental-health/trauma-sensitive-schools.

24. "Moving from Trauma-Informed to Trauma-Responsive: A Training Program for Organizational Change," Hazelden (n.d.), www.hazelden.org/store/item/520203?Moving-from-Trauma-Informed-to-Trauma-Responsive.

25. Bloom and Farragher, *Destroying Sanctuary*. This is an overall theme throughout this excellent book that, while not focused on education per se, is focused on a caring profession.

26. Allie Bidwell, "Study: FAFSA 'Nudges' Are Cheap, and They Work," National Association of Student Financial Aid Administrators, March 23, 2017, www.nasfaa.org/news-item/11626/Study_FAFSA_Nudges_Are_Cheap_And_They_Work.

27. Greta Anderson, "Nudging Doesn't Scale Nationally," *Inside Higher Ed*, August 20, 2019, www.insidehighered.com/news/2019/08/20/national-nudging-campaign-produced-no-increase-fafsa-applications-college-enrollment. Nudges remain important and I return to them later. They are the creation of Sunstein and Thaler in their groundbreaking book, *Nudges*. Dan Kopf, "It's Been 10 Years Since Behavioral Economics Hit the Mainstream," Quartz, October 13, 2018, qz.com/1418336/its-been-10-years-since-behavioral-economics-hit-the-mainstream/.

28. This observation reinforces a common teacher refrain (actually derived from the Pareto Principle): 20% of the students take 80% of the time. The consequence is that the well-behaving students get way less teacher time than the badly behaving students, a result that is harmful to many students who can succeed.

29. "Our Method," Children's Psychological Health Center (n.d.), www.childrenspsychologicalhealthcenter.org/rnt/our-method/. This is based on the work of Gilbert Kliman.

30. Punishment and discipline in education are different, but both are problematic, depending on how they are defined. Amy Morin, "The Difference Between Punishment and Discipline," *Verywell Family*, June 30, 2019, www.verywellfamily.com/the-difference-between-punishment-and-discipline-1095044. See also Chapter 9.

Chapter 7

1. "Fifty Years of Change, 1964–2014," in National Center for Chronic Disease Prevention and Health Promotion (US) Office on Smoking and Health, *The Health Consequences of Smoking—50 Years of Progress: A Report of the Surgeon General* (Atlanta, GA: Centers for Disease Control and Prevention [US], 2014), www.ncbi.nlm.nih.gov/books/NBK294310/; "Smoking and Tobacco Use: Economic Trends in Tobacco," Centers for Disease and Prevention (n.d.), www.cdc.gov/tobacco/data_statistics/fact_sheets/economics/econ_facts/index.htm.

2. "Civil Rights Acts (1964, 1968)," in *A Brief History of Civil Rights in the United States*, Georgetown Law Library, updated August 16, 2019, guides.ll.georgetown.edu/c.php?g=592919&p=4172702; "The Civil Rights Act of 1964: A Long Struggle for Freedom; Legal Timeline," Library of Congress (n.d.), www.loc.gov/exhibits/civil-rights-act/legal-events-timeline.html.

3. Ashley Crossman, "Malcolm Gladwell's 'The Tipping Point,'" ThoughtCo., updated May 25, 2019, www.thoughtco.com/malcolm-gladwell-tipping-point-theory-3026765.

4. I suspect, although it is way too early to tell, that the COVID-19 pandemic could be a key factor in moving the cultural change with respect to trauma forward. We'll just have to wait and see what the coming 18 months bring.

5. History.com Editors, "Patriot Act," History, updated August 21, 2018, www.history.com/topics/21st-century/patriot-act.

6. Liz McNeil and Kathy Ehrich Dowd, "Meet the Teens Who Were Born After Their Fathers Died on 9/11," *People*, September 11, 2018, people.com/human-interest/children-of-911-meet-the-teens-who-were-born-after-their-fathers-died/; Laura King, "Their Young World Crumbled: Now the Children of 9/11 Look Back," *Los Angeles Times*, September 11, 2016, www.latimes.com/nation/la-na-911-anniversary-montclair-snap-story.html; Mo Costandi, "Pregnant 9/11 Survivors Transmitted Trauma to Their Children," *Guardian*, September 9, 2011, www.theguardian.com/science/neurophilosophy/2011/sep/09/pregnant-911-survivors-transmitted-trauma.

7. Dean Balsamini, Sara Dorn, and Susan Edelman, "13 Children of Fallen 9-11 Firefighters Joining FDNY," *New York Post*, September 7, 2019, nypost.com/2019/09/07/13-children-of-fallen-9-11-heroes-becoming-nyc-firefighters/.

8. Stefan Armitage, "13 Children of Fallen 9/11 Firefighters Are Joining the FDNY," *VT*, September 8, 2019, vt.co/lifestyle/relationships/13-children-of-fallen-9-11-firefighters-are-joining-the-fdny/.

9. Simon H. Pincus, Robert House, Joseph Christenson, and Lawrence E. Adler, "The Emotional Cycle of Deployment: Military Family Perspective," Military.com, 2019, www.military.com/spouse/military-deployment/dealing-with-deployment/emotional-cycle-of-deployment-military-family.html; Anna Sutherland, "How Deployment Affects Military Families," Institute for Family Studies, April 21, 2016, ifstudies.org/blog/how-deployment-affects-military-families.

10. Joshua Axelrod, "Veterans Are Committing Suicide in VA Parking Lots: Report," Military Times Reboot Camp, February 7, 2019, rebootcamp.militarytimes.com/news/transition/2019/02/08/veterans-are-committing-suicide-in-va-parking-lots-report/.

11. "Weather-Related Disasters Are Increasing," *Economist*, August 29, 2017, www.economist.com/graphic-detail/2017/08/29/weather-related-disasters-are-increasing; "Are Natural Disasters Getting Worse?" *The Borgen Project*, March 10, 2018, borgenproject.org/are-natural-disasters-getting-worse/; Kimberly Amadeo, "How Hurricanes Damage the Economy: Why Harvey, Maria, Florence, and Other Hurricanes Were So Destructive," *The Balance*, updated June 25, 2019, www.thebalance.com/hurricane-damage-economic-costs-4150369.

12. Carolyn Kousky, "Impacts of Natural Disasters on Children," Semantic Scholar, 2016, www.semanticscholar.org/paper/Impacts-of-Natural-Disasters-on

-Children.-Kousky/e72d88a8b2880a1edb5d553d7499b7d46732a540; Billy Briggs, "Education Under Attack and Battered by Natural Disasters in 2018," Relief Web, December 27, 2018, reliefweb.int/report/world/education-under-attack-and-battered-natural-disasters-2018.

13. Karen Gross, "Why We Need Trauma Trained Educators for National and Regional Disaster Teams," Medium, December 8, 2017, medium.com/@KarenGrossEdu/why-we-need-trauma-trained-educators-for-national-and-regional-disaster-teams-3f6835595a4a; Lauren Greubel, Xanthe Ackerman, and Rebecca Winthrop, "Prioritizing Education in the Face of Natural Disasters," *Up Front* (blog), October 31, 2012, www.brookings.edu/blog/up-front/2012/10/31/prioritizing-education-in-the-face-of-natural-disasters/.

14. Terri Erbacher, "Could Schools Help Identify Troubling Behavior Before a Mass Shooting?" *Philadelphia Inquirer*, updated September 5, 2019, www.inquirer.com/health/expert-opinions/mass-shooting-school-prevent-20190905.html.

15. "The 11 Mass Deadly School Shootings That Happened Since Columbine," Meghan Keneally, ABC News, April 19, 2019, abcnews.go.com/amp/US/11-mass-deadly-school-shootings-happened-columbine/story?id=62494128.

16. "Gunfire on School Grounds in the United States," Everytown for Gun Safety Support Fund, February 11, 2019, everytownresearch.org/gunfire-in-school/#12594; see also Michelle Lou and Christina Walker, "There Have Been 22 School Shootings in the US So Far This Year," CNN, updated July 26, 2019, amp.cnn.com/cnn/2019/05/08/us/school-shootings-us-2019-trnd/index.html, with somewhat different numbers. Again, definitions matter.

17. Amy Rock, "College Campus Shooting Statistics You Should Know," Campus Safety, January 15, 2019, www.campussafetymagazine.com/university/college-campus-shooting-statistics/; German Lopez and Kavya Sukumar, "After Sandy Hook, We Said Never Again. And Then We Let 2,237 Mass Shootings Happen," *Vox*, updated September 28, 2019, www.vox.com/a/mass-shootings-america-sandy-hook-gun-violence.

18. Amy Novotney, "What Happens to the Survivors," *Monitor on Psychology* (American Psychological Association) 49, no. 8 (2018): 36, www.apa.org/monitor/2018/09/survivors; Jared Keller, "The Psychological Aftermath of Surviving School Shootings," *Pacific Standard*, March 25, 2019, psmag.com/education/the-psychological-aftermath-of-surviving-school-shootings.

19. Rebecca Harrington and Michael Kranz, "It's Been 6 Years Since the Sandy Hook Shooting. Here Are the Names and Pictures of the 27 Victims, Including 20 Children, Who Were Murdered That Day," *Business Insider*, December 14, 2018, www.businessinsider.com/who-were-the-victims-of-the-sandy-hook-shooting-2017-12.

20. Patricia Mazzei, "After 2 Apparent Student Suicides, Parkland Grieves Again," *New York Times*, March 24, 2019, www.nytimes.com/2019/03/24/us/parkland-suicide-marjory-stoneman-douglas.html; John Bacon, "Father of Sandy Hook Victim Latest Apparent Suicide After Deadly School Shootings," *USA Today*, March 25, 2019, www.usatoday.com/story/news/nation/2019/03/25/suicides-school-shootings-sandy-hook-father/3267514002/; Tovia Smith, "Father of Sandy Hook Shooting Victim Dies by Apparent Suicide," NPR, March 25, 2019, www.npr.org/2019/03/25/706602331/father-of-sandy-hook-shooting-victim-dies-by-apparent-suicide.

21. Greg Allen, "Suicides in Parkland Leave Community in Shock," *All Things Considered*, March 25, 2019, www.npr.org/2019/03/25/706598774/suicides-in-parkland-leave-community-in-shock.

22. Rafael Maravilla, "Trump Administration Announces $1.8 Billion in Funding to States to Continue Combating Opioid Crisis," *ACES Connection*, September 9, 2019, www.acesconnection.com/blog/trump-administration-announces-1-8-billion-in-funding-to-states-to-continue-combating-opioid-crisis-hhs-gov.

23. "Opioid Abuse Is Devastating Families—*and* America's Middle Class," *The Catalyst*, Fall 2018, www.bushcenter.org/catalyst/opportunity-road/winnefeld-opioids-addiction.html.

24. "The Opioid Crisis Explained in Black and White," Focus for Health (n.d.), www.focusforhealth.org/the-opioid-crisis-explained-in-black-and-white/.

25. Taylor N. Santoro and Jonathan D. Santoro, "Racial Bias in the US Opioid Epidemic: A Review of the History of Systemic Bias and Implications for Care," *Cureus* 10, no. 12 (2018), e3733, www.ncbi.nlm.nih.gov/pmc/articles/PMC6384031/.

26. Gary Galles, "Self-Interest Is Not Selfishness," Mises Institute, April 15, 2015, mises.org/library/self-interest-not-selfishness; Bryan Walsh, "Why We Don't Care About Saving Our Grandchildren from Climate Change," *Time*, October 21, 2013, science.time.com/2013/10/21/why-we-dont-care-about-saving-our-grandchildren-from-climate-change/.

27. While early in the unraveling of the impact of the COVID-19 pandemic, there is already a sense that we are forever changed by this virus and the threat it presents to each and every person across the globe. Longer term, I think it can contribute to the movement to create more trauma-responsive educational systems. Bill McKibben, "With the Coronavirus, Hell Is No Other People," *The New Yorker*, March 11, 2020, www.newyorker.com/news/daily-comment/with-the-coronavirus-hell-is-no-other-people.

28. *Identifying, Preventing, and Treating Childhood Trauma: A Pervasive Public Health Issue That Needs Greater Federal Attention*, House Committee on Oversight Reform Hearing, July 11, 2019, oversight.house.gov/legislation/hearings/identifying-preventing-and-treating-childhood-trauma-a-pervasive-public-health.

29. United States Government Accountability Office (GAO), *Children Affected by Trauma: Selected States Report Various Approaches and Challenges to Supporting Children*, GAO, April 2019, www.gao.gov/assets/700/698684.pdf.

30. A hearing and briefing were subsequently scheduled in the Senate. Elizabeth Prewitt, "Hearing to Be Held This Week on Education and Trauma in House of Representatives Ed and Labor Subcommittee," *ACES Connection*, September 9, 2019, www.acesconnection.com/blog/hearing-to-be-held-this-week-on-education-and-trauma-in-house-of-representatives-ed-and-labor-subcommittee.

31. "Clark, Quigley & Fitzpatrick Introduce Bill to Expand Trauma-Informed Practices in Schools" (press release), Katherine Clark, July 26, 2019, katherineclark.house.gov/2019/7/representatives-clark-quigley-fitzpatrick-introduce-bill-to-expand-trauma-informed-practices-in-schools. *A Bill to Amend the Elementary and Secondary Education Act of 1965 to Provide Criteria for Use of Federal Funds to Support Trauma-Informed Practices in Schools, and for Other Purposes*, 116th Congress, 1st Session, July 25, 2019, traumasensitiveschools.org/wp-content/uploads/2019/08/Trauma-Informed-Schools-Act-7.26.19-f.pdf. Quibbles include that the bill is limited

to elementary and secondary schools and thus is too narrow. We need attention across the entire educational pipeline. It also ignores the impact of trauma on student health, focusing instead on learning, behavior, and relationships in schools. Funding for these efforts would seem to come through the federal government through the Elementary and Secondary School Act of 1965.

32. *S. 1770: RISE from Trauma Act*, GovTrack, June 10, 2019, www.govtrack.us/congress/bills/116/s1770/text; Leah Harris, "Bipartisan 'RISE from Trauma Act' Introduced to Address Childhood Trauma in America," Mad in America, June 17, 2019, www.madinamerica.com/2019/06/address-childhood-trauma-america/.

33. This bill is comprehensive in the sense that it speaks to trauma in many settings, including education and health care. I worry that its breadth will make its implementation less effective and it is contingent on major funding. There is an explicit push for a federal center to distribute information and models, something that concerns me given the amount of money to be expended and the likelihood of success. The legislation also funds pilots, and as noted in Part I, replication of programs is tough sledding in the context of trauma. What is relevant is shared values, something not identified in the legislation. Note too that there is inconsistent and undefined terminology with respect to trauma; that leads to confusion in both implementation and empirical assessment. I also note some very particular provisions, such as the inclusion of the arts to deal with trauma. While a good idea, it is but one of many such suggestions where trauma can be addressed in the educational arena.

34. David Washburn, "Q&A: California's First-Ever Surgeon General on Her Plans to Tackle Toxic Stress in Children," EdSource, March 27, 2019, edsource.org/2019/qa-californias-new-top-doc-on-her-plans-to-tackle-toxic-stress-in-children/610449.

35. See www.dhcs.ca.gov/provgovpart/Pages/TraumaCare.aspx. As a point of information, I completed this training and received a Statement of Participation from the Postgraduate Institute for Medicine on January 20, 2020. The adequacy of this training and the ways in which the ACE score will be used in California are a topic for another day, but it is a conversation surely worth having in the relative near term.

36. E.g., Nadine Burke Harris, "The Toxic Stress of Detention Can Dramatically Alter Kids' Lives," *Salt Lake Tribune*, updated July 11, 2019, www.sltrib.com/opinion/commentary/2019/07/11/nadine-burke-harris-toxic/; "California Surgeon General Dr. Nadine Burke Harris Launches Statewide Listening Tour" (press release), California Health and Human Services Agency, April 2, 2019, www.chhs.ca.gov/blog/2019/04/02/california-surgeon-general-dr-nadine-burke-harris-launches-statewide-listening-tour/.

37. Melissa Hellmann, "This Town Adopted Trauma-Informed Care—And Saw a Decrease in Crime and Suspension Rates," *Yes!*, February 22, 2017, www.yesmagazine.org/people-power/this-town-adopted-trauma-informed-care-and-saw-a-decrease-in-crime-and-suspension-rates-20170222. For how to replicate the Walla Walla trauma-informed high school, see Jim Sporleder and Heather T. Forbes, *The Trauma-Informed School: A Step-by-Step Implementation Guide for Administrators and School Personnel* (Boulder, CO: Beyond Consequences Institute, 2019).

38. Jennifer Hossler, "The Journey from Me to We: The Walla Walla Way," *Becoming Trauma Informed and Beyond,* March 9, 2018, www.acesconnection.

com/g/becoming-a-trauma-informed-and-beyond/blog/the-journey-from-me-to-we-the-walla-walla-way. Other towns wanted to be the first to be trauma informed. See Jane Ellen Stevens, "Tarpon Springs, FL, May Be First Trauma-Informed City in U.S.," *ACES Too High*, February 13, 2012, acestoohigh.com/2012/02/13/tarpon-springs-may-be-first-trauma-informed-city-in-u-s/. Still other towns are moving forward. Julia Werth, "To Be a Trauma-Informed City Takes a Cultural Shift and Partnership," *CT Mirror*, August 28, 2017, ctmirror.org/2017/08/28/to-be-a-trauma-informed-city-takes-a-cultural-shift-and-partnership/.

39. For a collection of the voices of the Parkland survivors, people.com/crime/voices-of-parkland-student-survivor-videos-exclusive/. For an individual, poignant voice, listen to voice of survivor turned activist David Hogg at www.youtube.com/watch?v=3fIeE8x-wXU.

40. Lois Beckett, "'We Can't Let Fear Consume Us': Why Parkland Activists Won't Give Up," *Guardian*, modified June 5, 2019, www.theguardian.com/us-news/2019/feb/11/parkland-student-activists-march-for-our-lives-year-later-2019.

41. Emily Taguchi, Stephanie Wash, Alexa Valiente, and Jake Lefferman, "At the March for Our Lives, Parkland Students Found Their Voices as Activists Against Gun Violence," ABC News, March 26, 2018, abcnews.go.com/US/march-lives-parkland-students-found-voices-activists-gun/story?id=54026989.

42. Alex Harris, "'This Is a Generational Thing Now': 19 Years After Columbine, Parkland Kids Walk Out," *Miami Herald*, April 20, 2018, www.miamiherald.com/news/local/community/broward/article209205434.html.

43. Chuck Schilken, "Simone Biles Gets Emotional Speaking About Larry Nassar Scandal," *Los Angeles Times*, August 8, 2019, www.latimes.com/sports/story/2019-08-08/simone-biles-larry-nassar-usa-gymnastics.

44. Gregory Wallace, "Jeffrey Epstein's World of Wealth and Powerful Friends," updated CNN, August 10, 2019, www.cnn.com/2019/07/08/politics/jeffrey-epstein-bio/index.html.

45. Marci A. Hamilton, "Jeffrey Epstein and His Enablers Are Evil, but Not Special: He's Just the Latest Example of a Toxic Culture for Children," *Verdict*, July 15, 2019, verdict.justia.com/2019/07/15/jeffrey-epstein-and-his-enablers-are-evil-but-not-special.

46. Ronan Farrow, "How an Élite University Research Center Concealed Its Relationship with Jeffrey Epstein," *New Yorker* (n.d.), www.newyorker.com/news/news-desk/how-an-elite-university-research-center-concealed-its-relationship-with-jeffrey-epstein?cid=pt&source=ams&sourceId=4231050; Allison Quinn, "'He Who Must Not Be Named': MIT Media Lab Rocked by New Jeffrey Epstein Revelations," *Daily Beast*, September 7, 2019, www.thedailybeast.com/mit-media-lab-rocked-by-new-jeffrey-epstein-revelations; Colleen Flaherty, "Another Harvard Professor Addresses Jeffrey Epstein Ties," *Inside Higher Ed*, August 15, 2019, www.insidehighered.com/quicktakes/2019/08/15/another-harvard-professor-addresses-jeffrey-epstein-ties.

47. Jan Ransom, "Harvey Weinstein's Stunning Downfall," *New York Times*, March 11, 2020, www.nytimes.com/2020/03/11/nyregion/harvey-weinstein-sentencing.html; and Taralê Wulff, "I Testified Against Harvey Weinstein: No Sentence Can Heal His Victims, but It's a Start," *The Guardian,* March 11, 2020, www.theguardian.com/commentisfree/2020/mar/10/testified-against-harvey-weinstein-trial-victims.

48. Maggie Fitzgerald, "The CEOs of Nearly 200 Companies Just Said Shareholder Value Is No Longer Their Main Objective," CNBC, August 19, 2019, www.cnbc.com/amp/2019/08/19/the-ceos-of-nearly-two-hundred-companies-say-shareholder-value-is-no-longer-their-main-objective.html.

49. Robert Putnam, *Our Kids: The American Dream in Crisis* (New York: Simon and Schuster, 2016).

50. Sandra L. Bloom and Brian Farragher, *Destroying Sanctuary: The Crisis in Human Service Delivery Systems* (New York: Oxford University Press, 2011), 355–364.

Chapter 8

1. Anthony Abraham Jack, "I Was a Low-Income College Student. Classes Weren't the Hard Part," *New York Times Magazine*, September 10, 2019, www.nytimes.com/interactive/2019/09/10/magazine/college-inequality.html.

2. TeachThought Staff, "20 Things Educators Need to Know About Learning Spaces," TeachThought, December 8, 2015, www.teachthought.com/pedagogy/20-things-educators-need-to-know-about-learning-spaces/.

3. Karen Gross, "Reopening Schools Post Disaster," February 20, 2019, Medium, medium.com/@KarenGrossEdu/reopening-schools-post-disaster-d3892ac88f.

4. Hayley Glatter, Emily Deruy, and Alia Wong, "Reimagining the Modern Classroom," *Atlantic*, September 2, 2016, www.theatlantic.com/education/archive/2016/09/reimagining-the-modern-classroom/498224/.

5. A recent example demonstrates how teachers are incorporating the coronavirus topic into their courses and classes, all without using the terms *trauma* or *trauma responsive* or recognizing that their efforts are, in fact, trauma-responsive pedagogy. Had the teachers had a language to identify their efforts, these efforts might have had even more directed and powerful. Shawna De La Rosa, "Educators Find Applications for Coronavirus Across Curriculum," *EducationDive,* March 11, 2020, www.educationdive.com/news/educators-find-applications-for-coronavirus-across-curriculum/573890/.

6. For a discussion of the impact of trauma on higher education in particular, see Shannon Davidson, "Trauma-Informed Practices for Postsecondary Education: A Guide," *Education Northwest,* educationnorthwest.org/sites/default/files/resources/trauma-informed-practices-postsecondary-508.pdf. (No date). While I disagree with certain aspects of this report, including the attention paid to resiliency and the particular focus on subgroups of students who are likely to be traumatized since I believe as noted herein that all students are susceptible, this is a worthy read.

7. "Salford Museum," *Talking Chairs* (blog), January 2012, www.talkingchairs.co.uk/2012/02/salford-museum.html; Abbi Matheson, "Talking Chair Installation Opens at Robbins Library," Wicked Local Arlington, April 6, 2018, arlington.wickedlocal.com/news/20180406/talking-chair-installation-opens-at-robbins-library.

8. Katelyn McAdam, "5 Best Colleges with Non-traditional Schedules," College Raptor, updated September 6, 2019, www.collegeraptor.com/find-colleges/articles/college-search/colleges-with-non-traditional-schedules/.

9. Elizabeth Chuck, "Active Shooter Drills Are Scaring Kids and May Not Protect Them. Some Schools Are Taking a New Approach," NBC News, updated

April 15, 2019, www.nbcnews.com/news/us-news/active-shooter-drills-are-scaring-kids-may-not-protect-them-n992941.

10. Nicole S. Simon and Susan Moore Johnson, "Teacher Turnover in High-Poverty Schools: What We Know and Can Do," *Teachers College Record*, 117, no. 3 (2015), eric.ed.gov/?id=EJ1056722.

11. Rachel M. Cohen, "The True Cost of Teach for America's Impact on Urban Schools," *American Prospect*, January 5, 2015, prospect.org/article/true-cost-teach-americas-impact-urban-schools.

12. An obvious corollary is that the cancellation of these events is destabilizing, something that has occurred in the context of school closures as a consequence of COVID-19. See Karen Gross, "We Are Messing Up by not Thinking Through School Closure Issues, *Medium*, March 12, 2020, https://medium.com/age-of-awareness/were-messing-up-by-not-thinking-through-school-closures-2d0057d2d62e.

13. As noted earlier, this book does not deal with trauma to students that is caused by teachers, administrators, and staff. That said, safety would, were that topic covered, be expanded to include adult behaviors that threaten and traumatize students.

14. Deborah Smith, "Harassment in the Hallways," *Monitor on Psychology* (American Psychological Association) 32, no. 8 (2001): 38, www.apa.org/monitor/sep01/harassment.

15. Lea Winerman, "The Mind's Mirror," *Monitor on Psychology* (American Psychological Association) 36, no. 9 (2005): 48, www.apa.org/monitor/oct05/mirror.

16. Toni Airaksinen, "Columbia Sets Aside Meeting Space for POC, LGBTQ Students Only," *Campus Reform*, April 3, 2017, www.campusreform.org/?ID=9007; Rudo Ellen Kazembe, "5 Reasons Why Safe Spaces Are Important on Campus," *FreshU,* 2019, www.freshu.io/rudo-ellen-kazembe/5-reasons-why-safe-spaces-are-important-on-campus.

17. Jesse Singal, "Why the University of Chicago's Anti–'Safe Space' Letter Is Important," *Intelligencer*, August 26, 2016, nymag.com/intelligencer/2016/08/the-university-of-chicagos-anti-safe-space-letter-matters.html.

18. Quoted in Karen Gross, "Aging Educators: Still Valuable?" LinkedIn, August 16, 2019, www.linkedin.com/pulse/aging-educators-still-valuable-karen-gross/.

19. Selena Simmons-Duffin, "Positive Childhood Experiences May Buffer Against Health Effects of Adverse Ones," NPR, September 9, 2019, www.npr.org/sections/health-shots/2019/09/09/759031061/positive-childhood-experiences-may-buffer-against-health-effects-of-adverse-ones.

20. Karen Gross, "First Day of School: The Questions Our Teachers Should Not Ask," August 13, 2019, Medium, medium.com/@KarenGrossEdu/first-day-of-school-the-questions-our-teachers-should-not-ask-57421bec4cf1.

21. Andre Audette, "Selecting Groups for Collaborative Learning," *Notes on Teaching and Learning*, March 20, 2017, sites.nd.edu/kaneb/2017/03/20/selecting-groups-for-collaborative-learning/.

22. "How Can I Compose Groups?" Eberly Center (n.d.), www.cmu.edu/teaching/designteach/teach/instructionalstrategies/groupprojects/compose.html.

23. For young people, adult involvement is protective against the damage of trauma. Positive role models preceding a trauma can mitigate trauma's effects on young people. See Simmons-Duffin, "Positive Childhood Experiences."

24. Gary G. Abud Jr., "Student Trauma Is Real. But Connection Can Heal," *Education Week Teacher* (blog), July 11, 2017, blogs.edweek.org/teachers/teacher_leader_voices/2017/07/trauma_is_real_but_connection_.html.

25. Shannon Davidson, *Trauma-Informed Practices for Postsecondary Education: A Guide*, Education Northwest (n.d.), educationnorthwest.org/sites/default/files/resources/trauma-informed-practices-postsecondary-508.pdf.

26. Jessica Lahey, "How Teachers Help Students Who've Survived Trauma: One out of Every Four Children Sitting in American Classrooms Has Experienced Significant Personal or Emotional Distress," *Atlantic*, December 2, 2014, www.theatlantic.com/education/archive/2014/12/how-teachers-help-kids-heal/383325/.

27. Christina Bethell, Jennifer Jones, Narangerel Gombojav, Jeff Linkenbach, and Robert Sege, "Positive Childhood Experiences and Adult Mental and Relational Health in a Statewide Sample Associations Across Adverse Childhood Experiences Levels," *JAMA Pediatrics*, September 9, 2019, jamanetwork.com/journals/jamapediatrics/fullarticle/2749336; Christopher Bergland, "Seven Early Experiences with Potential Benefits in Adulthood," *Psychology Today*, September 9, 2019, www.psychologytoday.com/sg/blog/the-athletes-way/201909/seven-early-experiences-potential-benefits-in-adulthood.

28. Christopher Bergland, "A 17-Item Checklist Geared to Neutralize Early Life Distress," *Psychology Today*, September 17, 2019, www.psychologytoday.com/us/blog/the-athletes-way/201909/17-item-checklist-geared-neutralize-early-life-hardship; "For Kids Who Face Trauma, Good Neighbors or Teachers Can Save Their Longterm Health," *ScienceDaily*, September 16, 2019, www.sciencedaily.com/releases/2019/09/190916144004.htm.

Chapter 9

1. See Jim Sporleder and Heather T. Forbes, *The Trauma-Informed School: A Step-by-Step Implementation Guide for Administrators and School Personnel* (Boulder, CO: Beyond Consequences Institute, 2019).

2. This is an issue for traumatized parents who may struggle to play (and enjoy that play) with their own children. For a remarkable document on this topic (among others), see Ana Sofia Joanes's documentary *Wrestling Ghosts* (2018), available for viewing in a variety of settings. www.wrestlingghosts.com.

3. Karen Gross and Marc Wine, *Lady Lucy's Laugh Giraffe Journey* (Manchester Center, VT: Shires Press, 2018); Karen Gross, "Read, Read, Read: The Gift That Keeps on Giving," Medium, December 13, 2018, medium.com/@KarenGrossEdu/read-read-read-the-gift-that-keeps-on-giving-15f5961f1fe2; Karen Gross, "Heat Surrounds Us; Some Less Well-Known Consequences and Some Uncommon Solutions," Forest of the Rain Productions, July 1, 2018, www.forestoftherain.net/our-blog-your-voice/heat-surrounds-us-some-less-well-known-consequences-and-some-uncommon-solutions-by-karen-gross-esq.

4. Grant Hilary Brenner, "How Adverse Childhood Experiences Cost $1.33 Trillion a Year," *Psychology Today*, September 14, 2019, www.psychologytoday.com/us/blog/experimentations/201909/how-adverse-childhood-experiences-cost-133-trillion-year.

5. Ghislaine Boulanger, Linda M. Floyd, Kathryn L. Nathan, Deborah R. Poitevant, and Elsa Pool, "Reports from the Front: The Effects of Hurricane Katrina on Mental Health Professionals in New Orleans," *Psychoanalytic Dialogues* 23,

no. 1 (2013): 15–30, https://www.researchgate.net/publication/232529481_In_the_Aftermath_of_Hurricane_Katrina_A_Personal_Story_of_a_Psychologist_From_New_Orleans.

6. Boulanger et al., "Reports from the Front," 20.

7. Sophia Richman, *Mended by the Muse: Creative Transformations of Trauma* (New York: Routledge, 2014).

8. Id. (article) at 21.

9. Karen Gross and Anne Myrka, "'Roving' Interdisciplinary Professors," *Chronicle of Higher Education*, January 23, 2009, www.chronicle.com/article/Roving-Interdisciplinary/24505.

10. Gross and Myrka, "'Roving' Interdisciplinary Professors."

11. Hanover Research, *Optimal Scheduling for Secondary School Students*, February 2014, www.gssaweb.org/wp-content/uploads/2015/04/Optimal-Scheduling-for-Secondary-School-Students-1.pdf.

12. For an excellent discussion of why kicking a child out of school does not help the child, see the 2015 documentary *Paper Tiger*, about a high school for "troubled" kids (KPJR Films, www.papertiger.com). See also implementation guide book cited in fn—in Chapter 7.

13. The concept of authenticity is referenced in *Paper Tiger*, mentioned earlier.

14. Brad Wolverton, "As Students Struggle with Stress and Depression, Colleges Act as Counselors," *New York Times*, February 21, 2019, www.nytimes.com/2019/02/21/education/learning/mental-health-counseling-on-campus.html.

15. Manlu Liu and Max Cohen, "CAPS Executive Director Gregory Eells Died by Suicide Monday Morning," *Daily Pennsylvanian*, September 9, 2019, www.thedp.com/article/2019/09/caps-director-gregory-eells-dies-penn.

16. Janelle Griffith, "Head of Mental Health Services at University of Pennsylvania Dies by Suicide," NBC News, September 10, 2019, www.nbcnews.com/news/us-news/head-mental-health-services-university-pennsylvania-dies-suicide-n1052156; Brian Pascus, "Head of University of Pennsylvania Mental Health Services Dies by Suicide," CBS News, September 11, 2019, www.cbsnews.com/news/gregory-eells-death-director-university-of-pennsylvania-mental-health-services-dies-by-suicide-in-philadelphia/.

17. Devon Frye, "What to Know When Asking About Suicidal Thoughts," *Psychology Today*, June 11, 2018, www.psychologytoday.com/us/blog/brainstorm/201806/what-know-when-asking-about-suicidal-thoughts; Pooky Knightsmith, "Asking About Suicide Does Not Cause Harm, In Fact It May Help," The Mental Elf, July 20, 2018, www.nationalelfservice.net/mental-health/suicide/asking-about-suicide-does-not-cause-harm-in-fact-it-may-help/.

18. These observations are not meant to undermine the serious risks to mental health professionals who deal with troubled students, which can also affect educators working with traumatized students, as described in Chapter 5. See Alexander C. Kafka, "Overburdened Mental-Health Counselors Look After Students. But Who Looks After the Counselors?" *Chronicle of Higher Education*, September 18, 2019, www.chronicle.com/article/Overburdened-Mental-Health/247159.

Chapter 10

1. Richard B. Joelson, "Managing Difficult Life Transitions," Richard B. Joelson (n.d.), richardbjoelsondsw.com/articles/managing-difficult-life-transitions/;

Renee Fabian, "How to Stay Balanced During Major Life Changes," *Talk Space* (blog), July 23, 2018, www.talkspace.com/blog/major-life-changes-stay-balanced/.

2. See, e.g., Conor P. Williams and Rosario Quiroz Villarreal, "Back to School but Nothing's Normal. Schools Mobilize to Help Children of Immigrants After Traumatic Summer," *LA School Report*, September 16, 2019, laschoolreport.com/back-to-school-but-nothings-normal-schools-mobilize-to-help-children-of-immigrants-after-traumatic-summer/.

3. Tamara Glenz, "The Importance of Learning Students' Names," *Journal on Best Teaching Practices* 1, no. 1 (2014): 21–22, teachingonpurpose.org/wp-content/uploads/2015/03/Glenz-T.-2014.-The-importance-of-learning-students-names.pdf; Ambereen Khan-Baker, "Why Pronouncing Students' Names Is Important to Building Relationships," National Board for Professional Teaching Standards, August 12, 2016, www.nbpts.org/why-pronouncing-students-names-is-important-to-building-relationships/; Corey Mitchell, "A Teacher Mispronouncing a Student's Name Can Have a Lasting Impact," *PBS News Hour*, May 16, 2016, www.pbs.org/newshour/education/a-teacher-mispronouncing-a-students-name-can-have-a-lasting-impact.

4. These observations and others below are drawn from Karen Gross, "First Day of School: The Questions Our Teachers Should Not Ask," August 13, 2019, Medium, medium.com/@KarenGrossEdu/first-day-of-school-the-questions-our-teachers-should-not-ask-57421bec4cf1.

5. On the key questions to ask, see James Ryan's *Wait, What? And Life's Other Essential Questions* (New York: HarperOne, 2017). See also James Ryan, "Good Questions," Harvard Graduate School of Education, May 26, 2016, www.gse.harvard.edu/news/16/05/good-questions; Karen Gross, "A Wee Bright Light: The T. M. Landry School Saga," LinkedIn, November 30, 2018, www.linkedin.com/pulse/wee-bright-light-tm-landry-school-saga-karen-gross/.

6. Karen Gross and Debbi Wraga, *Teach Our Children Well* (Manchester Center, VT: Shires Press, 2017). They appear on numerous pages within this book; they can be recognized because of the quality of the art and the frequency with which they appear and are recognized.

7. AP tests aren't available in many schools, and some colleges do not accept the scores as an alternative to a college course.

8. I have made this suggestion to teachers working in the context of the coronavirus. Karen Gross, LINKEDIN, March 2020, www.linkedin.com/feed/update/urn:li:activity:6639909483252379648/.

9. This is central to the Montessori approach to education. Although not designed to address trauma specifically, many components of the Montessori method, including team activity, individualized learning, contextualized learning, and combining ages in classes, have benefits for traumatized students. "What Is Montessori Education?" Montessori Northwest (n.d.), montessori-nw.org/what-is-montessori-education.

10. See David S. Cohen, "Can Sports Help Young People Heal from Trauma?" *Culture of Health Blog*, April 11, 2016, www.rwjf.org/en/blog/2016/04/can_sports_help_youn.html; Perri Klass, "Team Sports May Help Children Deal with Trauma," *New York Times*, July 8, 2019, www.nytimes.com/2019/07/08/well/family/team-sports-may-help-children-deal-with-trauma.html; M. C. Easterlin, P. J. Chung, M. Leng, and R. Dudovitz, "Association of Team Sports Participation with Long-Term Mental Health Outcomes Among Individuals Exposed to Adverse Child-

hood Experiences," *JAMA Pediatrics* 173, no. 7 (2019): 681–688, doi: 10.1001/jama pediatrics.2019.1212.

Chapter 11

1. Kristen Bialik and Richard Fry, "Millennial Life: How Young Adulthood Today Compares with Prior Generations," Pew Research Center, February 14, 2019, pewsocialtrends.org/essay/millennial-life-how-young-adulthood-today-compares-with-prior-generations; Lauren M. Troksa, *The Study of Generations: A Timeless Notion Within a Contemporary Context* (undergraduate honors thesis, University of Colorado, Boulder), Spring 2016, /scholar.colorado.edu/concern/undergraduate_honors_theses/9z903038m.

2. See Jill Novak, "The Six Living Generations in America," Marketing Teacher (n.d.), www.marketingteacher.com/the-six-living-generations-in-america/.

3. "The Whys and Hows of Generations Research," Pew Research Center, September 3, 2015, www.people-press.org/2015/09/03/the-whys-and-hows-of-generations-research/.

4. Linette Lopez, "How Baby Boomers Became the Most Selfish Generation," *Business Insider*, November 30, 2016, www.businessinsider.com/how-baby-boomers-became-the-most-selfish-generation-2016-11.

5. Kristen Bialik and Richard Fry, "Millennial Life: How Young Adulthood Today Compares with Prior Generations," Pew Research Center, February 14, 2019, pewsocialtrends.org/essay/millennial-life-how-young-adulthood-today-compares-with-prior-generations/.

6. See, e.g., Mimi An, "Content Trends: Preferences Emerge Along Generational Fault Lines," *Hub Spot* (blog), updated October 1, 2019, blog.hubspot.com/news-trends/content-trends-preferences; Sarah Schmidt, "7 Market Research Reports on the Millennial Consumer," *Market Research Blog*, May 24, 2017, blog.marketresearch.com/7-market-research-reports-on-the-the-millennial-consumer.

7. David Costanza, "Can We Please Stop Talking About Generations as If They Are a Thing?" *Slate*, April 13, 2018, slate.com/technology/2018/04/the-evidence-behind-generations-is-lacking.html.

8. Costanza, "Can We Please Stop Talking"; AMA Staff, "The Myth of Generational Differences in the Workplace," American Management Association, January 24, 2019, www.amanet.org/articles/the-myth-of-generational-differences-in-the-workplace/; Jessica Kriegel, "Why Generational Theory Makes No Sense," *Forbes*, September 29, 2015, www.forbes.com/sites/oracle/2015/09/29/why-generational-theory-makes-no-sense/#22a107558eaa.

9. Jonah Engel Bromwich, "Tell Us What to Call the Generation After Millennials (Please)," *New York Times*, January 23, 2018, www.nytimes.com/2018/01/23/style/generation-names.html; Matt Rosenberg, "Generational Names in the United States," ThoughtCo, updated February 12, 2020, www.thoughtco.com/names-of-generations-1435472; Adrienne LaFrance, "How Generations Get Their Names," *Atlantic*, February 3, 2016, www.theatlantic.com/technology/archive/2016/02/how-generations-get-their-names/459720/.

10. William Strauss and Neil Howe, *Generations: The History of America's Future, 1584 to 2069* (New York: William Morrow, 1991); Samantha Sharf, "What Is a 'Millennial' Anyway? Meet the Man Who Coined the Phrase," *Forbes*,

August 24, 2015, www.forbes.com/sites/samanthasharf/2015/08/24/what-is-a-millennial-anyway-meet-the-man-who-coined-the-phrase/#197b220e4a05. See also Troksa, *The Study of Generations*.

11. Josh Sanburn, "How Every Generation of the Last Century Got Its Nickname," *Time*, December 2, 2015, time.com/4131982/generations-names-millennials-founders/.

12. John Donovan, "Why We Insist on Labeling Generations," MNN, July 1, 2015, www.mnn.com/lifestyle/arts-culture/stories/why-we-insist-labeling-generations; Rebecca Onion, "Against Generations," Aeon, May 19, 2015, aeon.co/essays/generational-labels-are-lazy-useless-and-just-plain-wrong; "Strauss-Howe Generational Theory," CenSAMM (n.d.), censamm.org/resources/profiles/strauss-howe-generational-theory.

13. Jean Twenge, "How Are Generations Named?" *Trend*, January 26, 2018, trend.pewtrusts.org/en/archive/winter-2018/foreword-how-are-generations-named.

14. See Tom McBride, "The Mindset List: Class of 2022," The Mindset Lists, August 20, 2018, themindsetlist.com/2018/08/beloit-college-mindset-list-class-2022/.

15. Chanel Miller, *Know My Name: A Memoir* (New York: Viking, 2019); Concepción de León "'It Will Always Be a Part of My Life': Chanel Miller Is Ready to Talk," *New York Times*, updated Sept. 24, 2019, www.nytimes.com/2019/09/22/books/chanel-miller-know-my-name-emily-doe.html.

16. Michael James, "Brock Turner, Ex-Stanford University Swimmer Convicted of Sexual Assault, Denied New Trial," *USA Today*, updated August 10, 2018, www.usatoday.com/story/news/2018/08/08/stanford-university-swimmer-convicted-assault-denied-new-trial/943186002/.

Chapter 12

1. See, e.g., Scott Barry Kaufman, "The Will and Ways of Hope," *Psychology Today*, December 26, 2011, www.psychologytoday.com/us/blog/beautiful-minds/201112/the-will-and-ways-hope.

2. Readers might be interested in this piece, highlighting the themes in *Don Quixote*. Rachel Hildebrandt, "Don Quixote de la Mancha: Timeless Message of Hope and Chivalry," Global Literature in Libraries Initiative, October 19, 2017, glli-us.org/2017/10/19/don-quixote-de-la-mancha-timeless-message-of-hope-and-chivalry/.

3. Finding hope is a theme in James Fallows and Deborah Fallows's *Our Towns: A 100,000-Mile Journey into the Heart of America* (New York: Vintage, 2019). They note the presence of educational institutions and a belief in them as a sign of hope (404–406) and add in two variables central to the present book: connections and engagement (411–412).

4. Robert Sege, "New Report: Positive Childhood Experiences Make for Healthier Adults," Health Resources in Action, May 14, 2017, hria.org/2017/05/14/new-report-positive-childhood-experiences-make-healthier-adults/; C. D. Bethell, M. R. Solloway, S. Guinosso, S. Hassink, A. Srivastav, D. Ford, and L. A. Simpson, "Prioritizing Possibilities for Child and Family Health: An Agenda to Address Adverse Childhood Experiences and Foster the Social and Emotional Roots of Well-Being in Pediatrics," *Academic Pediatrics* 17, no. 7S (2017): S36–S50, www.ncbi.nlm.nih.gov/m/pubmed/28865659/?i=5&from=/31362100/related; Selena Simmons-Duffin, "Positive Childhood Experiences May Buffer Against Health Effects of Adverse Ones,"

NPR, September 9, 2019, www.npr.org/sections/health-shots/2019/09/09/759031061/positive-childhood-experiences-may-buffer-against-health-effects-of-adverse-ones; "Positive Childhood Experiences Can Negate Harmful Health Effects in Traumatized Children," *Medical Life Sciences News*, September 17, 2019, www.news-medical.net/amp/news/20190917/Positive-childhood-experiences-can-negate-harmful-health-effects-in-traumatized-children.aspx; Christina Bethell, Jennifer Jones, Narangerel Gombojav, Jeff Linkenbach, and Robert Sege, "Positive Childhood Experiences and Adult Mental and Relational Health in a Statewide Sample Associations Across Adverse Childhood Experiences Levels," *JAMA Pediatrics*, September 9, 2019, jamanetwork.com/journals/jamapediatrics/fullarticle/2749336; Christopher Bergland, "Seven Early Experiences with Potential Benefits in Adulthood," *Psychology Today*, September 9, 2019, www.psychologytoday.com/sg/blog/the-athletes-way/201909/seven-early-experiences-potential-benefits-in-adulthood; Christopher Bergland, "A 17-Item Checklist Geared to Neutralize Early Life Distress," *Psychology Today*, September 17, 2019, www.psychologytoday.com/us/blog/the-athletes-way/201909/17-item-checklist-geared-neutralize-early-life-hardship; "For Kids Who Face Trauma, Good Neighbors or Teachers Can Save Their Longterm Health," *Science Daily*, September 16, 2019, www.sciencedaily.com/releases/2019/09/190916144004.htm.

5. There is increasing research on additional avenues to pursue to ameliorate trauma symptomology based on new understandings within neuroscience, neurobiology, and neurochemistry as well as immunology and psychiatry. We are also seeing new therapeutic approaches for treating trauma symptomology that may have positive effects for some traumatized individuals. Use of brain waves to retrain the patterns in our brains, eye movement desensitization, acupoint tapping, remapping memories, and meditation are all being tested and tried, alone and in combinations, to alleviate trauma symptomology. New drugs are being developed with the promise of better outcomes with fewer negative side effects. Indeed, in many senses, we are only at the beginning of our learning on how to improve the lives of traumatized individuals. For those interested in seeing some of these newer approaches in action, the movie *Wrestling Ghosts*, directed by Ana Sofia Joanes (2018), is well worth seeing. How and if these new approaches will impact trauma-responsive schools is something yet to be determined with any certainty.

6. Robert D. Sege and Charlyn Harper Browne, "Responding to ACEs with HOPE: Health Outcomes from Positive Experiences," *Academic Pediatrics* 17, no. 7S (2017): S79–S85, www.academicpedsjnl.net/article/S1876-2859(17)30107-9/pdf; Robert Sege, Christina Bethell, Jeff Linkenbach, Jennifer A. Jones, Bart Klika, and Peter J. Pecora, *Balancing Adverse Childhood Experiences (ACEs) with HOPE: New Insights into the Role of Positive Experience on Child and Family Development* (Boston: Medical Foundation, 2017), hria.org/wp-content/uploads/2017/05/Balancing-ACEs-with-HOPE.pdf; Christina Bethell, "The New Science of Thriving: Our Well-Being—Individually and as a Society—Depends on Mindfulness," *Johns Hopkins Public Health*, Spring 2016, magazine.jhsph.edu/2016/spring/forum/rethinking-the-new-science-of-thriving/index.html; Christopher D. Connors, "The Science of Hope—World Renowned Psychologists Explain Its Power," Medium, June 1, 2017, medium.com/the-mission/the-science-of-hope-world-renowned-psychologists-explain-its-power-b914dd0da631.

7. Bethell, Jones, et al., "Positive Childhood Experiences"; Bethell, Solloway, et al., "Prioritizing Possibilities"; "For Kids Who Face Trauma."

8. Ghislaine Boulanger, *Wounded by Reality: Understanding and Treating Adult Onset Trauma* (Mahwah, NJ: Analytic Press, 2007); Nancy Sherman, *Afterwar: Healing the Moral Wounds of Our Soldiers* (New York: Oxford University Press, 2015); Eva Alisic, "A Quarter of Cases of Posttraumatic Stress Disorder Is with Delayed Onset," *Trauma Recovery Lab* (n.d.), trauma-recovery.net/2012/06/14/a-quarter-of-cases-of-posttraumatic-stress-disorder-is-with-delayed-onset/amp/.

9. Elaine K. Howley, "Statistics on PTSD in Veterans," *U.S. News and World Report*, June 28, 2019, health.usnews.com/conditions/mental-health/ptsd/articles/ptsd-veterans-statistics.

10. MSW@USC Staff, "Service Members Speak Out on Difficulties of Transitioning to Civilian Life," University of Southern California, Suzanne Dworak-Peck School of Social Work, September 26, 2017, msw.usc.edu/mswusc-blog/transitioning-out-of-the-military/; *Common Challenges During Re-adjustment*, U.S. Department of Veteran Affairs (n.d.), www.mentalhealth.va.gov/communityproviders/docs/readjustment.pdf; *St. Louis Post-Dispatch*, "Veterans Returning to College Face Unique Challenges," Military.com (n.d.), www.military.com/veteran-jobs/career-advice/military-transition/veterans-in-college-face-challenges.html; Gillian Kiley-Brown, "After Combat, Veterans Need Help Getting Back to 'Normal,'" *Futurity*, February 14, 2017, www.futurity.org/veterans-transitions-1358692-2/.

11. Fallows and Fallows in *Our Towns* reinforce the observation that schools are part of communities.

12. Jeremy Bauer-Wolf, "A Lingering Tradition," *Inside Higher Ed*, August 29, 2019, www.insidehighered.com/news/2019/08/29/lingering-tradition-freshman-beanie-south-dakota-school-mines.

13. Jacqueline Schall, Tanner LeBaron Wallace, and Vichet Chhuon, "'Fitting In' in High School: How Adolescent Belonging Is Influenced by Locus of Control Beliefs," *International Journal of Adolescence and Youth* 21, no. 4 (2014): 462–475, www.tandfonline.com/doi/full/10.1080/02673843.2013.866148.

14. Mike McCiag, "High School Graduation Rates by State," *Governing*, December 3, 2012, www.governing.com/gov-data/high-school-graduation-rates-by-state.html; Joel McFarland, Jiashan Cui, Amy Rathbun, and Juliet Holmes, *Trends in High School Dropout and Completion Rates in the United States: 2018* (NCES 2019-117), U.S. Department of Education, National Center for Education Statistics, December 2018, nces.ed.gov/pubs2019/2019117.pdf; Child Trends Databank, "High School Dropout Rates," Child Trends, 2018, www.childtrends.org/indicators/high-school-dropout-rates.

15. Ghislaine Boulanger, "Seeing Double, Being Double: Longing, Belonging, Recognition, and Evasion in Psychodynamic Work with Immigrants," *American Journal of Psychoanalysis* 75, no. 3 (2015): 287–303, link.springer.com/article/10.1057%2Fajp.2015.27.

16. Brianna Wiest, "Connection Is a Core Human Need, but We Are Terrible at It," *Forge*, December 4, 2018, forge.medium.com/if-connection-is-our-core-human-need-then-why-are-we-so-bad-at-it-a904ae486a48.

17. Usable Knowledge, "The Value of Listening," Harvard Graduate School of Education, September 7, 2017, www.gse.harvard.edu/news/uk/17/09/value-listening.

18. "Balancing Adverse Childhood Experiences (ACEs) with HOPE," Alliance for Strong Families and Communities (n.d.), www.alliance1.org/web/resources/pubs/balancing-adverse-childhood-experiences-aces-hope.aspx.

19. Manica F. Ramos and Sarah Shea Crowne, "Home Visiting and Early Childhood Education Can Benefit Families by Broadening Their Strategies for Family Engagement," *Child Trends Blog*, February 12, 2019, www.childtrends.org/home-visiting-early-childhood-education-benefit-families-broadening-strategies-family-engagement; Christina Caron and Katherine Zoepf, "Pre-K Teachers Are Making House Calls. It's Helping Kids Succeed," *New York Times*, August 22, 2019, parenting.nytimes.com/preschooler/preschool-home-visit. See also Ann Schimke, "For This First-Grade Teacher, Visiting Students at Home Is Part of the Job," *Chalkbeat*, August 31, 2017, www.chalkbeat.org/posts/co/2017/08/31/for-this-first-grade-teacher-visiting-students-at-home-is-part-of-the-job/; Peggy Barmore, "To Smooth Transitions from Home to Pre-K to Kindergarten, States Must Invest in Every Aspect of Early Ed," *Hechinger Report*, July 8, 2019, hechingerreport.org/to-smooth-transitions-from-home-to-prek-to-kinder-states-must-invest-in-every-aspect-of-early-ed/; Madeline Will, "Can Visiting Students at Home Make Teachers Less Biased?" *Education Week Teacher* (blog), January 8, 2018, blogs.edweek.org/teachers/teaching_now/2018/01/can_visiting_students_at_home_reduce_teachers_implicit_biases.html.

20. *Are We Trauma-Informed? Tools to Measure Progress in a Program, School, or Organization*, Issue Brief 72, Child Health and Development Institute, October 1, 2019, www.chdi.org/index.php/publications/issue-briefs/issue-brief-72-are-we-trauma-informed-tools-measure-progress-program-school-or-organization.

21. See, e.g., "ARTIC Scale: Attitudes Related to Trauma-Informed Care," Traumatic Stress Institute (n.d.), traumaticstressinstitute.org/the-artic-scale/.

22. The Daily Take Team, the Thom Hartmann Program, "A Rising Tide Only Lifts All Boats When Everyone Has a Boat," *Truthout*, August 27, 2014, truthout.org/articles/a-rising-tide-only-lifts-all-boats-when-everyone-has-a-boat/.

23. The best way to contact me is through my website, which has a contact form: www.KarenGrossEducation.com. This address can also be used to provide added trauma symptomology that readers observe, as noted in Chapters 3 and 4. Finally, feel free to reach out in response to this book more generally, including if some of its suggestions have been of particular value to you and those you serve.

Further Readings

Alexander, Jen. *Building Trauma-Sensitive Schools: Your Guide to Creating Safe, Supportive Learning Environments for All Students* (Baltimore: Paul H. Brookes, 2019).

Boogren, Tina H. *Take Time for You: Self-Care Action Plans for Educators (Using Maslow's Hierarchy of Needs and Positive Psychology)* (Bloomington, IN: Solution Tree Press, 2018).

Chapman, Linda. *Neurobiologically Informed Trauma Therapy with Children and Adolescents: Understanding Mechanisms of Change* (New York: W. W. Norton, 2014).

Courtois, Christine A., and David Sack. *It's Not You, It's What Happened to You: Complex Trauma and Treatment* (N.p.: Elements Behavioral Health, 2014).

Craig, Susan E. *Trauma-Sensitive Schools: Learning Communities Transforming Children's Lives, K–5* (New York: Teachers College Press, 2016).

Craig, Susan E., and Jim Sporleder. *Trauma-Sensitive Schools for the Adolescent Years: Promoting Resiliency and Healing, Grades 6–12* (New York: Teachers College Press, 2017).

Curran, Linda. *101 Trauma Informed Interventions* (Eau Claire, WI: PESI, 2015).

Fisher, Janina. *Healing the Fragmented Selves of Trauma Survivors: Overcoming Internal Self-Alienation* (New York: Routledge, 2017).

Goldman, Linda. *Raising Our Children to Be Resilient: A Guide to Helping Children Cope with Trauma in Today's World* (New York: Routledge, 2006).

Goodyear-Brown, Paris. *Trauma and Play Therapy: Helping Children Heal* (New York: Routledge, 2019).

Herman, Judith. *Trauma and Recovery: The Aftermath of Violence—from Domestic Violence to Political Terror* (New York: Basic Books, 2015).

Herman, Judith Lewis, Diya Kallivayalil, and Members of the Victims of Violence Program. *Group Trauma Treatment in Early Recovery: Promoting Safety and Self-Care* (New York: Guildford Press, 2018).

Jennings, Patricia A. *The Trauma-Sensitive Classroom: Building Resilience with Compassionate Teaching* (New York: W. W. Norton, 2018).

Johnson, Jean. *The Bio-psychological Impact of Trauma on Children and Adolescents: Suggestions for Assessment and Treatment in the Jamaican Context* (self-published, 2013).

Levine, Amir, and Rachel S. F. Heller. *Attached: The New Science of Adult Attachment and How It Can Help You Find—and Keep—Love* (New York: Penguin, 2015).

Levine, Peter A. *In an Unspoken Voice: How the Body Releases Trauma and Restores Goodness*. Foreword by Gabor Maté (North Atlantic Books, 2010).

Loss, Christopher P., and Patrick J. McGuinn, eds. *The Convergence of K–12 and Higher Education: Policies and Programs in a Changing Era* (Cambridge, MA: Harvard Education Press, 2016).

Perry, Bruce D., and Maia Szalavitz. *The Boy Who Was Raised as a Dog: And Other Stories from a Child Psychiatrist's Notebook* (New York: Basic Books, 2017).

Rose, Mike. *Back to School: Why Everyone Deserves a Second Chance at Education* (New York: The New Press, 2012).

Solomon, Marion F., and Dan Siegel, eds. *Healing Trauma: Attachment, Mind, Body, and Brain* (New York: W. W. Norton, 2003).

Sorrels, Barbara. *Reaching and Teaching Children Exposed to Trauma* (Lewisville, NC: Gryphon House, 2015).

Walker, Rodney J. *A New Day One: Trauma, Grace, and a Young Man's Journey from Foster Care to Yale* (Charleston, SC: Advantage, 2016).

Webber, Jane M., and J. Barry Mascari. *Disaster Mental Health Counseling: A Guide to Preparing and Responding* (Alexandria, VA: American Counseling Association Foundation, 2018).

Wrestling Ghosts. 2018. Directed by Ana Sofia Joanes. United States: New Day Films.

Index

NAME INDEX

SUBJECT INDEX

Note: Page numbers followed by *f* indicate figures.

About the Author

Karen Gross is a Washington, D.C.–based author and educator, as well as an advisor to nonprofit schools, organizations, and governments. Her work focuses on student success, with a specialization in trauma, its symptomology, and approaches to its amelioration. She has worked with institutions planning for and dealing with person- and nature-made disasters, including shootings, suicides, immigration detention, family dysfunction, hurricanes, and floods.

She currently serves as senior counsel to Finn Partners. She is an instructor in continuing education at Rutgers University Graduate School of Social Work and also sits on the Advisory Council at the Center for Minority Serving Institutions at Rutgers. She is a visiting professor at Bennington College and artist-in-residence at Molly Stark Elementary School (VT).

She is the award-winning author of *Breakaway Learners: Strategies for Post-Secondary Success* (Teachers College Press, 2017) and *Failure and Forgiveness: Rebalancing the Bankruptcy System* (Yale University Press, 1996). She is also the author of a trauma-sensitive children's book series, *Lady Lucy's Quest.* She has read to more than 3,000 children across the globe.

She served for 8 years as president of Southern Vermont College and as senior policy advisor to the U.S. Department of Education during the Obama administration. Prior to that, she was a tenured law professor for 22 years in New York City. She has also served on numerous local, regional, and national boards, including Campus Compact, New England Board of Higher Education, and the Sage Colleges.

A frequent voice on education issues across the PreK–20 pipeline, she has written for numerous publications, among them *University Business, Age of Awareness, The Hechinger Report, New England Journal of Higher Education, LinkedIn, Forest of the Rain Productions, Inside Higher Ed*, and *Chronicle of Higher Education.*

Added information is available at www.karengrosseducation.com